## Advance praise for *White Flights*

"In *White Flights* Jess Row performs [...] American writers' attempts to evad[...] [...]resentation and racism in the US. The landscape of the imagination, like the country itself, he argues with rich insight and brio, is neither equal nor free."

—John Keene, author of *Counternarratives*

"*White Flights* confirms Jess Row's ability to quickly grasp large political issues and conflicts; it shows, too, a reflexive distrust of received wisdom, and a bracing honesty. I am convinced that it will be a major literary and intellectual intervention, clarifying the real stakes in what we too complacently call 'identity politics' and insisting on a fresh reckoning with American history and its main beneficiaries."

—Pankaj Mishra, author of *Age of Anger*
and *Temptations of the West*

"In *White Flights* Jess Row searches the unconscious construction of his own whiteness consciously, as something of a literary game with the most serious stakes and yet played with a seemingly light touch. The essays here are like snakes dancing along the blade of a knife, or tight-rope walkers bursting into laughter, mid-rope, or the deep plunge into a topic that takes you, thrillingly, out the other side, to places familiar and strange at the same time. These are brilliant, sweeping, intimate delights—and afterward, you may never read the same way again."

—Alexander Chee, author of *The Queen of the Night*
and *How to Write An Autobiographical Novel*

"With care and complexity, *White Flights* furthers a crucial national conversation on whiteness, white spaces, and racism, and how these concepts define American literature. More than just provoking thought, this book will provoke dialogue and discussion—exactly what we all need."

—Beth Bich Minh Nguyen, author of *Pioneer Girl*
and *Stealing Buddha's Dinner*

"*White Flights* is required reading for white readers and white writers. The rest of us can learn something, too, about how whiteness is not just a privilege, a norm, and a benefit, but also a burden. With these superb essays, Jess Row reveals himself to be an insightful critic of both literature and the American condition."

—Viet Thanh Nguyen, author of *The Refugees* and *The Sympathizer*

"Gutsy, capable, urgent, innovative, and timely: these elegant essays think and write across lines of race in American culture. The perception of whiteness in this country is charged and complex, and the author's project is to address these complexities and further the critical conversation. The essays move the ball down the field, mixing personal humility with a deep and resourceful reading of critical race theory, literature, and American history. Row examines strenuous naiveté, white flights of fancy, and unreconciled and avoidant imagination, and suggests an intriguing concept of reparative writing. The breadth and erudition of this project are convincing. Fully realized, this will be a soul-searching treatise on the way race underpins our stories in life and on the page."

—Judges' citation, Whiting Creative Nonfiction Grant

# White Flights

## Also by Jess Row

*Your Face in Mine*
*Nobody Ever Gets Lost*
*The Train to Lo Wu*

# White Flights

*Race, Fiction, and the American Imagination*

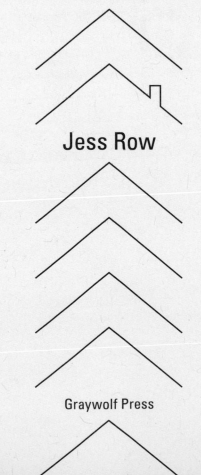

## Jess Row

Graywolf Press

This publication is made possible, in part, by the voters of Minnesota through a Minnesota State Arts Board Operating Support grant, thanks to a legislative appropriation from the arts and cultural heritage fund. Significant support has also been provided by Target, the McKnight Foundation, the Lannan Foundation, the Amazon Literary Partnership, and other generous contributions from foundations, corporations, and individuals. To these organizations and individuals we offer our heartfelt thanks.

Published by Graywolf Press
250 Third Avenue North, Suite 600
Minneapolis, Minnesota 55401

www.graywolfpress.org

Published in the United States of America

ISBN 978-1-55597-832-7

2 4 6 8 9 7 5 3 1
First Graywolf Printing, 2019

Library of Congress Control Number: 2018958158

Cover design: Oliver Munday

For Mina and Asa

Is this the
first time
I've seen the color of this room?

Is this the
first time
I've seen the size of these walls?
— Rites of Spring, "Hidden Wheel"


Writing and reading require being mindful of the places where imagination sabotages itself, locks its own gates, pollutes its vision.
— Toni Morrison


To a greater or lesser degree every man is suspended on *narratives*, on *novels*, which reveal to him the multiplicity of life. Only these narratives, often read in a trance, situate him before his fate. So we ought to seek passionately what *narratives* might be. How to orient the effort through which the novel renews, or, better, perpetuates itself.
— Georges Bataille


This is not freedom, but a question of how to work the trap that one is inevitably in.
— Judith Butler

# Contents

# White Flights

# Eating the Blame
## The Question of Reparative Writing

## 1

One day the head cook in the monastery of Fugai Ekun was cutting vegetables in the garden for dinner, and without noticing it, sliced off the head of a snake, which fell into his vegetable basket. Later, he emptied the basket into the soup pot. The monks thought the soup had never tasted more delicious, but Fugai was suspicious. Probing with his chopsticks in the soup pot, he lifted out the head of the snake and asked the cook indignantly, "What is this?"

"Oh, thank you, Roshi," the cook said immediately, took the head of the snake with his fingers, and ate it.

## 2

These essays are about race in the imaginative life of Americans from the end of the civil rights era to the present. They're about fiction in the proper sense of the word—novels, short stories, films, plays—and also the larger, boundaryless, improper sense, in which our collective life is a series of overlapping fictions, fantasies, dream states. They're about the ways fiction in the first sense reflects and sustains the fictions of the second.

Because it couldn't be otherwise—because I couldn't write it any other way—this is also a book about the dimensions and complications of my own racial identity, and particularly about my life as a white writer, and how I learned, without consciously learning it, to represent whiteness and identify with whiteness, while at the same time believing

I was practicing something called "imaginative freedom." I'm trying to undertake what might be called white autoethnography—a way of writing that should never take itself entirely seriously. Because whiteness is a category that is both laughable and lethal. Writing about race as a white man means I have to move beyond the understanding of what words like "sincerity," "earnestness," and "dignity" mean. The worst thing a book like this could be is polite.

And why write it in the first place? Why add another book attached to the adjective "white" to the pile? Consider this, as a strange and possibly unacceptable starting point: one of my favorite statements about the purpose of art, from the liner notes to the Operation Ivy album *Energy*, recorded in 1989, written by the singer Jesse Michaels (incidentally, son of the novelist Leonard Michaels):

> Music is an indirect force for change, because it provides an anchor against human tragedy. In this sense, it works towards a reconciled world. It can also be the direct experience of change. At certain points during some shows, the reconciled world is already here, at least in that second, at that place.

All art aspires to the condition of music, Joyce said, though he wasn't picturing a ska-punk band playing in a warehouse in Berkeley, or Prince asking us what it means when a rocket ship explodes and everybody still wants to fly, or Ornette Coleman writing, in the liner notes to *Skies of America*, "Why, where and what is the purpose of a country that has the essence of mankind and the blessing of the skies?" But I'll take it, I've felt it, I've known it: the reconciled world, the other world that is not just possible but here. It took me a long time to admit to myself that fiction could partake in this spirit, that it could be so relentlessly public and intentionally uplifting; but that was my own problem, because the evidence was and is in plain sight. There's no other way to describe the repetition of "Yes" at the end of *Ulysses* than to call it "life-affirming." Let alone the quasi-religious endings of *Franny and Zooey*, or *Another Country*, or *Infinite Jest*, or *Beloved*: what some contemporary critics, like Amy Hungerford, call "belief in belief," what Thomas Merton once described as "raids on the unspeakable."

When I talk about the longing for reconciliation I'm talking about a quality that cuts across the normative distinctions that rule contemporary American fiction: dystopian technomodernism versus immigrant narratives; "lower-middle-class realism" versus neofabulist fairy tales; popular, so-called middlebrow novels versus Dalkey Archive cult classics. Desire for reconciliation is built into the structure of narrative itself; it's another way of talking about the gesture known as "closure," which was supposed to have been eliminated by modernism, but wasn't. Then why is it so difficult to talk about? Or, to make the question more specific: why is it so difficult to imagine the readers of American fiction as subjects, both real and imagined, who might want to be brought together, who might *want* to be reconciled, or at the very least, truly recognize one another? Could fiction, to paraphrase Nina Simone, be a way of knowing what it feels like to be free? Or, if this is not possible—and I sometimes doubt it is—what is the nature and shape of that impossibility, that final (or not so final) estrangement?

Here's one attempt at an answer, borrowed from political theory: reconciliation is not a single event in time but a process that never actually ends; it's not something that comes from one person but an exchange, an interplay, that happens between people, in stages, as long as memory persists. In South Africa—whose history and political culture are more like those of the United States than most Americans want to admit—part of the process of recovery after apartheid was administered by a government body called the Truth and Reconciliation Commission. This was an act of collective narration, literally: testimonies collected from all sides, including apartheid-regime torturers, Umkhonto we Sizwe terrorists, Zulu royalists, ordinary citizens, and heads of state. There was no Ken Burns standing by to present a synthetically balanced narrative, as he did in his 2018 PBS documentary on the Vietnam War, insisting in the face of the available evidence that the war was begun "in good faith on all sides." The transcripts of the Truth and Reconciliation Commission are harrowing reading not just because of the staggering violence and waste of the apartheid era but because there is no way to narrate them other than to look to the future, and say, as John Berger wrote in his novel *G.*: never again will a story be told as if it is the only one.

The United States has never undergone the process of *officially* collecting the truth about itself, let alone the even more difficult process of figuring out how to balance opposing truth claims within something that calls itself a single society. This is an obvious and maybe even self-explanatory observation, given the large number of Americans who claim to believe in the literal truth of Armageddon and/or are positive that the government is still hiding what happened at Area 51, juxtaposed with the smaller number who can name one of the three branches of the federal government. But it's an observation that deserves to be marked, even for those who don't accept the nation-state as an acceptable or useful social construct. It means that, in some pregnant sense, many self-identified Americans remain in a kind of dream state—what the scholar Lauren Berlant calls "infantile citizenship"—about their common past, always open to deliberation and more often than not vulnerable to erasure and denial. The United States has only rarely issued a national apology for crimes committed in the name of the state, and only in a few cases paid material reparations to the victims of these crimes. Reparations to African Americans, in particular, has often been treated in the conventional wisdom as an absurdity or a comic fantasy: "Would the descendants of an Athenian helot of the fifth century B.C. . . . have a claim today on the Greek government?" asked Robert Penn Warren in 1965 in *Who Speaks for the Negro?* "The whole thing is a grisly farce. . . . It smacks not of fantasy, but of Bedlam."

In some ways this is an ideal situation for fabulists and mythmakers, dream historiographers; it's given us Mark Twain, William Faulkner, Henry Dumas, Thomas Pynchon, Ishmael Reed, Robert Coover, and George Saunders's *CivilWarLand in Bad Decline*. But the postures these writers adopt (tongue-in-cheek oblivion, hallucinatory prophecy, manic paranoia, selective memory) have never been all that satisfying to me. There was a period after September 11, 2001, when I all but stopped reading American fiction and turned instead to Nadine

Gordimer, Yvonne Vera, Danilo Kiš, Milan Kundera, Gao Xingjian, Eduardo Galeano, David Grossman, Roberto Bolaño, Manuel Puig—writers for whom "the personal" and "the political" were not separable, whose work was saturated with history by necessity, because there was no possibility of living otherwise. Reading James Baldwin, specifically the overwhelming experience of *Another Country*, turned me around, so to speak, and made me *want* to imagine another kind of American writing. To do that, I realized, about ten years ago, that I had to look very closely at this American (and particularly white American) quality of innocence or unknowing, which for lack of a better term could be called "closure without resolution." This is fictive closure, a fiction enforced by state power, de facto claims of possession, threats of communal violence, and, more than anything else, sheer wishful thinking. I recently visited the Kȟe Sapa or Black Hills of South Dakota, where my family has lived since my great-great-grandparents arrived there as illegal settlers during the gold rush of the 1870s. When I asked my cousin Bill, a prominent local historian, about the continuing Lakota claims on the Black Hills, he flatly replied, "That history is over. It's settled."

If "white flights" in the context of this book means only one thing, it means exactly that: wishful thinking as a way of life, a way of seeing, and a way of making art. The fictions I write about here represent an era when most white writers, like white Americans in general, consciously or unconsciously retreated from the "subject" of race, while writers of color did not; the result is that it often seems like there are two American literatures: one in which race is always marked, and almost always tied to the identity of the author, and one in which race seems to play no part at all. I don't think this is actually the case: stories not only deny but undeny, tell but untell themselves.

Kierkegaard wrote that life must be lived forward, but can only be understood backward; this may or may not be true of life, but it's unquestionably true of stories. "Understanding backward" is what allows us to stop and see the gaps, the internal silences, the ironic substitutions and double entendres, that make narratives so interesting and frustrating and continuously alive. It's a kind of ebb and flow that often reveals alternate, even opposed, meanings, or significations, or gestures, in the same text. You can call that ebb and flow deconstruction, or dialogism, or dialectics, or whatever; my point, in this case, is that reading with a different kind of alertness, with eyes truly open, reveals that even writers who would seem to have almost nothing to say about race (Anne Tyler, for example) are saying a great deal.

Sontag famously closed "Against Interpretation" with the line, "In place of a hermeneutics we need an erotics of art." Without foreclosing the question of the pronoun (who is it that needs these things?) I want to argue that the search for an erotics of art is not over; in fact it may never have even begun. In my particular corner I wonder about the libidinal and erotic possibilities of that backward-and-forward movement, which writers and readers both engage in, as a possible ground for reparation, reconciliation, mutual comprehension, and—this may sound unforgivable, but bear with me—as play. Art always operates, on some level, as play. As in, "I wonder what'll happen if I turn this object so it faces the other way."

3

Let's try this with an example: Aimee Bender's 2005 short story "End of the Line," which begins, "The man went to the pet store to buy himself a little man to keep him company."

The little man is a miniature human being, with his own house, television, chandeliers, and silverware; he was captured by "little-men bounty hunters" on his way to work, and tells his new owner that he misses his wife and children terribly. After a few weeks, the owner grows tired of talking to the little man—who is much more sophisticated and worldly than he is—and begins to torture him instead. He tosses him in the air; puts soap in his water; slips the little man down his pants while he's watching TV. Finally, growing bored with inflicting pain, he demands that the little man take him to see where little people live, but the little man refuses, and asks to be killed instead. "I'm the end of the line for you," he says.

Frustrated once again, the owner lets him go, but tries to follow him, driven by curiosity, and something arguably worse than curiosity: a kind of acquisitive protectiveness. "I don't want to harm you!" he shouts. "I just want to be a part of your society." But the little man has disappeared forever, and the world of the little people is invisible to the former owner's eye; all he can find is a tiny yellow hat left on a rose. Now the perspective switches: a group of little people huddles behind a rock, waiting for the giant to lose interest and go away:

> It was not up to them to take care of all the world, whispered the mother to the daughter, whose yellow dress was unmatched, whose hand thrummed with sweat, who watched the giant outside put her hat on his enormous head and could not understand the size of the pity that kept unbuckling in her heart.

Is "End of the Line" "about" enslavement and its dehumanizing, deforming effects, about the horror of human ownership? Obviously, in the most literal sense: Bender has taken great pains to make the "little people" the mimetic equivalent of their enemies. Moreover, the story is narrated not just from the perspective but from the scale of the owner, who thinks of his property as "little." (At the end of the story: "Everything about him felt disgusting and huge. Where are the tall people, the fatter people? he thought. Where are the aliens the size of God?") But in the undergraduate and graduate classes where I've taught this story—at least twenty times, over more than a decade—no student has ever named the allegorical nature of the story out loud, or used the words "whiteness" or "race" in discussing it. Maybe because of my own presence at the end of the table.

What could this story mean, if I situate it in the context of whiteness? Hannah Arendt reached for a phrase to describe Adolf Eichmann's diminished and pathetic affect, as he appeared on trial in Jerusalem, and called it "the banality of evil"; here Bender is evoking something even more terrible, in close-up: the banality of ownership. Acting out a state of absolute supremacy, in which the human object literally becomes a toy, deforms, even destroys, the psyche of the actor. The owner in "End of the Line" longs to return to the community of human friendship, of actual relationships, or "society," but can't; he's left to try on the tiny yellow hat alone, pathetically diminished by his giantness, that which makes him lethal.

Where does whiteness *not* live in this description? The owner's fascination with the little man's genitals; the frustrated homoerotic longing and envy of the little man's culture and mannerisms; the desperate need to "forgive and forget," exchanging torture for paternalism; and the yellow hat, an emblem of failed racial disguise, almost like a precursor of minstrelsy—what Eric Lott famously called love and theft. It would be reductive to call "End of the Line" "a story about whiteness," only in the sense that it would be reductive to call "In the Penal Colony" "a story about totalitarianism"; a great work of fiction will always resist being reduced to a predicate. The more interesting question is, why is it so easy to miss the story's most obvious analogy, its conceptual ground, even among people who read and write and interpret for a living? To me, at least, this resistance and the story's own pessimism seem interwoven. What work does that missing do?

# 4

Many contemporary American writers sincerely believe art begins where the sense of accountability stops, that art lives from whence we dream, that the point of art is to evade and/or transcend the realm of the political. Which, for what it's worth, is a pretty accurate description of the conditions of art production today. There have never been more ways to publish a text, or circulate an image, a film, a performance, yet, at the same time, very little contemporary American art or writing of any kind produces public discussion, let alone reaction from state authorities or people in positions of power. As state violence and attacks on civil liberties proliferate under the current regime, American artists and writers for the most part have been left unscathed. Contemporary controversies about "censorship" in the West are mostly debates about offense, harm, and the rules of discourse. (In the rest of the world—Russia, China, Turkey, Pakistan—the situation is, of course, very different.) In this climate there seems to be an inverse correlation between the threat of state censorship and the degree to which the public takes art seriously. "Upholding the inalienable right for art to be anything," Ian F. Svenonius writes in *Censorship Now!!*, "has made art—instead of being the shield, weapon, and broadside pamphlet of the otherwise disenfranchised, available to anyone—into a holy bit of fluff, the well-being of which must be protected by all costs by the muscle of the militarized state."

Putting aside Svenonius's ironic call for a return to the "shadow of the cudgel and the blackout"—which stinks of the fashionable yearning for dictators so common in the early twentieth century avant-garde—many artists, critics, and activists, in the past decade, have turned to simple observations and obvious questions (for example: "What is the relationship between art galleries and gentrification?") as a way of making disinterestedness an object of interest. I hope these essays can be read alongside that larger project. But as a novelist first, I'm interested in something other than structural and institutional critique: maybe stylized more in the vein of the 1970s (*Free to Be You and Me*, *Songs in the Key of Life*). I want to raise the possibility of a new method, a conscious extension of something writers and readers already do. I'm proposing this term—reparative writing—semiseriously, because it can't exist until it exists in a community, as a process of dialogue and exchange; and it can't exist initiated by me alone (or, necessarily, me at all). In the spirit of "you have to start somewhere," I want it for the moment just to linger as a question.

Reparative writing to me includes two overlapping possibilities. First, writing that invokes the spirit of actual reparations, that is, the return of tangible resources to people who were (and/or still are) denied them: this could take many forms, from literary activism to collaborative projects to work in hybrid forms, which mostly fall outside the scope of this book. Second, and more central to the project of *White Flights*: writing that takes up the meaning of "reparative" proposed by Eve Kosofsky Sedgwick in her essay "Paranoid Reading and Reparative Reading." Sedgwick draws her definition of "reparative" from Melanie Klein's theory of the depressive position. Infants, Klein says, are capable not only of feeling but also of internalizing, intense hate and love, particularly toward the mother; this tension can result in the paranoid-schizoid position, which treats all objects as potentially threatening and hateful, or the depressive position, which acknowledges that an object can be loving and hateful. "The depressive position," Sedgwick writes, "is an anxiety-mitigating achievement that the infant or adult only sometimes, and often briefly, succeeds in inhabiting":

> This is the position from which it is possible in turn to use one's resources to assemble or "repair" the murderous part-objects into something like a whole—though, I would emphasize, *not necessarily like any previously existing whole.*

To put this in simpler terms: the depressive position is not what psychotherapists usually call "depression"; it's what happens when a sad person begins to take realistic steps to address the sadness at its source. The depressive and reparative work the white subject can undertake in response to racism is such a poorly understood, understudied subject that I can't say anything definite about it at all; like reparative writing, it's a question that remains outside, to be answered not by me. What I *can* say, from my own experience, is that white American writers are almost never asked to bring their own sadness or their own bodies into play when writing about race or racism; their dreams, their sources of shame, their most nightmarish or unacceptable or crippling fantasies, or their feelings of sadness, paralysis, isolation, or alienation. American culture has evolved a theory of the white psyche that rarely, if ever, considers racism as a direct or even proximate cause of its disorder and distress.

I'm convinced that struggling with feelings of shame, and the possibility of humiliation, is psychologically, politically, artistically meaningful. This is part of the necessary work of whiteness, or recovery from whiteness, which is an okay phrase as long as everyone accepts that the recovery is never really over and the repair is never complete; that's another part of the beautiful struggle. I'm convinced that part of resisting normative whiteness is resisting the urge to have a breakdown, or meltdown, confess my sins, and seek absolution—that is, to make my feelings a catastrophe that has to be dealt with. Coping with whiteness has to do with awareness but not necessarily wakefulness, as if white people have been asleep the rest of the time. White people, for the most part, know very well what it is to be white. The white subject position is not actually unconscious. If you identify as white, and are committed to reading and thinking enough to be reading these words, you already have all the tools you need to transform your relation to your subject position as an instrument of racism. But this transformation is not a *complete* transformation, is not an end in itself: it's just a new way of asking the questions writers and artists always ask:

What's next?

What can we do with the time we have?

It may be useful to think about whiteness in the Trump era using a term from the literary theorist Emily Apter: "impolitic." To be impolitic in conventional terms means to be rude or obnoxious, ungenteel, intentionally disruptive, not following the *politesse* of the moment. An impolitic politician refuses to follow the disinterested vocabulary (or "tact") of the administrative state and its enablers, the pundits, White House reporters, lobbyists, and policy experts who sustain the workings of what Americans usually call "politics."

There is another way of thinking about the impolitic, however, Apter says, and maybe the United States has already arrived there. This is not an argument from necessity, nor even a historical analysis. Impolitics—the refusal to behave politically—is when citizens say these existing categories are not enough. The impolitic happens when power relationships are exposed as they really are: sometimes it's signaled by a phrase like "real talk." "The Impolitical," she writes, "describes why democracy will always be incomplete; an infinite incompleteness positioned as the complement to a myth of organic community." This can be a terrifying plane of existence (because it includes 4Chan and GamerGate, as well as Black Lives Matter, Occupy, and Ai Weiwei), but it's *our* plane of existence, in the literary world as in the larger cultural and political world.

One of the stories I was told in my first fiction workshop—I was seventeen, at Yale Summer School in 1992—detailed "what happened to" William Styron after the publication of *The Confessions of Nat Turner* in 1968. I say "story" because it was relayed to us that way by our teacher, Lee K. Abbott, the way so much information is passed between writers in the workshop. I don't remember exactly how Lee framed it—it had something to do with his own relationship with a black professor in graduate school in the 1970s—but the conclusion was unambiguous: white writers, meaning all the writers in the room, had no business writing about race, because Styron had tried to do it, in good faith, and had been publicly attacked and scorned, and his career had never recovered. I remember the phrase "kiss of death." That was twenty-five years ago, and the same fatalism, the same fear of the impolitic, still circulates in American creative writing. The rawness of this fear comes back into view every time an artistic controversy "erupts" over race: most recently Kenneth Goldsmith's use of Michael Brown's autopsy as conceptual poetry, or Dana Schutz's painting of the famous image of Emmett Till's mutilated face. I don't comment on these controversies directly in *White Flights*, but I will say this much: controversy, argument, and hurt feelings are not the end of the world. They could even be described as artistically necessary. I prefer them to the ritualized postures of avoidance and denial that governed the white American literary community when I was in my twenties and thirties, and still govern it, wherever it thrives in isolation.

5

In 1992, the year I took my first writing workshop, Toni Morrison gave the William E. Massey Sr. Lectures in the History of American Civilization at Harvard, later published as *Playing in the Dark: Whiteness and the Literary Imagination*. Given Morrison's devotion to promoting black writers—going back to her pivotal days as an editor at Random House in the 1970s—she may have surprised some audience members by announcing her subject would be whiteness. "My work," she writes, "requires me to think about how free I can be as an African-

American woman writer in my genderized, sexualized, wholly racialized world":

> To think about (and wrestle with) the full implications of my situa-
> tion leads me to consider what happens when other writers work
> in a highly and historically racialized society. For them, as for me,
> imagining is not merely looking or looking at; nor is it taking one-
> self intact into the other. It is, for the purposes of the work, *becom-
> ing. . . .* My project rises from delight, not disappointment. It rises
> from what I know about the ways writers transform aspects of their
> social grounding into aspects of language, and the ways they tell
> other stories, fight secret wars, limn out all sorts of debates blan-
> keted in their text. And rises from my certainty that writers always
> know, at some level, that they do this.

Here Morrison is not talking about unconscious processes, the inter-
twining of the codes, the rustle of language: she assumes the writer is
aware, on some level, of the "secret wars" within the text. Which is to
say, too, that they are aware that they are working in a "highly and
historically racialized society."

It wouldn't seem like a stretch of the readerly intellect to accept
this observation about nineteenth- and early twentieth-century white
American fiction. Yet, as Morrison says, until the 1990s scholars of
American literature steadfastly ignored race and whiteness as a central
and defining dimension of the white American literary experience—
with the notable exception of the great "outlaw" critic Leslie Fiedler,
whose essay "Come Back to the Raft Ag'in, Huck Honey," caused a
scandal in the late 1940s by making another painfully obvious observation: that Huck and Jim's relationship is colored by an unresolvable,
unnameable homoerotic need.

In fact, Morrison goes on to say, the presence of race, and all its implications, in these classic texts is often what gives them their fundamental strangeness, their richness and dimension. Witness the end of
Poe's *Narrative of A. Gordon Pym*, when Pym, who has endured a series
of catastrophic misadventures after running away to seek adventure

at sea, reaches an uncharted island in the southern oceans, Tsalal, inhabited by people who are literally black—jet black, with black teeth, clothed in black skins. Like the natives in so many adventure stories, the black people of Tsalal appear gentle and kind at first but turn "treacherous," attacking the ship and its crew. Pym survives, with one companion, a former mutineer named Dirk Peters; the two manage to flee the island on a tiny boat, accompanied by one prisoner from the island, Nu-Nu. The boat drifts south, into waters that become pale and then white, unpleasantly hot to the touch. The air is filled with a fine, white, ash-like powder. Finally they find themselves drawn toward an immense waterfall so white that it casts an intense glare:

> Hereupon Nu-Nu stirred in the bottom of the boat; but upon touching him, we found his spirit departed. And now we rushed into the embraces of the cataract, where a chasm threw itself open to receive us. But there arose in our pathway a shrouded human figure, very far larger in its proportions than any dweller among men. And the hue of the skin of the figure was of the perfect whiteness of the snow.

According to the editorial note that follows, Pym and Peters survive this encounter, but Pym dies, mysteriously and distressingly, not long afterward, and the few remaining chapters of his narrative are lost. Whatever else is happening in the text—and Poe's texts, with their purloined letters, unspoken curses, and bricked-up passageways, are designed to lead the reader in interpretive circles—*Pym* ends with a nightmarish version of racial difference, like a child's painting, in which absolute blackness and "perfect whiteness" cancel each other out, and in which whiteness becomes indescribable and unbearable, too hot and too cold: burning snow.

"There is no romance free of what Melville called 'the power of blackness,'" Morrison writes, "especially not in a country in which there was a resident population, already black, upon which the imagination could play; through which historical, moral, metaphysical, and social fears . . . could be articulated." African Americans, free and enslaved, were everywhere in Poe's world; according to some sources, he himself once inherited and then quickly freed an enslaved man, Edwin, who had belonged to his aunt, Maria Clemm. In *Pym* Poe is, transparently, playing with the experience of living among subjugated black people, with the boundaries and consequences of absolute power.

In his 2011 novel *Pym*, Mat Johnson—who identifies as biracial—reverses the logic of Poe's plot, beginning with a record left behind by the enigmatic Dirk Peters. Chris Jaynes, Johnson's protagonist, is an African American literature professor who happens upon Dirk's narrative shortly after receiving a large settlement from his former employer over allegations of racism. Taking Peters's narrative as evidence that Tsalal actually exists—and may be the home of a last undiscovered African people—Jaynes organizes a sea journey to Antarctica, which inevitably goes awry, in the manner of *Blazing Saddles* or *Monty Python and the Holy Grail*, and includes the rediscovery of Arthur Gordon Pym himself, who now lives on an island of almost transparently pale giants. Pym accompanies Jaynes on his journey to Tsalal—but, not surprisingly, dies in the bottom of the boat when they finally reach the island, terrified by the appearance of an ordinary brown-skinned man, who, Jaynes reminds us, represents the majority of the world.

Like a lot of contemporary American fiction (including my own), *Pym* is so hyper-self-aware that it sometimes makes for exhausting reading; at times it can feel entirely like programmatic satire, a kind of point-by-point refutation. But at its best moments, as in Johnson's description of the albino giants—"I realized I had never seen truly pale blue eyes before . . . the lightest possible variant, which had more in common with the snow around us. . . . These darting, acute, haunting orbs bobbed over noses that were so long and pointy I assume they served some sort of evolutionary purpose that was at the moment unclear"—*Pym* is an essential counterpoint, a counterfantasy, that demonstrates the power of Poe's racial dreamscape. Fantasizing imaginary differences is one way of looking at what readers can't always appreciate (or admit to appreciating), which is to say one another's ordinary beauty.

Which is to say, echoing Morrison, it isn't "wrong" for white American writers or critics to address race. It's already happening. It happens everywhere you look, and often when you're not looking. Race is in the American DNA; so are racial mythology, displacement, mystification, stereotype, hallucination, fantasy. The strenuous effort *not* to see it makes American fiction seem more naive, more one-dimensional, more culturally inert and irrelevant, than it actually is. It continues a melancholic operation of what cannot be included and yet never be excluded.

In these essays I'm only interested in confessions, proclamations of guilt, sudden or absolute or unquestioned epiphanies, faultfinding, shaming, or scapegoating—in other words, the ritual dramas of American "race relations"—to the degree they can be named, understood, redescribed, even satirized. I'm not interested in restaging them. I turn instead to the inner racial life of Americans, the private and intimate and even unconscious life embodied in American fictions, which often sustains, and sometimes undermines, the political conditions of white supremacy the country still inhabits. I write from the ugly hope against hope of the depressive position. "For them," Morrison says, speaking of white writers, "as for me, imagining is not merely looking or looking at; nor is it taking oneself intact into the other. It is, for the purposes of the work, *becoming.*"

Another note, or acknowledgment, is important here. This is a book by a white writer, largely about representations and images of whiteness, and while I've tried to make it inclusive of and addressed to all readers, there's no avoiding the fact that "all readers," or "the general reader," is itself a fiction, and sometimes a hostile construct. Black and brown and white readers will experience this text, participate in it, perhaps even recognize themselves in it differently. I've worked on it in a state of scrupulous uncertainty, trying to take all perspectives into account, while knowing that the problem of perception—what the author sees versus what the reader sees, or, in a larger sense, what I imagine your mind to be like—may be the most unanswerable, and valuable, question fiction poses. Which is to say: if you are encountering this book in a state of questioning or wariness, you're not alone. Thank you for being here. Let me know what you think.

## 6

Go back for a second to the story about the Zen master, the cook, and the snake. This is a story about the difficulty of apologizing, but also about why apologies, by themselves, are essential but not sufficient. Something has to be done. This is my theory, returning again to Klein: apologies are so difficult because the subject saying "I'm sorry," expressing sorrow, is also expressing the depressive position: reparation is possible, but only if the people involved accept that the reparation will create something new, not restore the previous situation. The head can't go back on the snake.

This is particularly true in situations, like the American present, that have to do with unresolved historical and present culpability bearing down, in a disastrous way, on the daily lives of its citizens. Maybe the most primitive fantasy of justice is "If I don't talk about it, it didn't actually happen." This is an infantile response, in the most literal sense, and it's no wonder that when the culpability is named— for example, by the suggestion that the statue of a mass murderer should be removed from the grounds of a government building—the response is rage, woundedness, and an intense feeling of grievance in reverse. People who have spent time with young children know this pattern by heart, only because it's easier to recognize from that distance.

Which is another way of saying: What is the purpose of this book? What is the purpose of talking about attempted gestures of reconciliation and the tricky business of reparative writing—the psychic rather than the actual life of power—with an explicitly white supremacist government in power, negotiating for closed borders, mass deportations, and encouraging state and paramilitary violence against people of color? I began writing the essays that became *White Flights* in 2009 and 2010, in the early Obama years, because I felt Americans had no time to lose. Now I find I've written a slow book for fast times. Or maybe—this is even more terrifying—slow times, when the iconography of white terrorism and European fascism has reappeared everywhere at once in the public sphere, like a scattered fungal growth that suddenly spreads and overwhelms the host.

But what is the correct response? This is the largely unarticulated, nonnarrated space in the debate: part of the political struggle against the resurgent forces of white supremacy has to involve some understanding of the reality of whiteness itself. In particular, for those of us placed in the corner or trap of whiteness, the question is this: what could it mean, what is the practice, of being culpable, and how can that self-awareness become—for lack of a better description—a way of life, or making art, and being in the world?

There's another dimension to this question as well, perhaps the most uncomfortable of all: in the past decade writers of color have risen to positions of fame and power in American literary and cultural life, so much so that they could be said to dominate the scene. As I write this, the current poet laureate and the last two winners of the National Book Award and the Pulitzer Prize in Fiction (not to mention the last American novelist to win the Nobel Prize in Literature) are all people of color; *Black Panther* is the top-grossing movie of the year; four of the best-known literary celebrities in the United States are Ta-Nehisi Coates, Claudia Rankine, Roxane Gay, and Chimamanda Adichie. Is it necessary, in this climate, to go back to a previous generation of white writers and literary figures—Marilynne Robinson, Raymond Carver, Annie Dillard, Don DeLillo, Gordon Lish, Richard Ford, even David Foster Wallace—to trace the literary history of the present? To phrase the question in the most painful and obnoxious, but also useful, way: are these writers, and the literary world that produced them, still "relevant"? The obvious answer is yes: the US publishing industry, according to a survey produced by *Publishers Weekly* in 2016, remains 89% white. The vast majority of booksellers, book reviewers, graduate faculty and students in creative writing, and authors published every year are white. Robinson, Carver, Dillard, DeLillo, Lish, Ford, and Wallace are still considered seminal, foundational figures, still taught and read and respected almost universally. But I'm most interested in the zero-sum thinking that prompts the question, as an illustration of what Michael Chabon in 2012 called the "apartheid of consciousness" that constitutes American imaginative life. For a moment I want to stay in this place and consider what white American writers, I often hear, are most afraid of: being forgotten; being sidelined; being passed over. The rawness of these feelings matters, because real questions of power and authority are at stake. It's possible to look at this situation and feel pessimistic, or wildly optimistic, or paranoid, but I'm interested in another option: literature as a project for liberation where everyone is welcome. In *White Flights* I begin with white writers who emerged in the 1970s and 1980s because those were the writers I was supposed to inherit something from: a sensibility, an imaginative legacy, what Gordon Lish once called "the secret history of our life and times." And I did inherit it: as a series of silences, defensive postures, lacunae, conscious and unconscious self-limitations. Understanding and rewriting that racialized position is my way of trying to undo it.

Robert Aitken Roshi, who translates the story of Fugai in *The Mind of Clover*, writes that when you are challenged—confronted with your own culpability—"you have two options: One is to defend and the other is to dance." This sounds unbelievably facile on first reading, at least to me. Like many Zen texts, when read wildly out of context, it's so open-ended as to mean almost anything. On the other hand, sincerity and seriousness are never enough either. Reparative writing, in the way I'm beginning to imagine it, has to do something like what the cook does—using words but also gestures, that is, performance, the realm of the body and material life.

When he won the Booker Prize for *G.* in 1971, John Berger could have refused the award—which came, as he said in his acceptance speech, from the fortune accumulated by the firm of Booker McConnell from exploited labor in the Caribbean. Instead, he said, he would "turn the prize against itself," by using half for an extended study of migrant labor in Europe (which eventually became the *Into Their Labors* trilogy) and giving the other half to the London-based Black Panthers and Black People's Information Centre, which focused on the struggles of migrants from the Caribbean. "It is not a question of guilt or bad conscience," Berger said:

> It certainly is not a question of philanthropy. It is not even, first and foremost, a question of politics. It is a question of my continuing development as a writer: the issue is between me and the culture which has formed me.
>
> Before the slave trade began, before the European de-humanised himself, before he [sic] clenched himself on his own violence, there must have been a moment when black and white approached each other with the amazement of potential equals. The moment passed. And henceforth the world was divided between potential slaves and potential slavemasters. . . .
>
> The novelist is concerned with the interaction between individual and historical destiny. The historical destiny of our time is becoming clear. . . . In their struggle against exploitation and neo-colonialism—but only through and by virtue of the common struggle—it is possible for the descendants of the slave and the slavemaster to approach each other again with the amazed hope of potential equals.
>
> This is why I intend to share the prize with those West Indians in and from the Caribbean who are fighting to put an end to their exploitation.

Once you stop thinking of it as a literary prize, Berger noted, the five thousand pounds awarded with the Booker in 1971 is "extremely small." But there is a difference between extremely small and, as some might say, merely symbolic. In the case of *White Flights*, the money I have to share—the advance on royalties given to me by my publisher—is even smaller. Racing Magpie, a Native-owned artists' collective and gallery in Rapid City, South Dakota, on occupied land that belongs to the Lakota by treaty, will use it to pay rent so their artists can work one month of the year for free. The money is not intended to produce an outcome. It is in no way—this point has to be emphasised—

"reparations." (The land is still occupied; the land is not for sale.) If it's a statement at all, it's one of possibility: the idea of a new kind of writing. I don't assent to Berger's phrase "the amazed hope of potential equals"; or, rather, I like it but can't bring myself to believe in it. I might have struck it and ended the sentence with, ". . . to approach each other again." That sounds like a place for a book to start.

On Seeing, Waking, and Being Woke

# 1

I saw Edward Hopper's *Pennsylvania Coal Town* for the first time in a gallery on Madison Avenue in 1994. I was a freshman in college; I had come into New York on the train for the day, alone. It was February. I had never been in a New York art gallery before, but I had seen reproductions of *Nighthawks*, and I wanted to know more. The room where the paintings were displayed was not large—the size of an ordinary living room. Apart from the gallery attendant behind her desk, I was the only one there.

I loved all the paintings, but when I stopped in front of *Pennsylvania Coal Town*, it seemed to me, in that moment, that I was looking at a perfect work of art. The man, who has been stooped over raking leaves, raises his head to look in the direction of the setting sun. The curvature of his back is a little exaggerated, giving him a feeling of intense, though perhaps accidental, humility. He's raised his head almost in surprise, without expectation, but his gaze is fixed on whatever lies on the other side of the house: on the source of light, of course. You're not supposed to think about what *exactly* he's seeing; his head, his chin, is lifted, looking toward the horizon. The little alley, the side yard between these no-nonsense, matter-of-fact clapboard coal town houses, is flooded with light. It's an image of transfiguration. The accidental quotidian life, illuminated from another angle.

In those days I was thinking almost nonstop about transfiguration by light: or, to use a more familiar term to writers, "epiphany." I was thinking about it but not quite getting it to happen. I wanted my stories to have endings like Joyce's "The Dead," or Raymond Carver's "Cathedral," or Cheever's "Goodbye, My Brother":

> The sea that morning was iridescent and dark. My wife and my sister were swimming—Diana and Helen—and I saw their uncovered heads, black and gold in the dark water. I saw them come out and I saw that they were naked, unshy, beautiful, and full of grace, and I watched the naked women walk out of the sea.

"Seeing . . . establishes our place in the surrounding world," John Berger writes in *Ways of Seeing*. "We explain that world with words, but words can never undo the fact that we are surrounded by it. . . . The explanation . . . never quite fits the sight." That, I thought, was what I was writing for: to reverse the process of analysis and return the reader/viewer to the moment itself.

I was in love with this idea. It's hard to say things like that and still be taken seriously. I was convinced that I cared more about accomplishing this artistic task, this objective, than I did about any human being. I had the convenient fierceness of a nineteen-year-old with no financial obligations whatsoever. But young love is still love. It isn't that emotions get less intense over time; young adults just aren't as adept at concealing them. I had no scar tissue.

One of the pivotal moments in my writing life happened the following fall, when I was in a workshop with the novelist Robert Stone. Bob Stone was not—as he would have admitted himself—a gifted or terribly engaged teacher. He was uncontestably a writer who was paying the bills. But he presented the most formidable example of seriousness, commitment, and gravitas: a writer who had ridden on the bus with the Merry Pranksters, who had lived with Kerouac in a dog food factory in Mexico, who had taken every trip and walked down every dark alley. He said very little to me or anyone in the class about our work, but every word counted. At the end of the semester, almost trembling with emotion, he read us Conrad's famous preface from *The Nigger of the "Narcissus"*:

It is only through complete, unswerving devotion to the perfect blending of form and substance; it is only through an unremitting never-discouraged care for the shape and ring of sentences that an approach can be made to plasticity, to colour, and that the light of magic suggestiveness may be brought to play for an evanescent instant over the commonplace surface of words: of the old, old words, worn thin, defaced by ages of careless usage. The sincere endeavor to accomplish that creative task . . . is the only valid justification for the worker in prose. And if his conscience is clear, his answer to those who in the fulness of a wisdom which looks for immediate profit, demand specifically to be edified, consoled, amused . . . must run thus: —My task which I am trying to achieve is, by the power of the written word to make you hear, to make you feel—it is, before all, to make you see.

I don't remember every student who was in class that day. There was a short, very intense-looking man, with perpetual stubble and shoulder-length black hair, who might have been Israeli; there was a tall woman with short blond hair from the Midwest, who was a senior and already applying to MFA programs; there was a Chinese American woman who sat to my left, whose first name may have been Katherine. As far as I can remember, there were no black students in the class. We sat at an oval seminar table in Lindsay-Chittenden Hall, the dark, drafty battlement of a building on High Street that houses the Yale English department. At that moment, there were Conrad's words, and then, of course, somewhere in our perceptual memory, there was the word "n_____."[1]

What was that word doing there, on that day? By which I don't mean

---

1. I've chosen to reproduce this word within quotations from texts but not within my own text, where it will appear as "n_____." Words and performances of words are never neutral; and "n_____" in particular is never not being performed. (For me this has everything to do with NWA's *Straight Outta Compton*, where I first heard the word used in the idiom of hip hop; that would be another essay in itself.) Suffice it to say this: the word's impact is not diluted or diffused by repetition. So I choose not to repeat it, but rather to indicate its presence.

"how did it arrive there"—it arrived via the title of one of Conrad's lesser-known works, a novella from 1897—but, what *work* was it doing there, what effect did it have? Bob could have chosen to say, "I'm going to read a well-known passage from Joseph Conrad," but that's not what he did, nor anything he probably would have considered doing. Would it have been different, if black students were present?

There's no simple answer to this question. Or even any answer at all. The point is this: at the time, I would never have considered it a question worth asking. I would have considered it an affront to the effort Conrad (and Bob Stone) were making to establish a universal invocation, a "mission statement," for fiction. In 1994 I might even have said, dismissively, something like, "this is mere semantics." I might have pointed out that the word "n_____" meant something very different to Conrad and his contemporaries in the late nineteenth century than it means today. (Which, for what it's worth, is true: Conrad's American publisher, Dodd and Mead, refused to publish the book with its original title, not because the word "n_____" was offensive, but because American readers would never want to read a book that centered on a black person.)

At the time, sitting in that classroom, I would not have appreciated the irony of Conrad's statement that the function of the artist is to enable "seeing," to illuminate the world, juxtaposed with the title of his most famous work, *Heart of Darkness*. Let alone the many obvious aporias within the novella—places where Marlow loses heart, loses his descriptive capacities—or his inability to describe black Africans as having notable human characteristics.

Love, the cliché says, is blind. Or, maybe a better way of putting it: love is selective. What kept me from even thinking to ask the question was my love for Conrad—I had already devoured *Lord Jim*, *Victory*, and *Nostromo*, in addition to *Heart of Darkness*—and for Bob Stone, an impersonal love, a projection of myself, of the artist I imagined I wanted to be. I left class that day in a kind of rapture that had within it more than a tinge of self-righteousness.

Love, which drives us toward literature in the first place, may be the thing that prevents us from achieving it. Because love so often takes the form of magical thinking, or what John Berger calls "mystification." Mystification, he says, "is the process of explaining away what might otherwise be evident." So often, he says, it involves turning away from inconvenient details, glaring absences, or obvious contradictions, toward universal principles, formal symmetries.

It never occurred to me to wonder, as I moved through that room of Hopper's paintings, why nearly all of the people in them were white. Or to wonder, as I gazed at his all-but-deserted urban scenes: where is everyone else?

Flannery O'Connor, who admires this Conrad preface and quotes from it several times in *Mystery and Manners*, also adds a necessary caveat: Conrad's faith is entirely rooted in revelation through sensory detail, but as a Catholic novelist, O'Connor can't stop there. "St. Augustine wrote that the things of the world pour forth from God in a double way," she writes, "intellectually into the minds of the angels and physically into the world of things." Writing fiction, for her, is always preoccupied with the world of things, but also with the mind of angels: a vision she calls "anagogical" (from the Greek *anagoge*, "ascent"), a phrase derived from biblical hermeneutics, where it means, approximately, to discern invisible realities in the visible world.

Anyone familiar with O'Connor's fiction knows that her vision is not, in any conventional sense, uplifting. She doesn't do epiphanies. Acknowledging the spiritual confusion and indecision of her own time as a given, she nonetheless says, "The Christian novelist is distinguished from his pagan colleagues by recognizing sin as sin. . . . Either one is serious about salvation or one is not. And it is well to realize that the maximum amount of seriousness admits the maximum amount of comedy. Only if we are secure in our beliefs can we see the comical side of the universe."

It's possible, even if you have no inherent feeling for O'Connor's theology, to appreciate how her anagogical view of her immediate world—the Jim Crow South of the mid-twentieth century—gives her the language and feeling for comedy to describe the grotesque racism of the time in a way that her white contemporaries or near-contemporaries could not. There are many ways of thinking about "the maximum amount of seriousness" without, necessarily, getting into a contest about who has reached the max. Dogmatic as she was, O'Connor was actually a very eccentric Catholic; her particular view of religious revelation was never meant to qualify as dogma for anyone but herself. John Berger, a very serious Marxist, nonetheless warns in *Ways of Seeing* against a "pseudo-Marxist mystification" of the past, which is as faulty as any other distortion.

What O'Connor is doing is calling attention to the presence of the unseen—not "unseen" in the sense of diaphanous spirits or ghosts, but an unseen structure in the world, one that can be glimpsed, as it were, by looking upward. For her, "the maximum amount of seriousness" is attained when the reader recognizes the structure (that is, the hierarchy) of God, the angels, and the path to redemption as something just as real as the visible world.

There are other structures, too, glimpsable, palpably real, in the visible universe. They are not "extra." The word "n_____," with all its resonances, was as present in that room as any other word. The absence of black or brown faces at the table, or the fact that I have forgotten them, is a visual fact. These things too can be perceived through the senses. To do justice to Conrad's meaning, I can't leave them out.

Which in its own way is a good thing. It means that within the sensory world, not to mention in the books I've read again and again, there are still things that may surprise me. I can go on making art simply by noticing. I can still be transformed by the obvious.


2


"Amazing Grace," the song that informs all generic American notions of epiphanic thinking—even O'Connor's, who both embraced the Protestant concept of grace and savagely mocked it in stories like "A Good Man Is Hard to Find"—was written by the English curate and former slave trader John Newton in 1772. Newton's activity in the slave trade is well documented, including an incident when he was whipped aboard ship for insubordination, then actually himself enslaved and forced to work on a plantation in what is now Sierra Leone.

Neither that experience, nor a near-death experience during a ship-wreck, convinced Newton to leave the trade; he worked as a sailor until he was too physically injured to continue, at the age of thirty. Although "Amazing Grace" is almost universally interpreted as an epiphany about the evils of enslavement, and Newton campaigned for the abolition of the trade later in life, he never described the hymn that way; he wrote it as a meditation on 1 Chronicles 17:16–17, where the prophet Nathan promises David that God will keep his family line intact for all time—a promise Christian theology interprets as fore-telling the birth of Jesus.

What exactly is the quality of sight implied by the intercession of grace? Newton was a Calvinist who believed in predestination, mean-ing that anagogy was not, strictly speaking, accessible to him; in a sense the concept of grace itself is a way of leapfrogging over the dark-ness or occlusion of the Calvinist vision, in which salvation itself is a mystery. In late eighteenth-century England, Newton's use of the first person seemed crass and unsophisticated, and "Amazing Grace" went almost unnoticed until it reappeared forty years later in the United States during the Second Great Awakening. In a way that seems ob-vious if I step back a little from the overfamiliar language of the text, the song's insistence on the singular speaker is its most exaggerated feature: "me," "I," "I," "my," "my," "I," just in the first two verses. This is a text about seeing myself: as Newton emphasized, over and over, the wretchedness and disgrace of the individual sinner, and the gift of grace even when it is not desired, understood, or wanted.

In a way, "Amazing Grace" is not about seeing at all, but about being seen: about the spotlight falling on you, for a distinct moment, not unlike Warhol's fifteen minutes of fame, "the hour I first believed." In church revivals, where "Amazing Grace" plays a prominent part, the spotlight literally falls on the individual sinner making her way up the aisle to the pulpit. It's about the performance of humbling (which should be distinguished from humility) in the presence of God but also the public. This has made the song a useful and disarming tool in nonviolent resistance movements, as Mahalia Jackson used it in the 1960s, but it has also, concurrently, created a psychic model for self-transformation that Americans use in all possible contexts, from discovering a new makeup regime to choosing a health insurance plan: revelation beams down out of the sky, illuminates my present unhappy state, and changes my life inalterably, at that moment. This absolutism of the present, as Charles Baxter writes in "Against Epiphanies," always implies that messages come down to us on Jesus rays through the clouds, complete:

> The veil of appearances is pulled aside and an inner truth is revealed. A moment of radiant vision brings forth the sensation if not the content of meaning. An epiphany, in a traditional religious context, was the showing forth of the divinity of the Christ child. It was, quite literally, an awful moment. Awe governed it.

An epiphany is supposed to be immobilizing *and* transforming. It's supposed to point to the impoverishment or debasement or bad faith of the subject *and* give a direction for the future. This is an inherently faulty idea on any number of levels, but nonetheless an extremely potent one: the belief that change not only shapes the future but also obliterates the past.

Except metaphorically, John Newton did not in fact believe this about his own life. It would have been better if he had not survived to write "Amazing Grace" at all. His epiphany was bought with bodies. Isn't this true of so many of the epiphanies, or redemptive moments, held up as examples in American culture? The cost of this wisdom is extraordinarily high, yet it's supposed to be canceled or written off, like junk bonds or bad debts, when the viewer, or listener, or speaking subject stops paying attention to it.

*Pennsylvania Coal Town*, in its realist transfiguration of the everyday, transferring the formal properties of European art—beginning with the illumination of Christ—onto a man raking leaves in his yard, is all about what Baxter calls the sensation, not the content, of meaning. But an interesting property of formalist works of art is this: their nonformal properties, their "content," doesn't actually disappear because they're not highlighted or beside the point. A Campbell's Tomato Soup can painted by Warhol remains a can of soup, made of tomatoes, corn syrup, iodized salt, commercial-grade steel. The process of mystification, in which a material object, or experience, is flattened, fragmented, stylized, made reproducible, comes at a certain psychic cost.

So put it this way: the kind of seeing I'm interested in is the kind that measures the cost of my perceptions. What am I being asked *not* to see? What kind of seer, or artist, or person am I being asked *not* to be? The awkwardness of the syntax implies the torsion of the thought. It feels "unnatural." Or, you could say, it's a new muscle being tested.

## 3

Here's another moment of seeing-as-unseeing: the closest I've ever been to anagogy, structural or hierarchical insight, as O'Connor describes it. (Or, to use a term closer to my own background, *prajna*, the Buddhist Sanskrit word usually translated as "insight" or "wisdom.") I was driving east across the country, from Oregon to New York, with Sonya, in 1999. Just east of the Kȟe Sapa, where we had been visiting my uncle, on I-80 headed to Minnesota, we passed through Badlands National Park, a sea of desert gullies and buttes in the middle of the prairie, where the last of the Ghost Dances took place before the Wounded Knee massacre in 1890. We had to make it to Ann Arbor the next day; we were moving there so I could start graduate school in creative writing that fall. I had just moved back to the United States after two years teaching in Hong Kong. All the way from Eugene, Sonya and I had been listening to a box set of Studs Terkel radio interviews from the fifties and sixties, and as we passed through the park, she flipped the tape over and put on an interview with James Baldwin, in 1961:

BALDWIN: To be a Negro in this country is really . . . never to be *looked at*. What white people see when they look at you is not visible. What they *do* see when they *do* look at you is what they have invested you with.

You can see in the life of the country, not only in the South, what a terrible price the country has paid for this effort to keep a distance between themselves and black people.

[In Paris] I began to see this country for the first time. If I hadn't gone away, I would never have been able to see it; and if I was unable to see it, I would never have been able to forgive it.

Education demands a certain daring, a certain independence of mind. You have to teach some people to think ... you have to teach them to think about everything. There mustn't be something they can not think about.

Now, there is something in this country, of course, one can not think about—the Negro. . . . Time will prove the connection between the level of the lives we lead and the extraordinary endeavor to avoid black men.

TERKEL: So we don't even know our own names?

BALDWIN: No, we don't. This is the whole point. And I suggest this: that in order to learn your name, you are going to have to learn mine. In a way, the American Negro is *the* key figure in this country; and if you don't face him, you will never face anything.

While I was listening I was behind the wheel, with the white sunlight pouring down on my forearms. We were off the highway, in the Badlands, probably looking for a place to have lunch, or a bathroom. Passing more slowly among the buttes. That was the visible world; but something had changed my way of seeing it. It may be that after two years of living in a mountainside apartment—on a clear day, which was rare, you could see over the coastal mountains all the way to the Chinese border—I was used to seeing presence and absence, the vertiginous experience all expatriates have of alternating homesickness and euphoric happiness, longing and belonging. I had spent the past year reading Madhyamaka philosophy, the Buddhist school that most radically critiques any concept of inherent existence by undermining concepts themselves, and I was ready—in an unmistakably privileged, consequence-free way—to experience not-understanding.

This is what prepared me to hear Baldwin saying that what I thought was the real, or "realism," in the fiction I was writing was another form of fantasy. I was performing what Brecht calls formal realism, which is actually unrealism. This is another uncomfortable truth about actual moments of realization: they tend to arrive only when a person is ready for them. They require preparation, without necessarily knowing what the preparation is for. Americans, who often fetishize ignorance and treat it as synonymous with innocence, have trouble with this idea: it works against the idea of the wretched, debased subject, who receives grace without doing anything to deserve or even imagine it in advance. It's not that I had placed myself in a virtuous or privileged position, that day in the Badlands: just that, accidentally, what I was hearing at that moment resonated with what I had already been thinking and doing.

If I gained anything in that moment of listening to Baldwin's voice, it was an anti-epiphany or even a meta-epiphany; and in this sense it matters intensely that I was *listening* to Baldwin while looking at something else. The formalist faith in seeing, in the transfiguration of the described object, the basis of Conrad's dictum "to make you see," stated most categorically in Joyce's *Stephen Hero* ("First we recognise that the object is *one* integral thing, then we recognise that it is an organised composite structure, a *thing* in fact. . . . Its soul, its whatness, leaps to us from the vestment of its appearance") was something I had to give up, without knowing what new aesthetic I had to replace it.

A Zen master once stayed in an interview with his student until late at night, and then lit a candle so the student could walk back to his room. As the student stepped over the threshold, the master called to him; the student turned around, and the master blew out the candle. That was his enlightenment.

## 4

Without wanting to, without knowing what wanting to would mean, virtually all American children eventually wake up to knowing they are seen: as black, white, brown, "Asian," "Spanish," "Indian." My colleague Piper Kendrix Williams calls the lineage of these stories in African American life "epiphanal blackness." There is also such a thing as epiphanal whiteness, which begins, in the most classic sense, with a blissful state of innocence, an idyll. Wholeness. Solidity. A shelter. A canopy. A nest. A house. The house as a chrysalis, as an extension of the womb. That which is, in other words, natural, whole, appropriate, "fitting." "Like any child, I slid into myself perfectly fitted, as a diver meets her reflection in a pool," Annie Dillard writes in *An American Childhood*:

> Her fingertips enter the fingertips on the water, her wrists slide up her arms. The diver wraps herself in her reflection wholly, sealing it at the toes, and wears it as she climbs rising from the pool, and ever after.

The particular moment of childhood she's describing is the age of ten, where, according to her, a certain kind of reflective consciousness emerges for the first time: "They feel themselves to have just stepped off the boat, just converged with their bodies . . . to lodge in an eerily familiar life already well under way."

When I read this passage, I think of myself swimming—I did a lot of swimming at the age of ten, in my own pool at home, in the lake at summer camp, in the muddy Patuxent River down the bluff from our house in southern Maryland. I remember learning to water-ski that summer on the Patuxent, and the feeling of letting go of the rope, at the end of a run, and sinking slowly on my skis into the water, which was so warm it hardly felt like water at all. I can do this feeling, this easeful kind of prose.

And then I look again at the phrase "Like any child." Dillard is proposing a homology, a perfect identification, of the child and the child's reflection, that is, the way the child is reflected by the world. "The diver wraps herself in her reflection wholly." For a white or white-appearing child, in the United States, the smoothness of this transition makes perfect sense. The reflection I cast is also me. What occurs in nature is an obvious metaphor for what occurs inside me. (In the same passage, Dillard writes, "Consciousness converges with the child as a landing tern touches the outspread feet of its shadow on the sand.")

But this is manifestly not what happens with *any child*. The Supreme Court decision in *Brown v. Board of Education* was partly, but decisively, based on Kenneth and Mamie Clark's famous "doll test" experiments in the 1930s, which showed African American children as young as three choosing to play with white dolls, identifying the white dolls as the ones "most like themselves." This idea threads through American culture in any number of ways—*Imitation of Life, Invisible Man, The Bluest Eye.*

In conventional literary language, to call a text "imaginative writing" or "creative writing," privileging the faculties of creativity or the imagination, is to say that the writer is exempt from having to answer this kind of critique. Annie Dillard is not strictly speaking "wrong" in using the phrase "Like any child," in the sense that she could be legally wrong in saying, *Like any child, I had the right to own a firearm*, or logically wrong in saying, *Like any child, I was a fan of the Boston Red Sox.* When Tolstoy says, at the beginning of *Anna Karenina*, "Happy families are all alike, but each unhappy family is unhappy in its own way," no one accuses him of being an armchair sociologist. There's a special kind of declarative absolute in a work of fiction, an essay, or a poem that takes on a provisional status dependent on its context. When Dillard says "Like any child," she's generalizing, broadening the circle, of her own experience, her subjectivity.

Is it useful, as an observation, to look at that act of generalization, that expansive gesture, and call it "whiteness"? Annie Dillard, someone might say, is not writing *An American Childhood*, or any of her books, in continuous, conscious possession of a white identity. She's writing as a person, an individual, an observing imagination. Like any writer worth paying attention to, she has a highly distinctive, almost immediately identifiable presence on the page. She's best known for the qualities present in this passage: intimate, precise, elaborately metaphorical writing, often in the form of observations of minute objects (as in her essay "The Death of the Moth") and informed by an expansive sense of natural theology, via Emerson and Thoreau. Her writing tends to be fiercely solitary and idiosyncratic. Eudora Welty, in an otherwise flattering review of *Pilgrim at Tinker Creek*, voiced a common critique this way: "Annie Dillard is the only person in her book, substantially the only one in her world; I recall no outside human speech coming to break the long soliloquy of the author. Speaking of the universe very often, she is yet self-surrounded, and, beyond that, book-surrounded. Her own book might have taken in more of human life without losing a bit of the wonder she was after. Might it not have gained more?"

Given these conditions, it might be possible to say that focusing on Annie Dillard's whiteness is beside the point. Dillard is, as Welty puts it politely, antisocial. But *An American Childhood* is not oblivious to race; race, and racism, are palpable in it, from the very point of origin. Dillard's father was a dissatisfied businessman with family money, who loved Dixieland jazz, who once in New York had been friends with a black drummer in a Fifty-Second Street band named Zutty Singleton. When Dillard was a young girl, he abruptly left on a months-long trip on a cabin cruiser from Pittsburgh, hoping to reach New Orleans, "the big and muddy source of it all. . . . In New Orleans men would blow it in the air and beat it underfoot, the music that hustled and snapped." Then, just as abruptly, he gave up and returned to the family. "For all his dreaminess," she writes, "he prized respectability above all."

At around the same moment of life, Dillard is playing with some Irish Catholic kids, "from a steep part of the neighborhood," and one of them tells her, "Go tell your maid she's a nigger":

He repeated it, and I did it, later, when I got home. That night, Mother came into our room after Amy was asleep. She explained, and made sure I understood. She was steely. Where had my regular mother gone? Did she hate me? . . . I was never to use such words, and never to associate with people who did so long as I lived; I was to apologize to Margaret Butler first thing in the morning; and I was to have no further dealings with the Sheehys.

"I had put myself in danger," Dillard writes, "—I felt at the time, for Mother was so enraged—of being put out, tossed out in the cold, where I would go crazy and die like the dog."

Whiteness, in scenes like this in *An American Childhood*, takes on a kind of heaviness, a metonymic weight. To be white in the way the Doak family was white—as benevolent, liberal, somewhat eccentric, nonpracticing Presbyterian aristocrats—was to take on a weight of shame and grief along with noblesse oblige.

When I write these words, "shame and grief," I'm also referring to my own upbringing. I had an early experience of saying the same word, and being punished for it, not at all unlike Dillard's. I lifted this incident more or less straight from life and inserted it in my novel *Your Face in Mine*:

> There's something else I forgot. Or, rather, something else I can't remember. I can't remember what caused me to fight the boy; I was seven, we were at some school summer camp, not in Newton but nearby, he appeared out of nowhere, and like that we were grappling in the dust, the only fight I'd had in my life up to that time. He elbowed me in the shoulder, pushed me over, and walked off; I was blinded, howling. That nigger, I said, when my counselor picked me up, and he put me down, immediately and pinned me against the wall by my shoulders. Don't *ever* say that again, he said. He had greasy shoulder-length black hair, a knobby nose, a Ziggy Stardust T-shirt fraying at the collar. You understand? Say it again and I'll beat the shit out of you myself. I'll fucking *kill* you. You understand?
>
> How is anyone supposed to understand?

The default American term for talking about experiences like these is "white guilt." Usually when a white person is accused of "white

guilt," the assumption is that the guilt is unjustified or misplaced—
*I* didn't own slaves!—and that it is immobilizing, that the white person
is being treated badly (disproportionately) and won't respond because he or she feels too guilty. This has become a standard feature of
conservative orthodoxy, but scorn for the guilty white liberal is by no
means limited to conservatives: I think I first encountered this concept reading a collection of *Doonesbury* cartoons my parents had lying
around the house when I was a child, in which one of Gary Trudeau's
stock characters is bullied by Black Panthers demanding money for
their free breakfast program. The guilty white liberal has become a
standard American feature of comedies about race, too, from *Spanglish*
to *Soul Plane* to Dave Chappelle's comedy routines.

White guilt is a politically useful stereotype, or caricature, because it focuses attention on an imaginary absurdity. Guilt, in the
*Oxford English Dictionary*, means "the fact of having committed a speci-
fied or implied offense or crime." How can a person be declared guilty
of a crime they did not commit? Annie Dillard describes herself as a
child who didn't know what "n_____" meant, and I feel with her, again,
the mysterious injustice of being hated by her own mother for having
used a word in ignorance. Racism, in this context, in a Presbyterian
family, becomes associated with original sin, with predestination—
and thus is wrapped up in that most fundamental American conflict,
the struggle between Calvin and Rousseau, or Jonathan Edwards and
Emerson, between knowing you are damned—a sinner in the hands
of an angry God, or a wretch, as Newton put it in "Amazing Grace"—
and believing you can and will be born again, in innocence, or, better
yet, that you always *were* innocent, that you are one with the fecun-
dity of the landscape.

I come from a family that was Unitarian in practice but Calvinist
in spirit, and it's difficult for me to let go of the idea that racism is
America's original sin. The problem with viewing racism as sin is that
it then becomes subject to epiphanic forgiveness and redemption. It
becomes a personal failing, a transgression, which can (and should)
be confessed, and after which the sinner can return to innocence. Of
course, because racism is not *actually* sin, not actually subject to the

tribunal of the church—that is, because racism can't actually be for-given by Jesus, or his worldly emissaries—the process becomes murky and frustrating, the state of innocence almost never achieved.

White guilt and its far more powerful counterpart, white innocence—as theory, or theology, or fantasy—is hugely destructive as a feature of American public life, and what makes it destructive, in part, is that it's not descriptive or accurate in practice. Guilt doesn't explain why Annie Dillard's father, Frank Doak, befriended Zutty Singleton in New York, or why he temporarily abandoned his family to follow Huck Finn down the river to New Orleans. It doesn't explain the intimate re-lationship between a young white girl and the middle-aged African American woman, Margaret, who cares for her and who has known her since birth. It's an overlay in Dillard's way of thinking about race, but it doesn't describe the *weight* of race, the deep psychic wound, a fun-damental sadness, even grief, that is difficult, or impossible, to articu-late fully.

In his 1917 essay "Mourning and Melancholia," Freud drew a criti-cal distinction between a healthy response to a traumatic loss, in which a person is able to mourn and then move on with life, and mel-ancholia, in which a person returns again and again to the traumatic loss, unable to fully process it. A person trapped in the cycle of mel-ancholia, Freud says, has actually confused the lost object—a person who has died, for example—with a part of his or her own self, with the ego. Once this happens, it's impossible for the melancholic person to transfer that attachment to any other object. The "shadow of the ob-ject," as Freud puts it, exists within oneself, in a kind of limbo, neither fully satisfying as something to be loved or fully *unsatisfying*, as some-thing that needs to be expelled. The worst part of melancholia, then, is the inability even to wish that the lost object would return. The melancholic person, as it were, has "consumed" the object. It has be-come part of that person's psyche. If the object reappears in the out-side world, it is actually intolerable.

This might sound abstruse and speculative if there weren't so many situations and narratives in American racial history that correspond to the same pattern. As Anne Anlin Cheng puts it in *The Melancholy of Race*:

American national idealism has always been caught in this melancholic bind between incorporation and rejection. . . . Like melancholia, racism is hardly ever a clear rejection of the other. . . . Racist institutions in fact often do not want to fully expel the racial other; instead, they wish to maintain that other within existing structures. . . . Segregation and colonialism are internally fraught institutions not because they have eliminated the other but because they need the very thing they hate or fear. . . . *It is this imbricated but denied relationship that forms the basis of white racial melancholia.* [italics mine]

How is it possible to describe the ways American whiteness needs American blackness? It's such a fraught question, so simultaneously obvious and grievous, that it's hard to know where to begin. Enslaved Africans were commodified as labor, as the economic engine that created American capitalism as it is known today; in his recent book *The Half Has Never Been Told*, Edward Baptist documents how the slave trade was intrinsic to the market economy that transformed luxuries into necessities and created patterns of consumption that still exist today. As enslaved people and as free laborers, or servants, African Americans were also intimately intertwined with the lives of many white families, especially (but of course not only) in the South, as personal servants and caregivers, nurses, nannies. African and African American women, throughout the entire history and prehistory of the United States, have been subjected to the sexual needs of white men, which is why so many white and black Americans are actually related, as family.

But there's an even more fundamental way to answer this question: whiteness needs blackness to confirm that it is white. The concept of whiteness, the use of the word "white" to refer to a group of people, dates to the early seventeenth century, and originates alongside the enslavement of Africans for transport to the New World. In Europe the construct of a "white race" was one small part of the larger project of racial classification during the Enlightenment—the scientific division of humans into those who resembled animals and those who were capable, in Kant's terms, of transcendent rationality. Only in a country founded on a model of continuous immigration, assimilation, and geographic expansion did whiteness come fully into its own; before there was an American nation, it was crucially necessary to have a term that connoted solidarity in power, over and above national origin, culture, or language.

To drill down into this history is to conclude that the role of blackness in the formation of the white ego—the shadow of blackness, or nonwhiteness, in the white mind—is much more fundamental, and more complicated, than the words "racism" or "race" imply. When Dillard, as a young girl, performs a racist act toward a black woman she loves and then is chastised for it, she awakens to three separate groups of people in the world: black people, who she can never be; racist whites, who she is in danger of becoming; and nonracist whites, who she is supposed to be. She feels the power of the word, the label, but also the power of judgment. Using a racial word is dangerous and wrong; therefore it must have some special power, even magic, but a magic that is forbidden. Power and goodness are associated with *withholding* the word, with not mentioning or acknowledging race at all. This is a power that is, obviously, reserved only for white people.

Judith Butler has argued for decades that melancholia, the absorption-then-rejection of the object, plays a key role in how power consolidates itself around normative heterosexual identity. In Butler's formulation, heterosexuality emerges only after a primary homosexuality, attraction to the same, is rejected: "Masculinity and femininity," she writes, "emerge as the traces of an ungrieved and ungrievable love." This leads to a "culture of gender melancholy," in which envy, thwarted love, becomes rejection, then subjection, then violence. And the melancholic operation becomes a way of understanding how power of all kinds operates. "Dominant white identity in America operates melancholically," Cheng writes in *The Melancholy of Race*, "as an elaborate identificatory system based on psychical and social consumption-and-denial":

Both racist and white liberal discourses participate in this dynamic, albeit out of different motivations. The racists need to develop elaborate ideologies in order to accommodate their actions with official American ideals, while white liberals need to keep burying the racial others in order to memorialize them. Those who do not see the racial problem or those who call themselves nonideological are the most melancholic of all.

It would be reductive to say that Dillard's isolation, from which she derives so much wonder and joy, can be limited to a diagnosis of racial melancholia. On the other hand, reading the narrative of *An American Childhood* in the stages she carefully lays out, it is all but impossible to ignore the way in which love for, and engagement with, black people is taken up and then discarded, buried, in her early memories.

In one pivotal scene—the most significant moment in the book, in many ways—Dillard makes this departure absolutely explicit:

The Homewood branch of Pittsburgh's Carnegie Library system was in a negro section of town—Homewood. This branch was our nearest library; Mother drove me to it every two weeks for many years, until I could drive myself. I only very rarely saw other white people there. . . . Beside the farthest wall, and under leaded windows set ten feet from the floor, so that no human being could ever see anything from them . . . stood the last and darkest and most obscure of the tall nonfiction stacks: NEGRO HISTORY and NATURAL HISTORY. It was in Natural History, in the cool darkness of a bottom shelf, that I found *The Field Book of Ponds and Streams.* . . .When I checked out *The Field Book of Ponds and Streams* for the second time, I noticed the book's card. It was almost full. There were numbers on both sides. My hearty author and I were not alone in the world, after all. . . . The people of Homewood, some of whom lived in visible poverty, on crowded streets among burned-out houses—they dreamed of ponds and streams. They were saving to buy microscopes. In their bedrooms they fastened plankton nets. But their hopes were even more vain than mine, for I was a child, and anything might happen; they were adults, living in Homewood. . . . I no more expected anyone else on earth to have read a book I had read than I expected someone else to have twirled the same blade of grass. I would never meet those Homewood people who were borrowing *The Field Book of Ponds and Streams*; the people who read my favorite books were invisible or in hiding, underground.

In *The Psychic Life of Power*, Butler writes, "Power not only *acts on* a subject but, in a transitive sense, *enacts* the subject into being." Here, in real time, as it were, that process is taking place. Like so many writers-to-be, the young Annie Dillard enters the library, the "vaulted marble edifice," to find a world that is both limitless and unthreatening, where she can wander freely and at ease. But a sacrifice has to take place first: somehow she has to convince herself that the black people who, like herself, "dreamed of ponds and streams" are actually "invisible or in hiding, underground." Probably every fiction writer who has ever lived has realized she or he prefers the company of imaginary people, living or dead. John Barth, in the last line of his classic story "Lost in the Funhouse," writes of his younger self, "He wishes he had never entered the funhouse. But he has. Then he wishes he were dead. But he's not. Therefore he will construct funhouses for others and be their secret operator—though he would rather be among the lovers for whom funhouses are designed."

But the pact Dillard has made with herself, the pact so many white American writers have made—the pact I made with myself, in my early twenties—is much more profound, and particular, than that: at this moment of artistic awakening, she has sealed off from herself both the secret and the public lives of black people, as a necessary step in achieving her own imaginative selfhood. What remains for her is a kind of detached feeling of troubled guilt and mourning and isolation that is not immediately locatable as a "racial" feeling. But it is one.

# 5

My ancestors, the Cushmans and the Clarks, were settler colonial-ists; they were among the first wave of white pioneers who entered the northern Kȟe Sapa in the 1870s, while the US Army fought a cav-alry war with the Lakota and the Cheyenne, over control of terri-tory that belonged to them by treaty. My great-grandfather Horace Clark went to work in Deadwood at fourteen, after his father was murdered; an entrepreneurial genius, he began buying and selling real estate while still a teenager, and by the 1910s owned much of Deadwood and many properties around it. In a historically accurate HBO version of *Deadwood*, Al Swearengen would be just like him: a Congregationalist teetotaler who raised his family in a neat Victorian house, high up on the hillside and far away from the saloons—who hated smoking, loved picnics in the country and the *Saturday Evening Post*, and ran the school board with an iron first, while still profiting, as landlord, from most of the brothels in town.

My father was named after Horace Clark, and inherited his grand-father's uncanny abilities in math; he participated in the Westinghouse Science Competition, became class valedictorian, and was the second student from South Dakota ever admitted to Yale. Afterward, apart from summers in college, and occasional visits, he never returned. Before his death from cancer in 2013 I never asked him directly how he felt about the Lakota: whether he personally felt a sense of guilt or historical responsibility, or whether he'd ever calculated the value of our family's fortune, the money that paid for his excellent schools, that put him through college, that helped put *me* through college and my brother through law school, or our debt to the original inhabitants of the Kȟe Sapa, from whom the land was forcibly taken. He was an en-vironmental economist whose work involved estimating the value of natural resources for populations over time; if I had asked him, he could have sketched out on a napkin the value of all the gold ever mined out of the Kȟe Sapa, the land sales, the buildings, the gambling revenues, the tourism, the Sturgis Rally. The word "incalculable," more often than not, means "I would rather not calculate." After all, the invasion of the Black Hills happened less than a century and a half ago. The records have been kept.

I'm reluctant to speak for him now. When we visited my family in Lead and Deadwood in the 1980s I heard "the Indians" described with violent, racist contempt: a constant stream of jokes and offhand remarks about drunks, welfare cheats, toothless braves, dirty squaws. The federal government's supposed threat to return the Black Hills to the Sioux was imminent, according to my cousins and great-uncles. When I was five or six we visited a family friend near Lead whose living room had four glass corner cabinets filled with rifles, and who talked constantly about the government coming to take his land. On those visits I never saw a single Native American. They were close by, but out of sight.

It seems obvious to me—though perhaps it wouldn't have to him—that my father left South Dakota not merely to escape its narrow aspirations but to embark on an entirely new kind of life. He became an environmental economist, specializing in forest management; working for the Forest Service in Washington in the 1960s, he met my mother, who at the time had just left politics (she was a legislative aide to Walter Mondale) to start a career in hospital administration. I was born in 1974; I remember the seventies mostly as colors, shapes, music—a kind of hazy yellow sunshine, a smoggy, diffuse, but still palpable light over everything. We lived in Woodley Park, near the National Zoo, a neighborhood of large, handsome houses and imposing trees, a neighborhood often described as "prosperous" and "leafy." Some of my favorite memories are of the days my father would take us downtown on the Metro—then new and gleaming—across the Mall, with its impossibly tall monuments and somber-faced museums, to his office in the Department of Agriculture, a building so big it occupied two city blocks. The hallway that led to his office was so long that to me it seemed to reach a vanishing point and then actually vanish. If he had told me it was the Department of Infinity, I would have believed him.

This was a world that seemed to me grand, solemn, and old, but it was also 1978, '79, '80; my nursery school teachers were unabashed hippies, and my first songs, along with "Puff the Magic Dragon," were

"John Henry," "If I Had a Hammer," and "We Shall Overcome." Every Friday, when I was a few years older, my school's chapel services, in the National Cathedral, were led by Bishop John Thomas Walker, the second black bishop in the Episcopal Church, who spoke often of his friendships with Martin Luther King and Desmond Tutu. In my mind Bishop Walker was a combination of Martin Luther King, Mr. Rogers, and Jesus, in purple silk robes, his baritone echoing through St. Joseph's Chapel, where we sat cross-legged on the stone floor in our turtlenecks and corduroys. The cathedral smelled like balsam candles and incense and the dusty undersides of velvet cushions. We had no black friends in my family—none at all. No neighbors. No business associates of my parents I ever met. But we had an entire pantheon of black heroes. And the rhetoric of the civil rights movement—the pre-1968 civil rights movement—was as close as we came to gospel.

In our stereo cabinet, I found a copy of the Floyd Westerman record *Custer Died for Your Sins*, a popular folk-rock album inspired by Vine Deloria's book of the same name and by the American Indian Movement. (I believe it belonged to my mother.) I loved that album; I played it over and over, alongside *Free to Be You and Me*. At the same time I loved the TV show *The Chisholms*, about a settler family on the Oregon Trail; I loved to put on cowboy boots and gallop around the house to the theme music: Copland's *Appalachian Spring*.

This is the life, the symbolic order, I woke up to: what I associate with home, with comfort and happiness. It's no more or less complicated than that. Children, if they're lucky, believe the world they inhabit is the given world, the way things have always been. Of course the world of my childhood was not something my parents inherited but something they constructed, consciously and unconsciously, out of the conditions and circumstances available to them. To choose the simplest starting place, the actual ground we were standing on: they had both been traumatized—without ever using that word—by the riots in Washington in 1968. My mother remembers vividly returning home to her apartment in Adams Morgan, only to find the streets cordoned off by the National Guard, with smoke and sirens only a few blocks away.

Woodley Park, where they bought a house only a few years later, was not a suburb in the postwar sense; it was a "streetcar suburb," or a "garden suburb," names given to upscale subdivisions developed within city limits (often in an area set apart from the rest of the city by elevation or some physical feature, in this case Rock Creek Park) around the turn of the twentieth century, usually by a single company, with powerful "citizens' associations" and often with restrictive bylaws or covenants prohibiting African American, Jewish, Asian, or other nonwhite residents—in addition to unspoken relationships and practices, in noncovenanted areas, that kept neighborhoods racially "pure." In 1971, when my parents moved in, these covenants and practices had been invalidated by the Fair Housing Act, but Woodley Park was still, at least in my memory, entirely white.

The term "white flight," when used by demographers and political scientists, refers to the abandonment by whites of a downtown area, an urban core, for surrounding communities—garden suburbs, inner-ring postwar suburbs, planned and gated subdivisions, formerly rural "exurbs." To me it has at least three crucial additional meanings. It describes my father's effort to escape the violent and explicitly racist atmosphere of his childhood and both my parents' responses to the riots of the late sixties—which is to say the effort of a generation of white Americans to escape scenes and situations of racialized violence, whether on Native American land, in the South, in cities like Washington and Detroit and Baltimore and Newark. It implies the abandonment of the ideals of integration, coexistence, brotherhood, racial harmony that my parents' generation cherished in their early adulthood. But it also represents a flight *toward* a kind of perverse ideal, represented by the world in which I grew up: an overwhelmingly white world that tried to become colorblind, somehow innocent, but ultimately dissolved and sublimated and assimilated racial self-consciousness and culpability until it was no longer recognizable as itself.

In *Margins of Philosophy* Jacques Derrida describes the Western philosophical tradition as a "process of metaphorization which gets carried away in and of itself. Constitutionally, philosophical culture will always have been an obliterating one." Consider, he says, the way Hegel assumes the movement of the sun—from East to West—to be the obvious metaphor for the movement of the Spirit in the course of history. So obvious that we forget how arbitrary it is; we forget it's a metaphor at all. This, Derrida says, is "white mythology":

> Metaphysics—the white mythology which reassembles and re-flects the culture of the West: the white man takes his own mythol-ogy, Indo-European mythology, his own *logos* . . . for the universal form of that he must still wish to call Reason. . . . Metaphysics has erased within itself the fabulous scene that has produced it, the scene that nevertheless remains active and stirring, inscribed in white ink.

The order of the world I inherited and inhabited, inscribed in white ink on white paper: "an invisible design," Derrida says, "covered over in the palimpsest." Think of the word "fabulous," which contains the root *fabula*, meaning the chronology of events that can be turned into a story but are not yet one. The fabulous scene of whiteness in my fam-ily's history, "active and stirring," the scene of theft and warfare and massacre, of righteousness, of self-erasure, shame, avoidance.

When I say "the Black Hills," I perform the world as my father explained it to me, and as it was explained to him. I say it with the flat, terse, slightly nasal accent of the northern Plains: my father's voice, spacing out the words. I say the place-names of his childhood, the places to which my family belongs. Spearfish. Deadwood Gulch. Sturgis. The Homestake. Harney Peak. Rapid. To say "Khe Sapa," the familiar Lakota name for the same geographical place, enacts some-thing entirely different, as translated by Russell Means, the Lakota leader of the American Indian Movement:

> Our origin story takes a full year to explain, because you have to utilize all four seasons. The sacred Black Hills have two descrip-tions in the Lakotah language. Paha Sapa and Khe Sapa. . . . The

word "Pa-ha" is broken up into two meanings: Pa describes the
mountains emerging from the earth. Paha Sapa all together gives
you a picture and a description of our sacred mountains as seen
from a distance. The Ponderosa Pine gives the illusion of black
from a distance and the mountains emerging from the earth. Paha
Sapa. Therefore, what you see is holy. The words "Kȟe Sapa" also
gives you a description of what the sacred mountains look like
close up, with the white stone cliffs, the meadows and the trees
and the valleys. Therefore, you know it is holy.

When *I* say Kȟe Sapa, instead of "Black Hills," what does that mean?
Is it a self-conscious and ludicrous performance of guilt, a necessary
corrective, an attempt to Indianize myself? Maybe I sound like Kevin
Costner in *Dances with Wolves*, running around the Hollywood version
of a Sioux hunting camp, poking his fingers away from his head and
shouting "Tatonka! Tatonka!" I'm good with that. There are only more
or less awkward ways for me to name it. Which is to say that I don't
know another way to rupture the mythology I was raised in. My great-
grandparents are the indifferent dead; the family fortune is nearly all
spent, the buildings long sold, and the family itself dispersed. What
remains is the mutilated land, and the need of the Lakota, who are
real, present, and organized, to reclaim it. This represents a turn, to
invoke Freud again, away from melancholy and toward actual mourning. The best I can do at the moment is to try to change the words, and
try to convince others to do the same. The register has to be comic
and also deeply serious. Because there is no way, in words, to put it to
rest or do it justice.

# 6

"Getting woke is like being in the Matrix and taking the red pill," one
commenter writes on Urban Dictionary. "You get a sudden realization of what's really going on." Another commenter responds: "'Woke'
means the day a progressive realizes everything they accuse the right

of is actually what they are guilty of." The conversation redirects to "stay woke": "To keep informed of the shitstorm going on around you in times of turmoil and conflict."

I published *Your Face in Mine*—a novel in which a young white man undergoes "racial reassignment surgery" to become black—in August 2014, only a few days after Michael Brown was murdered in Ferguson, Missouri. Something changed, in those few weeks, and the country has never been, will never be, the same. In the era of a new liberation movement, new terms are required; though it's existed as an idiom for years, "woke" seems completely of this moment, simultaneously ironic and in earnest, unquestionably and critically aware that Americans, and white Americans in particular, have narcoleptic tendencies. "Stay woke" can have the tone of a command and an admonition or a reminder or a joke. If the image of epiphany and awakening has to stick around—and let's face it, it isn't going anywhere—it seems to me it belongs in this register. This is the language of courage in the face of fear: where, as Nas once said, sleep is the cousin of death. The nightmare politics of whiteness, hardly ever discussed in my lifetime, are now everywhere and unavoidable and terrible. ("Their distinguishing characteristic, however, is the far-reaching distortion to which the returning material has been subjected as compared with the original," Freud wrote in 1939, describing the return of the repressed.) Explicit whiteness has reentered the realm of struggle, in the language of the administration and its paramilitary supporters. People are dying.

I want to think for a second about what it means "to stay," not as a main verb but as an auxiliary: to stay looking, to stay thinking. In formal linguistic terms, "stay" stays a common iterative/continuative aspect marker in African American English, meaning something like "living in the state of," and may be increasing in popularity in so-called Mainstream American English, as so many elements of AAE have been absorbed and normalized over time. (This also needs to be seen, named, and honored.) To stay, to live in the state of, in the continuous or habitual present, is exactly what the force of an epiphany is supposed to disrupt; which makes "stay woke" sound like an oxymoron. But it isn't: it's more like a vocation. And a form of psychic survival, in an era of metastatic lying. It means, to begin with, never settling for the visual plane alone. "Surely i am able to write poems," Lucille Clifton wrote, late in life, "celebrating grass and how the blue / in the sky can flow green or red":

>     but whenever i begin
>   "the trees wave their knotted branches
>   and . . . "  why
>   is there under that poem always
>   an other poem?

This was also Flannery O'Connor's vocation, which, as her early prayer journal reveals, she struggled to keep alive among her urbane and skeptical classmates at the Iowa Writers' Workshop in 1946–47. "Dear God," she wrote, "please give me as much air as it is not presumptuous to ask for":

> Let me get away dear God from all things thus "natural." Help me to get what is more than natural into my work—help me to love & bear with my work on that account. . . . I would like to be intelligently holy.

I rarely think of myself as a "religious writer," certainly not in the sense O'Connor would have accepted, but in this sense, I absolutely am: having very little confidence in my own powers, I resort to prayer. I need all the help I can get. The second of the four great vows we recite in my Zen school at every practice session is "Delusions are endless. We vow to cut through them all." Which is absurd. But it's an absurdity I want to live with.

# Beautiful Shame
## (or, What We Talk About When We Talk About White Writing)

Like my god Nick, how could this be here without my knowing?

Don DeLillo, *Underworld*

# 1

Here is the voice of a man telling a story. The man is a doctor; the story is about one of his patients, an elderly rancher who along with his wife has barely-survived a terrible car accident. Their names are Henry and Anna Gates. Because of their injuries, they have to recover in separate rooms, and Henry becomes severely depressed, even while knowing Anna is nearby and on the mend. When the doctor, Herb, visits him, Henry insists on telling him about his ranch outside Bend, Oregon, where he's lived with Anna since their marriage in 1927:

"We had a Victrola and some records, Doctor. We'd play the Victrola every night and listen to the records and dance there in the living room. We'd do that every night. Sometimes it'd be snowing outside and the temperature down below zero. The temperature really drops on you up there in January or February. But we'd listen to the records and dance in our stocking feet in the living room until we'd gone through all the records. And then I'd build up the fire and turn out the lights, all but one, and we'd go to bed. Some nights it'd be snowing, and it'd be so still outside you could hear the snow falling. It's true, Doc," he said, "you can do that. Sometimes you can hear the snow falling. If you're quiet and your mind is clear and you're at peace with yourself and all things, you can lay in the dark and hear it snow. You try it sometimes," he said. "You get snow down here once in a while, don't you? You try it sometimes. Anyway, we'd go to the dances every night. And then we'd go to bed under a lot of quilts and sleep warm until morning. When you woke up you could see your breath," he said.

Viewed within a piece of contemporary fiction, the feeling of this passage is one of density, or richness: a density of detail and lived experience (what Walter Benjamin, in his essay "The Storyteller," calls the informational purpose of traditional storytelling, which comes away in layers, like peeling an onion) and maybe a little too much sententiousness. Henry Gates here feels a little too wise and folksy for his own good. On the other hand, who would object to the haunting image of hearing the snow falling, the inner and outer quietness required for that kind of listening? For Herb, the doctor, in the context of a conversation about modern love, it's a moment of historical awe, of embeddedness in the passage of time in the American West—specifically the history of white settlement of the high deserts of Oregon, which required enormous effort, because the land itself was "unyielding," in resource terms, and isolation, because very few settlers wanted to stay there. The richness of Gates's language carries what might be called a spatiotemporal awareness of this moment: the sheer loneliness and strangeness, the perversity and beauty of that way of life, which few descendants of settlers (like me) remember. Or want to.

In this case, it's clear exactly who would object to this passage, in all its dimensions. The story quoted here is Raymond Carver's "Beginners," better known as the first draft of "What We Talk About When We Talk About Love." In "What We Talk About," intensely compressed by Carver's editor, friend, and mentor Gordon Lish, Henry and Anna no longer have names, and their recovery is described by the doctor—now named Mel—in a single, offhand paragraph:

I'd get up to his mouth-hole, you know, and he'd say no, it wasn't the accident exactly but it was because he couldn't see her through his eye-holes. He said that was what was making him feel so bad. Can you imagine? I'm telling you, the man's heart was breaking because he couldn't turn his goddamn head and see his goddamn wife.

What exactly is lost in this gesture of editing? Obviously, the density and richness of Henry Gates's speech, and the governing metaphor (if it was one) of the audibly falling snow. The story has lost the ability to pass out of Herb's (or Mel's) world and into the world of the remote Oregon plains of 1927. Lish's version, on the other hand, is much more sonically and structurally interesting: there's the weird repetition of "holes," making the injured man seem more material and less human, and then, in the next sentence, the odd repetitive construction, "that was what was." And then: "turn his goddamn head" and "see his god-damn wife." The rest of the text of the story (both the first draft and the final) features relatively short and terse paragraphs like this one; Lish's edit removes what was a tonal and linguistic detour and consoli-dates Herb/Mel's account into the overall narrative rhythm. The ef-fect of this kind of composition appears even more clearly in the story "View Finder," also from *What We Talk About When We Talk About Love*, which begins, "A man without hands came to the door to sell me a photograph of my house":

> "How did you lose your hands?" I asked, after he'd said what he wanted.
> "That's another story," he said. "You want this picture of the house or not?"
> "Come on in," I said. "I just made coffee."
> I'd just made some jello, too, but I didn't tell him that.

It's a story phrased almost like a joke without a punchline: a story made of non sequiturs, inhabited by characters who seem (like Beckett's characters) to have had little experience making casual con-versation. When I reread "View Finder"—a story I first read twenty-five years ago—I still feel a sense of giddy satisfaction, almost glee, at the gnomic declarative bravado of these sentences. There's a deeply American sense of strangeness tinged with a faint malice toward the audience, a new artistic invention announcing itself with no supplementary explanation. It's the same spirit you hear in Ornette Coleman's early albums, or Frank Zappa, or Captain Beefheart. I tend to think of the nineties noise-rock band Jesus Lizard, whose singer, David Yow, intoned lines like "He's a nice guy, I like him just fine . . . but he's a mouth breather."

There's a quality in Raymond Carver's early work that is a very American version of the "uncanny," which Freud, using the German equivalent *unheimlich*, "unhomely," describes as something both deeply familiar and troublingly estranged from the familiar, haunting because it is recognizable but somehow altered or doubled. Uncanny or *unheimlich* things have a strange, sometimes hypnotic power over the reader, which she may be at a loss to explain. This quality is often called "Carveresque," but the historical record demonstrates it's largely Lish. There is an agonized letter Carver wrote to Lish on July 8, 1980, begging him to stop production of the edited version of *What We Talk About When We Talk About Love*. "Even though they may be closer to works of art than the original and people be reading them 50 years from now, they're still apt to cause my demise," Carver writes. "I feel I've somehow too far stepped out of bounds, crossed that line." He requests, among other changes, that Henry and Anna Gates be added back into "What We Talk About When We Talk About Love." None of which actually happened; the book was published, as is, and became an enormous success, further cementing Carver's reputation as a master of the short story, an American Chekhov. (It was, however, the beginning of the end of their relationship: not long after this episode, Carver began to refuse Lish's edits, and eventually cut ties with him altogether.)

The Carver-Lish dispute is almost always described as a stylistic, editorial disagreement: which version, which choice, is "better" or "worse"; which edits "serve the story"? Lingering over this kind of questioning is the question of efficacy and worldy success: were Lish's changes the magic formula that made Carver Carver? (Lish thinks so: in a recent interview, he said, "I think the heroising of Carver is nuts. As is the defence. You take any cherished object and show, No, no, that was made by Morty Shmulevitch on a lunch break as a full-time jeweller, it's unacceptable to the fans. Nobody can quite process it, conceive of the case.") Typically the narrative goes something like this: Carver's earlier drafts were baggy, overwritten, conventional, maudlin, sentimental, and Lish bravely cut them, killing Carver's darlings, making them "tight," economical, "haunting," "telegraphic." This language—more or less the language of the fiction-writing workshop, of the lit biz—is itself highly coded and telegraphic. It implies values rarely if ever directly stated. Even Carver himself, in his desperate letter, seems reluctant to say what he means, using vague euphemisms instead: "stepped too far out of bounds, crossed over that line."

When a work of art seems deliberately self-obscuring and opaque, it's always worth asking: what is being hidden, and why? When a process of art making seems consumed with obscuration and secrecy, again: why? In the workshops and in the books I read obsessively as a young writer, editing was described in such violent and intimate terms that it became clear to me—though I never would have said so at the time—that the excised material, the "fat," was metaphorically part of my body, my selfhood, which meant the story was my whole body ("This essay needs to be put on a diet," one of my very first writing teachers said to the class, when I was thirteen). I've struggled with my weight since high school, so I'm particularly attuned to this correlation: you cut away the parts of the story body you're most ashamed of, the parts you want no one to see.

Which leads to another question: what was it about the specificity of Raymond Carver's version of "What We Talk About When We Talk About Love" that hurt so much when Lish cut it away—so much so that it threatened his sobriety, his carefully reconstructed life, his ability ever to write again? Think of Henry Gates as part of Carver's body, as one body substituted for or superimposed over another. Bring in the silence and the almost-imperceptible sound of snow falling (which is also the knowledge that the nearest neighbor is twenty miles away over dirt roads) and the government-sanctioned poverty that can easily be misread as "self-reliance," and you have a specific instance of whiteness made visible—painfully, embarrassingly, even sentimentally visible. Or cut it away, drench it in feedback, lose the name and the story, turn the sufferer into an object with holes for mouth and eyes. More than one kind of violence is at work here.

## 2

Aphasia, the loss of the ability to speak, can range from an everyday annoyance—"what's the word, it's on the tip of my tongue"—to a lifelong disability, most often caused by a stroke or traumatic brain damage. Even today, in the era of PET scans and MRIs, aphasia is poorly understood; in 1956, when the Russian linguist and philologist Roman Jakobson wrote the paper "Two Aspects of Language and Two Types of Aphasic Disturbances," he presented it as a challenge to the Western understanding of language itself. So Jakobson began at the beginning. Language, he says, works on two axes: the horizontal axis is syntagmatic, from the Greek *syntagma*, or "arrangement"; it represents the way speakers arrange words in order to make sentences, each word dependent on its connection to the previous word, each sentence dependent on the previous sentence. This horizontal axis operates on the principle of combination, where the speaker combines words out of a preexisting vocabulary, according to the context and purpose of the utterance. Sometimes these word arrangements are rote and involve very little flexibility, as when I say to my students at the end of class, "See you on Monday," or "Have a good weekend." In other situations, where the context is less obvious—where the speaker feels more pressure to say something original or introduce something new—the pressure to choose individual words can be overwhelming, and there is a whole category of aphasics who break down exactly when they can no longer produce utterances from a fixed context.

The vertical axis, the paradigmatic, represents the entire stock of possible words and expressions in a language, only one of which can be used at a given time. Roland Barthes, applying Jakobson's theory to fashion, described the "garment system" in this way: the paradigmatic axis is all the possible wearable objects in every category (e.g., hats, shoes, skirts, skorts), while the syntagmatic axis is how these objects are combined to make a single ensemble. If language works on the syntagmatic axis as combination, on the paradigmatic axis it operates as selection or association: bringing together words or expressions not in a sequential or syntactic combination but by understanding their underlying meaning and similarity to other related words. In choosing what kind of shirt to wear today, I look at my closet and pick the one that suits the weather, the places I'll be going, my mood, and, unconsciously or consciously, the message this shirt sends to the world; that's the selective process. Based on that selection, I select a pair of pants, and so on, until I look in the mirror and realize my shirt doesn't match my jacket; that's the syntagmatic process.

"Two Aspects of Language" is ostensibly a study of how language breaks down in the pathological sense: or more accurately, pathological in language the breaks sense how down. But Jakobson, like Freud in the *Psychopathology of Everyday Life*, isn't looking for a cure; rather the opposite: what does it mean to start with nonsense rather than sense, to construct a system out of its failures? In this case, what does it mean to use language as an active, conscious process, rather than a sequence of premade utterances—for its own sake, as a verbal art, that is, literature? When you think of these axes in literary terms, Jakobson writes, you're talking about the interdependence of metaphor—selection, substitution, similarity, analogy—and metonymy: combination, association, juxtaposition. Speaking in very broad terms, it's easy to see that poetry works primarily on the vertical axis of metaphor; but it's somewhat less easy to see the opposite:

> Following the path of contiguous relationships, the Realist author metonymically digresses from the plot to the atmosphere and from the characters to the setting in space and time. He is fond

of synecdochic details. In the scene of Anna Karenina's suicide Tolstoj's artistic attention is focused on the heroine's handbag; and in *War and Peace* the synecdoches "hair on the upper lip" and "bare shoulders" are used . . . to stand for the female characters to whom those features belong.

Of course, Jakobson never claims that one of these axes, metonym or metaphor, can work in isolation from the other. That exclusion is the place he started from: the two types of aphasia, which correspond either to an inability to produce words out of a fixed context, or to an inability to put words in order in a sentence. Verbal art in an individual case is a matter of "manipulating these two kinds of connection." A dysfunctional writer is one who can't strike the balance, who has a "similarity disorder." Jakobson refers to a now-forgotten nineteenth-century Russian novelist, Gleb Ivanovich Uspenski, who suffered from "a mental illness involving a speech disorder," and whose work involved such a penchant for synecdoche that according to one critic "the reader is crushed by the multiplicity of detail unloaded on him in a limited verbal space, and is physically unable to grasp the whole, so that the portrait is often lost."

This is the point where Jakobson's assumption that balance always wins—the assumption that aphasia is a disturbance, that a poem or story can't function in aphasic terms—begins to feel, in literary terms, a little naive, as if he didn't want to acknowledge how deeply the modernist literature of his own era was rooted in an antagonistic, even pathological, relation to ordinary language. Gordon Lish's great passion is keeping this antagonism alive. "I don't want to communicate," he said, speaking of his faith in sentences, in a 2015 interview with the scholar David Winters. "I want communion. I want mutuality. I want to enter the being of the other. I want unimprovable illumination." Although Lish has never stayed long in a single institution, and never anchored an MFA program, he has probably had more influence than any other single teacher of fiction in the past forty years, thanks to a series of remarkable seminars he's conducted in exactly the same way, by all accounts, since the 1970s. These seminars are founded on a technique called "consecution," summed up by his longtime student Gary Lutz: "a recursive procedure by which one word pursues itself into its successor by discharging something from deep within itself into what follows." (Or, even more pithily, by another former student, Christine Schutt: "Each sentence is extruded from the previous sentence; look behind when you are writing, not ahead. . . . The sentence that follows is always in response to the sentence that came before.") Lish has always refused to publish his teaching materials, or allow his lectures to be recorded, so the only way to capture his aesthetic is secondhand, as in Lutz's remarkable 2008 lecture, "The Sentence Is a Lonely Place":

> Once the words begin to settle into their circumstance in a sentence and decide to make the most of their predicament, they look around and take notice of their neighbors. They seek out affinities, they adapt to each other, they begin to make adjustments in their appearance to try to blend in with each other better and enhance any resemblance. Pretty soon in the writer's eyes the words in the sentence are all vibrating and destabilizing themselves: no longer solid and immutable, they start to flutter this way and that in playful receptivity, taking into themselves parts of neighboring words, or shedding parts of themselves into the gutter of the page or screen. . . . They begin to take on a similar typographical physique. The phrasing now feels literally all of a piece. The lonely space of the sentence feels colonized. There's a sumptuousness, a roundedness, a dimensionality to what has emerged. . . . The words of the sentence have in fact formed a united community.

The faith Lish professes—and it's clearly a faith—has to do with an immanent quality of words and sentences, a kind of radical non-instrumentalism, which insists on treating words not as dependent on what they refer to but as entirely self-sufficient and beautiful in themselves. A good sentence, for Lish, is one that actually carries with it "the being of the other." Its meaning, literal or figurative, is beside the point. "What the hell is wrong with solipsism?" he says to Winters.

"What I want when I'm in the presence of a writer is that person's soul. The more solipsistic the better." "A story," he's quoted as saying, "must be about what it is about, and continue to be about what it is about."

It's hard to encounter this aspect of Lish's thinking without hearing echoes—even deafening echoes—of Gertrude Stein, who wrote, in her 1926 lecture "Composition as Explanation," "One finds oneself interesting oneself in an equilibration, that of course means words as well as things and distribution as well as between themselves between the words and themselves and the things and themselves, a distribution as distribution. This makes what follows what follows and now there is every reason why there should be an arrangement made." Stein is even now such a radical figure as a prose writer that it's difficult to find a single "follower" of hers in a straightforward sense; like Beckett and Joyce, she is the ne plus ultra of her own particular project and era. She has had an enormous influence in contemporary poetry and avant-garde writing, visual art, performance art, and music, but fiction writers have kept themselves at more of a distance: partly because, as she labored to objectify words and make them artistic material unto themselves, she stopped writing fiction. Her important late works, *The Making of Americans, Three Portraits of Painters, Tender Buttons,* and *The Autobiography of Alice B. Toklas,* are a demonstration of the tautology of her own genius, less and less concerned with other lives or worlds in any recognizable way. In the early part of her career she taught her principles as an intense discipline to writers (Hemingway, most obviously) who found them transforming but also later confining. But Stein, especially in her later career, believed only in herself; Lish is an evangelist, a "coach," in his own words, who believes that tautology and repetition, "torsion" and "the swerve," are not only possible in fiction but necessary.

If I place Stein and Lish in the context of Jakobson's work—which became a fundamental text for literary structuralism and semiotics in the 1960s, and has been widely taught ever since—it's not difficult to see that "consecution," or what Stein calls "distribution," is another name for an extreme, even aphasic preference for synecdochic association as a compositional technique. I could even call it a kind of learned aphasia, a similarity disorder. If that seems like an extreme characterization, consider Ben Marcus's *The Age of Wire and String*, one of the last books Lish published as an editor at Knopf in 1995:

> Intercourse with resuscitated wife for particular number of days, superstitious act designed to insure safe operation of household machinery. Electricity mourns the absence of the energy form (wife) within the household's walls by stalling its flow to the outlets. As such, an improvised friction needs to take the place of electricity, to goad the natural currents back to their proper levels. This is achieved with the dead wife.

At first glance *The Age of Wire and String* reads like the highly descriptive notes taken by a person suffering a permanent state of hallucination or dementia: an obsessively detailed codex of a private, static universe, as in the visual worlds of so-called outsider artists like Henry Darger. Nothing could be further, it would seem, from the world of Lish's earlier authors, with their absorption in the mundane everyday. But viewed from the perspective of sentence composition alone, *The Age of Wire and String* represents Lish's ultimate aspirations: a work of prose that is pure syntax, pure combination, which "communicates" nothing and represents nothing. Many of the writers Lish championed in the 1990s and 2000s seem to operate in a state of permanent and unnamed verbal trauma, much closer to the kind of prose Lish himself has written since the late 1970s, in novels like *Extravaganza*, *Zimzum*, and *Peru*. (In *Peru*, the narrator describes himself as a child murdering another child: "To me it looked like he was interested in just lying there and watching it. Because isn't it interesting to watch it even if it's happening to you? That you're the one who's getting it doesn't make any difference. Actually, if my own personal experience can be counted for anything, that part of it—my opinion is that that part of it is the part of it which just makes you all the more interested in it.")

Here is a point where Lish's self-regard—the thesis, such as it is, that he presents to the world—and his literary record diverge. Over the years he has presented himself as a generalist and a chronicler (*The*

*Secret History of Our Times*) and a champion of humanist vitality, particularly against the more "cerebral" writers of the 1960s and 1970s he
claimed to abhor. As he put it in the foreword to his 1976 *Esquire* anthology, *All Our Secrets Are the Same*:

> My mother, a humanist if ever there was one, swore me to the faith
> that art breaks a trail for science. My father . . . said I'd never get
> rich backing a proposition like that.
>
> But science *did*—the richer for often finding its theory in the
> imagination's intransitive play. I think we will agree on that.
>
> But will we agree that my mother's gospel is losing its prophets?

There's something inherently odd, however, about being a humanist who doesn't believe in communication but rather the immanence
of the word, who wants "to enter the being of the other." One way of
understanding Lish's position would be to say he understands himself
not to be a humanist in the vein of Dewey or Carl Rogers or Habermas
but rather in the vein of Heidegger, who built his philosophy around
the inexpressibility of Being, and in particular the tautological, untranslatable selfhood of works of art situated in their proper context.
But a more likely explanation, given Lish's long-standing reverence
for Harold Bloom, is that Lish sees himself as a literary gnostic, a believer in the secret and inexpressible illumination that resides within
each of us, crusted over by the messy, inconvenient details of our lives,
our families, our relationships; our cultural, ethnic, racial significations; even our sense of "knowledge" as a set of communicable, relevant, important facts. In Bloom's view, gnosticism is key to America's
religious genius: distinctively American faiths, like Mormonism and
evangelical Protestantism, center on the belief in a personal angel,
or personal Jesus, untranslatable and intransitive, which can't be explained by science or mediated by any institutional authority. But
while Bloom views this as an almost catastrophic misreading of the
function of politics—justifying, for example, the religious right's worship of the fetus at the expense of government aid to actual children—

Lish has always seemed unwilling to translate his faith into the public realm. For him, the immanent word remains just as it is.

To me the most interesting way to see Lish is not necessarily the way he sees himself—as an otherworldly mystic, or a defender of a lost humanism overwhelmed by science—but as a highly social thinker whose practice of literary aphasia is also a kind of social aphasia, the deliberate exclusion of a certain kind of reference, observation, or sign. Virtually every writer closely associated with Lish's teaching and editorial style is white—from writers whose heyday was in the 1980s, like Carver and Amy Hempel and Barry Hannah, to writers very much still active and influential today: Schutt, Lutz, Diane Williams, Noy Holland, Sam Lipsyte, Deb Olin Unferth, Ben Marcus. The writers Lish promoted so forcefully at the beginning of their careers—Don DeLillo, Cormac McCarthy, Harold Brodkey, T. C. Boyle—are all white. While the past four decades have seen the emergence of "multicultural literature"—that ambivalent phrase, full of coded resentment—as a significant, even dominant, element of the American literary scene, Lish has operated in a parallel aesthetic universe that deals neither in culture nor multiplicity. You could call this a practice of conscious exclusion, but not in the way it may sound. Whether Lish deliberately avoided working with nonwhite writers is a significant question for his biographers. What concerns me—because I was taught it, and absorbed it, long before I'd ever heard his name—is how his aesthetic so easily translates into a radical practice of shame, rooted in the white body, that makes it so difficult for white writers to recognize race at all.

# 3

"The power and problem of whiteness as a subject of cultural critique lie in the treatment of white racial identity as a uniform cultural construct, a coherent, historically determined ideology of dominance," writes John Hartigan Jr. in his 2005 book *Odd Tribes: Toward a Cultural Analysis of White People.* Instead, he says, speaking as an anthropologist,

it's more accurate to understand whiteness as "a conflicted and heterogeneous social position"—and particularly conflicted in one way:
for almost as long as "white" has been in use as a racial marker for
groups of people, which is to say about as long as the concept of race
has existed at all, there has been a certain discomfort about the group
that populates the lowest end of the white class hierarchy. This group
has a million possible names ("Pineys" in south Jersey; "hillbillies" in
Appalachia; "crackers" in Florida, particularly north Florida and the
panhandle), but the oldest and most potent and animating name is, of
course, "white trash."

The idea of white trash—debased, permanently impoverished, "con-
taminated," disposable, uncivilized, unreliable people who are nonetheless white and similar to other whites, sharing visible whiteness
and therefore a heritage that somehow went wrong—has a long and
chameleonlike role in American history, fitting neatly into abolition-
ist narratives about the degradation of southern culture and eugeni-
cist arguments about the importance of proper breeding to maintain
the purity of the so-called Anglo-Saxon population. According to
the cultural historian Matthew Frye Jacobson, the American concept of whiteness was inherently "fractured" (the differences among
self-perceived white people were more important than their similari-
ties) during much of the nineteenth century, particularly during the
Civil War and Reconstruction. Although, in his reading, whiteness
became more monolithic as a racial identity in the 1910s and 1920s—
the heyday of the Ku Klux Klan and lynchings as mass spectacles;
also the presidency of Woodrow Wilson, an avowed white supremacist who rolled back many of the federal government's desegregation
policies—an anxiety over "good" and "bad" whiteness, often framed
around issues of etiquette and conduct, has persisted in American culture ever since.

The meaning of good or virtuous whiteness became particularly
important, and rigid, during the postwar expansion of the American
economy. The mass migration of the population from farming communities to cities, suburbs, and exurbs, the rise of the middle class
and unionized working class, and the emergence of the information

age all worked together to make white poverty, and its visible markers, more and more remote in the 1950s and '60s. The 1960s, in particular, saw a kind of consolidation of middle-class white identity as broad-minded, educated, cultivated, well spoken and tolerant—think of Walter Cronkite as its avatar—in contrast to the debased poor whites of the South, who screamed curses at black schoolchildren in Little Rock and shot at election workers from the cabs of pickup trucks. These are the "white trash" who curse Gregory Peck's Atticus Finch in *To Kill a Mockingbird* and blast Peter Fonda off his motorcycle at the end of *Easy Rider.*

The most significant vision of white trash from this era, Hartigan writes, is John Boorman's 1972 film version of James Dickey's novel *Deliverance*, in which four suburban, middle-class white guys on a weekend canoe trip in Georgia are attacked by gap-toothed, overalled mountain men who rape one of them (Ned Beatty) in what has to be one of the most horrifying, and bizarrely compelling, scenes ever filmed. One of the four, a weekend survivalist played by Burt Reynolds, manages to kill the rapist with a bow and arrow, drawing them into what appears to be a cat-and-mouse game of murder and retribution as they canoe frantically down the river to safety. *Deliverance* deliberately blurs the line between the civilized and the monstrous Other, the debased state of nature, which appears in the film to have no boundaries, not even heterosexual norms, and the secure state of bourgeois propriety, in which the four men are free to dream of getting "back to nature" but only for a short and protected visit. The film persists as a cultural signifier, Hartigan writes, because it represents a nightmare version of white fantasies—not only about nature but about whiteness itself:

> ... whether the Other is really, threateningly there or if it is a projection of a repressed Self that class, sexual, and racial decorums produce. In this regard, the figure of white trash exists as much in middle-class fears and fantasies as it does in the rural southern hill country or in the northern urban communities of migrant Appalachians. The figure gives dynamic shape to transgressions of

the intangible boundaries and decorums that constitute whiteness as a cultural identity.

This anxiety over what constitutes "appropriate" white behavior, or what qualifies as acceptably white—often called "boundary maintenance" or "boundary policing"—is ubiquitous in American cultural life. The entire genre of reality television, from *The Real World* to *Jersey Shore* to *Survivor* to the sagas of the Kardashians and the Duggards (and, obviously, the Trumps) would not exist without it. Neither, for that matter, would the "Southern Strategy," which dominated Republican politics from the Nixon era until Trump, through his unrepentant and explicit racism, shredded decades' worth of conventional wisdom about what constitutes acceptable white political behavior. Since the 2016 election—propelled by J. D. Vance's *Hillbilly Elegy* and Nancy Isenberg's *White Trash*—the specter of the white underclass, the monolithic Trump voter, opiate-addicted, culturally and geographically isolated, undereducated and heavily armed, has been a constant topic of what passes for American "cultural conversation," invoked once again as a fantasy and an object of virtuous juxtaposition, even while the granular demographic data and sociological research present a much more complicated picture of Trump's support, which came from all sectors of the white population, including many prosperous and presumably virtuous households in upscale suburbs and supposedly liberal cities.

I was raised in a household that embraced white boundary policing with real fervor, particularly during the years in the mid-1980s when we lived in a rural community in southern Maryland, close to Chesapeake Bay. In the tiny private school I attended, I remember joining in when my class mocked my friend Brian, who came from a farming family, for saying "Sa'erday" instead of "Saturday." I loved the pit beef from John's Barbecue; I could eat a dozen blue crabs in one sitting; and I loved the landscape of the Chesapeake and its tributaries; at the same time I mercilessly made fun of rednecks and hicks, with their rattails, gold chains, three-wheelers, and Air Jordans with the tongues hanging out. Rednecks, of course, were racist, and we were not. Rednecks bought flashy boats and gigantic trucks; we bought a secondhand motorboat that hardly ever worked. Rednecks never left Calvert County; we were "really" from somewhere else. My mother often said of her job—she was the CEO of the local community hospital—that it was like providing health care in a third world country. And yet the people I would have described as rednecks were just as obsessed with boundary policing themselves: their word for the boundary was "common." I myself never really understood what was "common" and what wasn't, but there was no question that it meant trashy, poor, inferior. No eleven- or twelve-year-old had invented that idea, just as I had not invented my own forms of ridicule. I had adapted them. Power works that way: it constantly translates itself into new vocabularies, new symbolic orders. People often rediscover it and imagine they invented it.

# 4

What, again, was Gordon Lish doing when he struck the story of Henry and Anna Gates from "What We Talk About When We Talk About Love"? He was erasing, or policing, in part, a gesture toward the particularity of Carver's own whiteness. Carver wasn't white trash, by most definitions, but he was white and poor, raised in Yakima, Washington, by parents from Arkansas; his father worked intermittently at the local sawmill, but was a heavy drinker and barely able to provide for his family, and his mother was deeply depressed and self-sabotaging. Carol Sklenicka writes in *Raymond Carver: A Writer's Life* that as a child young Ray was an indifferent student but a passionate hunter and fisherman, whose first attempts at writing were "outdoor stories" that he tried and failed to sell to magazines.

This kind of specificity—A was born in B to parents C and D—is as far as most normative writers' biographies go, but of course there's much more one could add: not only Carver's parents, but his extended family and much of his community came from Arkansas, for example; his great-grandfather Abram, who died in 1860, was wealthy enough to own slaves, but the family's wealth collapsed after the Civil War, leaving them as sharecroppers and mill hands, until they left Arkansas for the Northwest in 1929. Carver's father, C. R. Carver, was a militant unionist who participated in a long and violent strike at the Biles-Coleman Lumbermill in 1936, and later worked hauling buckets of sand in the construction of the Grand Coulee Dam; throughout his life, according to Sklenicka, he was deeply affected by the memory of the forgotten workers who died there.

Carver was not a novelist, temperamentally, and likely would never have been a writer to construct a large-scale version of his own family history or to use Yakima as a wellspring—like Roth's Newark or Morrison's Lorain, Ohio. His family's experience of poverty and dislocation, and the poverty and dislocation of his own early adulthood, may have made him partly indifferent to individual places and their histories; but as "Beginners" demonstrates, it also made him keenly sensitive to that loss. Which is why it's not surprising that he experienced Lish's editing as what it really was: an aesthetic form of boundary policing, a kind of symbolic violence.

It was also a harbinger, strangely enough, of a new kind of American regional writing. In the late 1970s and through the 1980s, white American fiction—which had been dominated by urban or suburban characters and settings since World War II—experienced a remarkable return to the rural, and to wilderness itself. For the first time since the early twentieth century, it seemed, the most important new names were likely to be writers from rural Washington State, Kentucky, West Virginia, rural Florida, Iowa, Idaho, the oilfields of East Texas, a firehouse in Mississippi, a Masonic lodge in New Hampshire. But unlike other regionalist American literary movements and figures of the past—think Bret Harte, Sarah Orne Jewett, Willa Cather, the Southern Agrarians—this turn toward regional or rural or even wilderness writing didn't emphasize details of setting, speech, or "local color." Quite the opposite: the most visible of these writers, such as Carver, Barry Hannah, Tobias Wolff, Bobbie Ann Mason, Richard Ford, Larry Brown, and Joy Williams, were called "minimalists," or practitioners of "Kmart fiction," in which brand names associated with working-class or lower-middle-class American life essentially substituted for descriptions of landscape or regional particularity (note the Jell-O in "Neighbors"). Some of these writers produced small masterpieces, like Mason's "Shiloh," which uses a remarkable dexterity in point of view to describe a working-class couple in rural Tennessee helplessly feeling their marriage dissolve:

> Leroy takes a lungful of smoke and closes his eyes as Norma Jean's words sink in. He tries to focus on the fact that thirty-five hundred soldiers died on the grounds around him. He can only think of that war as a board game with plastic soldiers. Leroy almost smiles, as he compares the Confederates' daring attack on the Union camps and Virgil Mathis's raid on the bowling alley. General Grant, drunk and furious, shoved the Southerners back to Corinth, where Mabel and Jet Beasley were married years later, when Mabel was still thin and good-looking. The next day, Mabel and Jet visited the battleground, and then Norma Jean was born, and then she married Leroy and they had a baby, which they lost, and now Leroy and Norma Jean are here at the same battleground. Leroy knows he is leaving out a lot. He is leaving out the insides of history. History was always just names and dates to him. It occurs to him that building a house out of logs is similarly empty—too simple. And the real inner workings of a marriage, like most of history, have escaped him. Now he sees that building a log house is the dumbest idea he could have had. It was clumsy of him to think Norma Jean would want a log house. It was a crazy idea. He'll have to think of something else, quickly. He will wad the blueprints into tight balls and fling them into the lake. Then he'll get moving again.

From the perspective of three decades, part of what's so striking about these writers is not only how similar they are to one another—given how different their origins are—but also how similar their work is to that of other, much more cosmopolitan writers who emerged in the same era: Amy Hempel, Deborah Eisenberg, Mary Gaitskill, Bret Easton Ellis, Jay McInerney, Tama Janowitz, Mona Simpson. (Some of these writers—Gaitskill, Eisenberg, McInerney, Ford, Wolff—continued onto very different stylistic paths, as Carver did, which makes their earlier cohesion all the more interesting.) There is astonishingly little difference in tone between "Shiloh," for example, and this passage from the opening of Ellis's *Less Than Zero*:

> From where I'm standing I can see the dog lying by the pool, breathing heavily, asleep, its fur ruffled by the wind. I walk upstairs, past the new maid, who smiles at me and seems to understand who I am, and past my sisters' rooms, which still both look the same, only with different *GQ* cutouts pasted on the wall, and enter my room and see that it hasn't changed. The walls are still white; the records are still in place; the television hasn't been moved; the venetian blinds are still open, just as I had left them. It looks like my mother and the new maid, or maybe the old maid, cleaned out my closet while I was gone. There's a pile of comic books on my desk with a note on top of them that reads, "Do you still want these?"; also a message that Julian called and a card that says "Fuck Christmas" on it. I open it and it says "Let's Fuck Christmas Together" on the inside, an invitation to Blair's Christmas party. I put the card down and notice that it's beginning to get really cold in my room.

Underneath the outward passivity in these texts, there's a tremendous amount of tension: the sentences are under pressure to perform. They're not able to relax into something larger, even into idiomatic speech: the consecution method doesn't permit that. There is grace, but rarely what anyone would call effortless grace. What they are performing is a Morse code, a telegraphic effect: this is how we live, this is what the present entails. And: this is all that the present entails.

In his chapter "The Hidden Injuries of Craft," in *The Program Era: Postwar Fiction and the Rise of Creative Writing*, Mark McGurl describes this kind of writing (his name for it is "lower-middle-class modernism" or simply "minimalism") as driven by an intense experience of shame, intrinsically related to the dynamic of the writing workshop and the university itself. Drawing on the theories of Silvan Tomkins and Eve Sedgwick, he describes shame as "an emotion associated with involuntary subjection to social forces, and [it] marks the inherent priority and superiority of those forces to any given individual." Minimalism, he writes, "has very little to say about emotion . . . because it was engineered as a way . . . of beautifying shame":

> For the postwar student venturing into the hazardous space of the creative writing workshop, the minimalist aestheticization of "Dick-and-Jane prose" is a re-performance . . . of the original acquisition of . . . verbal self control. . . . Its impulse is toward something we could call autopastoral: an aesthetic appreciation of a simpler, slower, more controllable version of oneself. The excisions and understatements that are the hallmark of minimalism . . . can be understood as analogous to the self-protective concealments, like shielding the eyes, triggered before, during, and after the fact of shameful exposure. . . . If the modern world is a world of risk, a "Risk Society," then minimalism is an aesthetic of risk management, a way of being beautifully careful.

In the 1990s I recognized this code, in part, because it corresponded so perfectly with the way I had been taught to live. It was the cool version, figuratively and literally, of the code of whiteness. It elevated the ritual emptiness into something that actually felt like a ritual. It was replicated, particularly in the late 1980s and early '90s, in the emergent ironies of indie rock: bands that seemed to be working off the energy of various states of dementia, from Throwing Muses, Sonic Youth, Big Black, and Jesus Lizard, to Versus, Polvo, Red House Painters, Pavement, and, of course, Nirvana ("I take all the blame / I proceed from shame"). I imagined myself teaching a class on Literatures of the Pacific Northwest that would incorporate grunge music with Carver and Denis Johnson and James Galvin and with films like *Heathers* and *River's Edge* and *Twin Peaks*. My imagined Northwest—literally imagined, as I'd never been there—was stereotypically rain-washed, sullen, and economically depressed, but its most salient feature was working-class white people who spoke a kind of gnomic, sarcastic, Zen-like dissociated English ("I looked over at the side of the road and thought, yeah, that's my leg. I wonder if there's any beer left in that can"). It was not for nothing that *Heathers*'s most infamous line, repeated in a parody of Valley Girl speak, was "What's your damage?" Damage was assumed. Damage was normal, and also rhetorical; it bled into rhetoric itself.

## 5

In highly fraught conversations about race and creative writing—there often seem to be no other kind—the most common protest against foregrounding race or underrepresentation goes like this: when institutions—English departments, anthology editors, prize committees—start selecting writers or texts on the basis of identity, they stop thinking about "merit." There are at least two ways of reading this protest, the most obvious being that it's an intrinsically racist or sexist assumption that any set of writers of color, or women, or writers with disabilities have less merit, less inherent quality, than a parallel set of white writers. (In other words: if an awards panel assumes that what they have been doing in selecting writers for award $X$ is to prioritize merit only, then the lack of writers of color receiving award $X$ must demonstrate that they have less of it.) But it's important to consider another possibility too: this protest is really about a deeply rooted belief in what might be called the white autonomy of the imagination.

The white autonomy of the imagination is essentially a Kantian principle, derived from the *Critique of Judgment*, that assumes only certain people are capable of truly universal, disinterested aesthetic or artistic perception—those who belong to a *sensus communis*, a "community of taste." Drawing on the beginnings of European race science in the eighteenth century, Kant presented the *sensus communis* in strongly racialized terms, arguing that Africans, who clearly resembled animals, could never have the capacity for universal judgment. Generations of scholars (most recently Fred Moten, in *Stolen Life*) have detailed the ways Kant's association of whiteness and universal judgment have filtered down to public concepts of taste and quality in the present. Among fiction writers, white universality, or autonomy, is often presented as a theatrical ambivalence about that classic and useless bit of literary advice: "write what you know." There's a useful caricature of this drama in the otherwise forgettable 2002 movie *Orange County*: Shaun, a young white aspiring writer, can't wait to leave behind his brainless O.C. compadres and begin his artistic life at Stanford; when he discovers that his school guidance counselor has bungled his application, his ne'er-do-well uncle, played by Jack Black, takes him to Palo Alto and helps him break into the admissions office to correct the mistake, with predictably disastrous results (the admissions office, at the end of a long screwball sequence, burns to the ground). Rather than suffer any consequences, Shaun returns to Orange County unscathed; his fabulously wealthy parents decide to donate a new admissions building to Stanford, which gains him admission after all; but he chooses instead to stay in Orange County and turn his superficial and pampered milieu into art—that is, to write what he knows.

Shaun, of course, is free to make a choice, but it isn't really a choice at all: whether he goes to Stanford this year or NYU the next, whether he decides to find himself in Kathmandu or to remain on the scene in Laguna Beach, he's free to make or remake himself as he wishes. If he's able to make the leap into art, through the shaming vehicle of the workshop, he will be acclaimed as an individual, unrepeatable genius. (This is a pattern that has repeated itself, in recent years, in the reception of blockbuster debut novels by young white American men: Benjamin Kunkel's *Indecision*, Chad Harbach's *The Art of Fielding*, Garth Risk Hallberg's *City on Fire*.)

It's necessary, for comparison, to consider how differently this ideological formation works with writers of color, who are almost always encouraged or challenged to believe in an essentialist idea of collective representation, whether they go on to embody it or not. African American, Latinx, Asian American, and Caribbean American writers (to use the current and not entirely helpful categories) all inherit decades of literary debate about the politics of self-representation that white writers almost never see. To be a black writer in America in 2019 is to position oneself, or be positioned, in a debate about blackness and Americanness that extends back to W. E. B. Du Bois, Langston Hughes, Zora Neale Hurston, Sterling Brown, the Black Arts movement, and into the present, in debates about Afro-pessimism and Afro-futurism that invoke the existential terms set down more than a century ago.

Yet it's not enough to say, as has been said many times before, that writers of color carry a burden of self-representation white writers do not. Normativity is not weightlessness. Repressed identity, repressed shame, is itself a burden, reflected in prose that bears the traces of extreme pressure and self-denial. Normativity is itself a kind of facelessness. What the construction of the white autonomy of the imagination misses is that autonomy, which often feels like vacancy, is a state of oppression.

Among contemporary American writers no one has transformed this paradox—what might be called faced facelessness—into an aesthetic problem more fruitfully, more extravagantly, than Gordon Lish's close friend and artistic ally Don DeLillo. (Lish edited DeLillo at *Esquire* in the 1970s, and the two have remained inextricably linked ever since.) "I was an extremely handsome young man," says David Bell, the narrator of DeLillo's first novel, *Americana*. "I had almost the same kind of relationship with my mirror that many of my contemporaries had with their analysts. When I began to wonder who I was, I took the simple step of lathering my face and shaving. It all became so clear, so wonderful. I was blue-eyed David Bell. Obviously my life depended on this fact." Later in the novel, in the voice-over to the film Bell has created of his life, he relates himself—as a DeLillo character always will—to the symbolic order of his time: "The dream of the good life," he writes, "beginning for me as soon as I could read and continuing through the era of the early astronauts, the red carpet welcome on the aircraft carrier as the band played on":

> To achieve an existence almost totally symbolic is less simple than
> mining the buried metals of other countries or sending the pilots

of your squadron to hang their bombs over some illiterate village. And so purity of intention, simplicity and all its harvests, these were with the mightiest of the visionaries. . . . For the rest of us, the true sons of the dream, there was only complexity. The dream made no allowance for the truth beneath the symbols, for the interlinear notes, the presence of something black (and somehow very funny) at the mirror rim of one's awareness.

DeLillo was born in the Bronx in 1936 to Italian immigrant parents, originally from the town of Mongano in the Abruzzi region. His family were working-class and perhaps typical Italian Americans of their era; his grandfather, who lived in the United States for fifty years, never learned English, but his father, who arrived at the age of nine, had forgotten most of his Italian by the time he died. In the late nineteenth and early twentieth centuries, Italian immigrants endured vicious racism and overt discrimination throughout the United States, especially in large cities like New York, Boston, and Chicago; but by the time DeLillo was a child, Italian American identity had begun to permeate American white culture, through musicians and entertainers (Louis Prima, Tony Bennett), through food (spaghetti, pizza), and, perhaps more than any other way, through the sheer charisma of Frank Sinatra, who inspired the slogan "It's Sinatra's world; we just live in it." As Jennifer Guglielmo puts it in *Are Italians White? How Race Is Made in America*, Italian Americans "quickly learned that to be white meant having the ability to avoid many forms of violence and humiliation, and assured preferential access to citizenship, property, satisfying work . . . 'White' was a category into which they were most often placed, and a consciousness they both adopted and rejected."

But even to write of DeLillo in this minimal way, as ethnically marked, feels disingenuous and deflective, because the critical consensus about the kind of writer he is, the entire reading of the culture of fiction to which he belongs, is designed to defeat it. "What is characteristic about DeLillo's books," Frank Lentricchia writes in *Introducing Don DeLillo*, "is their irredeemably heterogeneous nature; they are montages of tones, styles, and voices that have the effect of

yoking together terror and wild humor as the essential tone of contemporary America. . . . It is the sort of mode that marks writers . . .
whose work is a kind of anatomy, an effort to represent their culture
in its totality." Writing in 1991, Lentricchia contrasts DeLillo's ambi-
tion, his apparent desire to "leave home (I don't mean 'transcend' it),
to leave your region, your ethnicity, the idiom you grew up with,"
with the "new regionalism" of Carver, McInerney, Anne Tyler, et al.,
where "the comforts of our stability require a minor, apolitical, domestic fiction of the triumphs and agonies of autonomous private individuals." Daniel Aaron, who founded the Library of America, writes
approvingly of DeLillo: "I think it's worth noting that nothing in his
novels suggests a suppressed 'Italian foundation'; hardly a vibration
betrays an ethnic consciousness." This confidence is even stronger
among critics who see DeLillo as the preeminent postmodern or "systems" novelist, whose work is perfectly in accord with the role of the
artist spelled out in Fredric Jameson's *Postmodernism, or, The Cultural
Logic of Late Capitalism* or, for that matter, Guy Debord's *The Society of
the Spectacle.*

What's so striking about these readings of DeLillo, when assembled
together, is their insistence on inscribing a master narrative—DeLillo
is a writer who has escaped race and locality, who never betrays an
"ethnic consciousness," who has become perfectly national, plural,
"essential"—over a body of work that obsessively picks apart the cer-
tainties those narratives require. DeLillo's best-known narrators exist
in a state of toxic exaltation over their own inherent falseness; his dialogue exists in a state where every word is in quotation marks. His
characters' bumper stickers might as well read *Aphasics R Us.* The
conventional and all-too-easy reading of his work is to describe this
paranoia as a mode of postmodern realism, as if DeLillo is simply re-
porting back on the normative state of the country, which overrates
his ability as a cultural chronicler and underrates his originality. It
would be more accurate to say that DeLillo's characters find themselves projected into symbolic systems they understand and define but
can't control; they are witnesses to history but only barely partici-
pants in it. More than anything else, they are under pressure to per-

form as makers of sentences themselves: each one a miniature student of Lish. Not surprisingly, they're often gripped by a paralyzing, obsessive nostalgia.

Nowhere is this truer than in *Underworld*, DeLillo's longest and most venerated novel. Nick Shay, formerly James Nicholas Costanza, was born and raised in the Bronx, abandoned in childhood by his father, Jimmy, a low-level numbers runner. As a teenager Nick accidentally killed an acquaintance with a shotgun and served more than a year in juvenile detention; as an adult he's moved to Phoenix, married a cheerful all-American woman, and worked his way up the ladder in a multinational waste management corporation. For Nick, waste is the controlling metaphor for all life at the end of the twentieth century, along with that ultimate waste-producing object, the hydrogen bomb; early in the novel, in a quintessential DeLillo moment, he's mesmerized by his former lover Klara Sax's art project: a work of landscape art painted directly on rows of decommissioned B-52 bombers in the Nevada desert.

But if these master images operate as the book's syntagmatic axis, so to speak, endlessly combining and recombining, there is another symbol that works as an unresolvable metaphor: the lost baseball hit by Bobby Thomson of the New York Giants to win the National League Championships at the Polo Grounds in 1951 (the game immortalized by the radio announcer shouting, "The Giants win the pennant! The Giants win the pennant!"). Nick Shay has purchased the ball, or what he believes to be the ball, for reasons he can't entirely understand. "My shame is deep enough," he says, when friends ask him about it. He adds, "I didn't buy the object for the glory and drama attached to it. It's not about Thomson hitting the homer. It's about Branca making the pitch. . . . It's about the mystery of bad luck, the mystery of loss." In fact, the ball functions like any MacGuffin or purloined letter, any narrative object charged with allusions and overdetermined associations: it disrupts the urgency of the sentences, the relentless movement of consecution, that animates DeLillo's earlier novels: *Mao II*, *White Noise*, *The Names*. Whole sections of *Underworld* move back to the Bronx and New York City of the 1950s and '60s and camp out there, in the world of muttered "Abruzzese," embittered nuns, failed chess players, small- and big-time mobsters, sidewalk knife grinders from Campobasso, wisecracking butchers teasing teenaged Nick about his girlfriend, Lenny Bruce performing in the Village.

*Underworld* is, in other words, an Italian American novel just as much as Gish Jen's *Typical American* is a Chinese American novel or Oscar Hijuelos's *The Mambo Kings Play Songs of Love* is a Cuban American novel; it vibrates with an ethnic consciousness that may be suppressed by historical and cultural forces, but is not extinguished and is all the more powerful for being so powerfully repressed, not only in one narrative, but throughout DeLillo's earlier career. Yet to say so surrounds the book, its characters, and DeLillo himself with radiating waves of shame. Here are, to somewhat inappropriately borrow a phrase from David Roediger, the wages of whiteness: *Underworld* as a novel is undermined, made static and sepulchral, by Nick's shamed inability to connect the dots about his past. Its need to perform the paranoid style, the DeLillean version of aphasia, makes its nostalgic sections gossamer thin, like rushes from an unmade movie.

# 6

What would it have been like, at the height of Lish's influence, to write fiction that not only named whiteness explicitly but also played with its various shades—of conscious solidarity, queasy difficulty and shame, obsessive guilt? If that sounds like a hypothetical question, it's because a certain stratum of white American fiction from the past forty years has been kept alive in college courses, or in particular communities, but otherwise held at the margins, well outside the canon. Allan Gurganus's *White People* and Dorothy Allison's *Trash* are both works that deal explicitly with shame, but the shame, the boundary in question, is much more likely to be identified as sexuality first and race a distant second. I have no choice but to read at a diagonal, which is to say an intersection, and to think hard about the afterechoes of a cultural event like *Deliverance*. Race in America has always been sexualized, and its avoidance is also sexualized. "What's wrong with you?"

the narrator's wife asks at the beginning of Gurganus's story "Nativity, Caucasian"; and he answers, "I was born at a bridge party. This explains certain frills and soft spots in my character. I sometimes picture my own genes as so many crustless multicolored canapes spread upon a silver oval tray."

The whiteness of *White People* is the bawdy comedy of a Richmond socialite giving birth on a damask tablecloth ("You couldn't have known, Irma. It was Grandmother Halsey's, 1870 or so. No problem"); it's a missionary couple killed during a coup in Africa; a woman listening to Eleanor Roosevelt compliment her soldier son in 1942 ("Though she acknowledged things graciously, she never started them. In this way, she had become an adult and then a wife and, quite soon after that, a mother"); and, most extraordinarily, in "Reassurance," a dying Union soldier writing to his parents about the nurse caring for him whose name is Walt Whitman. In this sense *White People* is a book about etiquette, exactly as John Hartigan Jr. uses the term in *Odd Tribes*: it's about whiteness as self-perceived virtue, status, idiom, and nuance. It's an unabashedly queer book, "excessive" in every way, reveling in kitschy details and performative turns, and also a highly sober and moral one. In its culminating moment, the novella "Blessed Assurance," an old man confesses the great sin of his life: he once worked as a door-to-door salesman and collector for a funeral insurance company, selling poor black people exploitative policies that could be canceled after a single missed payment:

> "Oh, it you. It the boy back for Assurance." I got squired indoors then. I didn't want this. Into shacks, lean-tos, quonset huts, through the smell of frying fat, toward backrooms of Mom and Pop grocery stores (mostly only Moms present). Through shanties, former stables, leaky bungalows. . . . In I went—ducking under low doorways—in against my better judgment. The nervier farmed-out grandkids and great-grandkids touched my hands ("They *hot*!"). Others trailed me, stroking my new shirt. . . . I let myself be led as kids commented, "Ain't he pink?" For a Whitie, I was sure a shy Whitie. Did they believe I couldn't understand our mother

tongue? Did they think that, even understanding, I wouldn't care how others saw me? —Downtown I'd overheard redneck white men speak loud about some passing black girl of real beauty. "Roy, is that the most purple dress you ever seen in your life, boy? My, but that'd be a fine little purple dress to take home late tonight, hunh, Roy?"

When I first read "Blessed Assurance," not long after *White People* was published, I cringed, inwardly, at the sheer closeness of the narrator's descriptions: the mixture of intimacy and alienness, the skin-crawling self-estrangement he feels at being viewed from inches away, with curiosity, desire, and friendly contempt. (As Melville once put it, "Envy and antipathy, passions irreconcilable in reason, nevertheless in fact may spring conjoined . . . in one birth.") Years later, I think I can say why: at first I imagined Gurganus's narrator to be someone like my own father, a white man of liberal sensibilities born in an unabashedly racist, segregated world, who feels driven—as my father sometimes did—to confess, in measured tones, how he inhabited that world without challenging it; but it was my father speaking with a kind of sensual self-knowledge, and openness, and irony that my actual father was never allowed. In which the narrator closes, having deprived an ancient woman of her policy over a balance of $12.15, "There, I've told you. I'll feel better. Thank you very much."

Dorothy Allison's *Trash* reignites a different narrative of southern whiteness, from the opposite perspective: as the title indicates, it's a book about the dispossessed and despised, and about actual, rather than fantasized, sexual violence. In her introduction to the 2002 edition, Allison writes that she was directly inspired by *The Bluest Eye*: "That book felt like a slap on the back from my mother's hand, as if a trusted, powerful voice were telling me, You know something about incest—something you fear, but had best start figuring out." And indeed the stories in *Trash* have more in common with Alice Walker or Toni Cade Bambara than with Bobbie Ann Mason or other white southern women writers of Allison's generation; they're explicitly autobiographical and discursive, often to "excess," set among feminist activists, small-town lesbians and gay men, rape survivors, and "re-covering," newly educated, self-estranged refugees from extreme pov-erty. This is a milieu in which the smallest of domestic ironies can have catastrophic consequences. In the story "A Lesbian Appetite," the narrator describes her imperfect education in nutrition, and its outcome:

> "Vitamin D," the teacher told us, "is paramount. Deny it to a young child and the brain never develops properly." . . . I imagined my soft brain slipping loosely in its cranial cavity shrunk by a lack of the necessary vitamins. How could I know if it wasn't too late? . . . I became a compulsive consumer of vitamin D. Is it milk? We will drink milk, steal it if we must. . . . If we can't afford cream, then evaporated milk will do. One is as thick as the other. Sweet is expensive, but thick builds muscles in the brain. Feed me milk, feed me cream, feed me what I need to fight them. Twenty years later the doctor sat me down to tell me the secrets of my body. . . . "Milk," he announced, "that's the problem, a mild allergy."

When I read a story like "A Lesbian Appetite," I still struggle with my own inclination to dismiss it as art. I hear, in the back of my mind, the shaming voice of all the critics I've read and internalized who would accuse—have accused—writers like Allison and Walker and Morrison of making a fetish of victimization, of "special pleading," of identity politics or politics at all, self-balkanization, blame ther-apy or simply therapy, misandry, or sappy melodrama. I'm aware, too, that in my mind I'm boundary policing: less willing to give Dorothy Allison, a white woman, the same benefit of the doubt I would give to a writer more conveniently stereotyped as an "other." When I first heard Eminem's violent and misogynistic fantasy rap "Kim," in 1999, I actually said, out loud, before self-correcting my own racism, "he's got no excuse." I still have a built-in vocabulary that allows black and brown writers to be partial, to be placed, situated, contextualized, but expects white writers to be whole and transcendent.

Read that last sentence again: the key word in it is "still." This essay has taken twenty-five years to write because it's taken me that long to describe straight whiteness not as a lack of artifice but as a different level of artifice or, more accurately, drag. (Years ago I heard RuPaul say, in an interview, "Anything above the skin is drag, it doesn't matter who's wearing it.") This is another way of saying that when I read *White People*, in the early 1990s, I thought I had been changed by it; I thought it had shown me something. But I never followed that thought: I was too afraid of being accused of that vaguest and worst of workshop sins, which is so transparently a rejection of the implied threat of queerness: "sentimentality." This fear of the sentimental, the artificial, the performance, or the mask, explains so much of the latent reluctance in American literary culture, and particularly the culture of the workshop—despite the sustained literary activism represented by groups like Cave Canem, the Asian American Writers' Workshop, VONA, and VIDA—to treat nonwhite writers, queer writers, or even women writers as central, default, defining models for the literature of the future. In this formulation, to be marked by an identity, to be vulnerable to being identified, is itself an artifice, something "extra"; the work of the workshop is to strip these vulnerabilities away, or, to use an apocryphal cliché, often incorrectly attributed to Faulkner, "kill your darlings." It's hard, or at least it's always been hard for me, as a straight man, not to believe this of myself: that I am the brave killer, the warrior against clichés (another cliché, courtesy of Martin Amis), the bullshit detector, the voice of reason, the pitiless text reducer and truth seeker. Or, rather, to believe these things without knowing it's an act, as transparently readable as any other.

## 7

White writing is writing under pressure: the pressure to perform while minimizing the risk of shame, to manage language under highly restricted conditions. It normalizes conditions of language restriction that would otherwise appear dysfunctional, even diagnosable; but it does this without describing those conditions as problematic. Instead, it treats them as normative, and often goes so far as to call them "realism." White writing is a covenant, a shared understanding, about what is sayable and what is shameful and not allowed. In the current era, the program era, it's often taught as a doctrine in writing seminars and workshops, which often explicitly or implicitly share a covenant about what is or is not up for discussion. It means to create an illusion and then write as if one's life, as DeLillo says, depends on it.

As a mode of writing, white writing derives much of its power from what might be described as its extreme efficacy: its repeated, demonstrable, sometimes immediate success. Gordon Lish pioneered the practice of simultaneously teaching a writing class and selecting material for publication, radically shortening the distance between apprenticeship and professional success; today MFA students in prestigious programs sometimes get substantial book contracts while still in school, or very shortly afterward. To publish under these conditions, in fierce competition with others, generates a highly noticeable uniformity among first books, and an enormous amount of what might be called magical thinking, a belief in the totemic power of certain combinations of words. Lish, of course, has always explicitly encouraged this kind of thinking.

Which perhaps explains his repeated invocations of secrecy, because secrecy, the belief in something invisible or not apparent, is the essence of magic or sorcery. It's also, as Karen Fields and Barbara Fields write in *Racecraft: The Soul of Inequality in American Life*, an excellent description of the operations of racism. Witchcraft and racism, they argue, both operate according to an "invisible ontology"—a set of beliefs in how things came to be the way they are, in origins, that cannot be demonstrated factually or empirically but remains pragmatically true and actionable. In this way witchcraft and racism retain much of their power—in modern African and Western societies, respectively—precisely because they provide a theodicy, an explanation of why things happen the way they do, why they are the way they are, that science and technology do not. Whether or not we endorse racism ourselves, the Fieldses say, the invisible ontology of racism "underpins a conceptualization of relations between persons as relations between races. . . . It, too, has provided a highly flexible yet deeply authoritative vocabulary in which to conceptualize good and evil, hence also the distribution of good and bad fortune."

The idea of an invisible ontology, an unspoken racial theodicy, forms the basis of so many forms of white etiquette and boundary policing: the efforts white people make not to draw attention to one another's social or economic circumstances, background, advantage or disadvantage, largely (if not entirely) because of their own discomfort with structures of power that are inherently, transparently, unfair. To act politely, in an American context, is to call everybody "sir" or "madam," "Mr." or "Mrs," "ladies" and "gentlemen," terms that originate in European aristocratic circles and are decidedly nonegalitarian. (Imagine Samuel Pepys observing a New York policeman in 2016 who says to a homeless man, "Sir, you'll have to get off this bench.") People who were raised with relatively strict rules of etiquette, like me, like to imagine that etiquette is disinterested and neutral, available to all equally, and in some ways that's true: unlike Chinese family names, or Korean hierarchical verb tenses, or rankings in *Debrett's Peerage*, it's not difficult to learn. In some situations, if delivered with real respect, etiquette can be a way of making unlikely encounters and conversations possible. But American etiquette is never separable from American value judgments; there is no such thing as politeness without an ideal of "polite society." If Americans view etiquette as morality, and morality as "goodness," they are already saying, consciously or not, that goodness involves learning a set of fixed rules for acting disinterested and neutral, while not recognizing that it is much easier for some people to feel disinterested and neutral than others. In this sense, etiquette becomes its own metaphysics, its own magic.

All art operates under restricted conditions, within imposed boundaries and borders, and in conversation with the conventions of its era. But conventions, all too easily, become their own metaphysics: under pressure to succeed, to find a formula that "works," artists reassure one another that what lies outside the border doesn't really matter or even isn't really there. This is what creates the theodicy, the racecraft, of American writing: the belief that because white writers can most easily pretend to possess disinterest, abstraction, and generality, that quality is necessarily and naturally white.

But white writing isn't actually a metaphysics, and doesn't have to be treated as one; it's a mode, an act, that can be learned and un-learned, manipulated, reversed, turned inside out. The story of con-temporary American fiction that's least likely to be mentioned by mainstream critics or scholars is the one in which writers outside whiteness have been using that tradition, those modes, against itself, rewriting the canon rather than separating themselves from it. This is true of Colson Whitehead's remaking of Don DeLillo's glassy detach-ment in *The Intuitionist*, Chang-rae Lee's mimickry of Cheever and Updike in *A Gesture Life* and *Aloft*, Martha Southgate's revision of the prep-school novel with a black protagonist, *The Fall of Rome* (which is itself indebted to Kazuo Ishiguro's virtuosic mirroring of English manners in *The Remains of the Day*). The most insidious and perhaps greatest of all these reversals is Monique Truong's *The Book of Salt*, which springs from a dismissive reference to a Vietnamese cook in Gertrude Stein's *The Autobiography of Alice B. Toklas*. Bình, Truong's narrator, serves as Stein and Toklas's cook in Paris for decades, say-ing very little but seeing everything; he understands Stein's hermetic genius, the fierceness of her privacy, her weakness for elegant surfaces and coded gestures, better than she does herself, and *The Book of Salt* acts as a substitute life, full of the things she was never able to write. In the end, he gives it to her as a gift.

## 8

In August 2014, a few days after Michael Brown was murdered in Ferguson, Missouri, Tobias Wolff published an online essay in the *New Yorker*, "Heart of Whiteness," about rereading letters he'd exchanged with Carver—one of his closest friends—in the 1980s. "I was dis-heartened by what I found there," Wolff writes. "Clumsy, effortful wit. Vulgarity. A racist joke. Sitting there alone, reading my own words, I felt humiliatingly exposed, if only to myself; naked and ashamed."

With this essay, Wolff made explicit what many people in the literary world had known for decades: in Carver's circle of friends and associates, who were almost exclusively white, it was not uncommon to hear racist jokes and racist terminology. "But this was always done with a dusting of irony," Wolff says:

> After a black family bought a house on Ray's block, an unredeemed neighbor complained to him that "a certain element" was taking over, and the word "element" immediately entered our lexicon as an irresistibly sublime piece of swamp-think. So, too, the word "Negro," as if delivered by an out-of-touch white alderman.

"Heart of Whiteness," as the title indicates, is Wolff's attempt to understand the role of race and racism in his life, but like its namesake, the essay is most notable for its omissions. Wolff concedes that he and Carver and their friends weren't as redeemed as they imagined themselves to be; he details his early life in segregated and all-white communities, describing how in a small rural town in Washington State, populated (like Carver's hometown) by immigrants from the South, he "acquired a store of racist expressions of which I was hardly conscious because just about everyone around me spoke this way, and in the entire valley there were no black people to make us choke on the words we used, or at least give us pause." Later, in high school and college, Wolff read Baldwin and Ellison and even participated in the March on Washington in 1963; as a soldier in Vietnam he served alongside black soldiers and attributes his survival to a black commanding officer. But in his adult life, he affirms without quite admitting, he has retreated from the company of people of color: "Even blinkered by alibis we can't blind ourselves entirely to the reality that the jolly mixed-nuts company of friends in television commercials is almost nowhere to be found," he writes. "We know better, and our discomfort with what we know makes us resentful, even angry. We feel it as a kind of accusation."

There's a term for the psychic state Wolff describes here, coined in a 2011 paper (and later a best-selling book) by the sociologist Robin

DiAngelo: "white fragility." White Americans, DiAngelo writes, "live in a social environment that protects and insulates them from race-based stress. This insulated environment . . . builds white expectations for racial comfort while at the same time lowering the ability to tolerate racial stress, leading to . . . a state in which even a minimum amount . . . becomes intolerable, triggering . . . anger, fear, and guilt." The root of this problem isn't just segregation, she says, but the kind of segregation white Americans have experienced over the past four or five decades:

> White people are taught not to feel any loss over the absence of people of color in their lives and in fact, this absence is what defines their schools and neighborhoods as "good"; whites come to understand that a "good school" or "good neighborhood" is coded language for "white." The quality of white space being in large part measured via the absence of people of color (and Blacks in particular) is a profound message indeed, one that is deeply internalized and reinforced daily. . . . Yet, while discourses about what makes a space good are tacitly understood as racially coded, this coding is explicitly denied by whites.

It's worth dwelling for more than a moment on that first sentence: white people are not taught to feel any loss over the absence of people of color in their lives. This is the essential mystery of white American culture in the wake of the civil rights movement: how did it come to reconstitute itself as a separate body, as something autonomous, isolated and deraced, in an era when race seemed to be everywhere? There's no way of understanding this without understanding the congealing powers of shame. To put it in Wolff's terms: Where exactly does the accusation come from? And what are the "self-absolving explanations and narratives" he alludes to, but doesn't describe? These are questions that, to a fiction writer, should have no easy answer or more likely no answer at all; they have to be worked through, or more accurately (in the case of a writer like Wolff, already near the end of his career) they have already been worked through, consciously or not. But Wolff, notably, never mentions his own fiction. "Heart of Whiteness" isn't really an essay about writing; it's part of another species of white American rhetoric, the confession long after the fact, the "reckoning" with race in the form of a footnote: an essay about remembering that really should be about its opposite, about the mechanics of forgetting and erasure.

By the time Raymond Carver died—of lung cancer, in 1988—he had broken the spell of shame and become a different kind of mystic, interested in much more explicit forms of redemption and palpable grace. Though he never wrote in detail about his own upbringing, and never mentioned race or racism explicitly, he became almost obsessed with reconciliation in a less particular sense; his later writings are filled with sacramental gestures, from the offering of bread at the end of "A Small, Good Thing" to the champagne Chekhov drinks on his deathbed in "Errand" to the baptismal river of his poem "When Water Comes Together with Other Water," which ends:

> Would anyone believe it if I said
> I was once 35?
> My heart empty and sere at 35!
> Five more years had to pass
> before it began to flow again.
> I'll take all the time I please this afternoon
> before leaving my place alongside this river.
> It pleases me, loving rivers.
> Loving them all the way back
> to their source.
> Loving everything that increases me.

This poem was written thirty years ago. I reread it now with a sense of amazement that white Americans—and particularly straight white men—are still being taught to write fiction, in workshops, in graduate programs, at conferences, without being asked to take their own bodies, their own subjectivities and limitations, into account. As if what matters is "craft," as if a sentence can ever be fully severed from the person and context that produced it. What would it mean, instead, for a white American writer actually to write according to this premise—to write as if love, rather than shame, were the final standard, that is, non-self-protectively, but rather expansively, out of joy, rather than terror, at an expanding universe? Out of all the formal experiments of the last century and change this may be the one that has never been tried.

I've given up trying to write perfect sentences in the interest of accuracy. My injuries are subtle and slight, compared to nearly every other person on Earth, but I have to mark them. I have wide feet, irritable bowels, bad eyesight, and am perennially thirty pounds overweight. I stand five four and a half in stocking feet. My clothes never fit perfectly, when they fit at all. Which has to stand, metonymically, for all the ways I've never fully inhabited the person, and the writer, I am supposed to be. But this isn't a posture of mourning, or loss, because sentences don't have to end where they begin. They need to be, in the phrasing of the classic Eric Dolphy album, outward bound. Out of their own loneliness and back into the world where they belong.

# White Flights

To flee within your own nation is to create a kind of captivity for
yourself.                                          Eula Biss, "Babylon"


# 1

This is an essay about space, which makes it difficult to know where to
begin. When I write the word "space" on the page, what am I doing?
You could be reading this in a security line at the airport, in the passenger seat of a car on the interstate in Nebraska, in a coffee shop
in Mexico City, by a rain-streaked window in Newark. Am I there,
in your space, with you, or are you here, in my space, with me? Or
are we both in some intermediate space, on the page, or the screen, a
little confused about our materiality but otherwise perfectly content
as long as the words scroll by? Writing and reading is an act of public
communication that is also private and intimate; this paradox seems to
bother exactly no one, but for a second I want to be bothered by it. As
a parent I'm haunted by the sight of my children reading. When they
read they often curl up like cats in small unlikely spaces; when she was
younger Mina especially loved to read in closets, with the door closed,
by flashlight. (Winnicott: "It is a joy to be hidden, but a disaster not to
be found.") When they read they share a private life with people who
are not me. They are elsewhere, in a solitude filled with (and joined
to) other people. Which, when I think about it, seems more and more
like a preparation for, a description of, adult life.

Or to put it another way: reading blurs the line between private and public; it should alter what the word "public" means. To learn to read is to learn to read the world, but also inhabit the world. These abilities often arrive, strangely, at the same moment. A five-year-old girl walks to school on the first day of kindergarten, holding her mother's hand. They arrive at school, but it's the wrong school, even if it's across the street from their church: the girl watches as the woman in charge, "out of the advertisements in *Ebony*," tells her mother to go elsewhere. At the other school, the strange school, her mother picks up a form, and asks one of the other mothers to help her fill it out:

> The woman asks my mother what she means.
> "This form. Would you mind helpin' me fill it out?"
> The woman still seems not to understand.
> "I can't read it. I don't know how to read or write, and I'm askin' you to help me." My mother looks at me, then looks away. I know almost all of her looks, but this one is brand new to me. "Would you help me, then?"
> The woman says Why sure, and suddenly she appears happier, so much more satisfied with everything.

That's it. The story—Edward P. Jones's "The First Day," in *Lost in the City*—leaves the girl there, in the auditorium, the threshold of knowledge and her life to come: "Somewhere in the room a child is crying, a cry that rises above the buzz-talk of so many people. Strewn about the floor are dozens and dozens of pieces of white paper, and people are walking over them without any thought of picking them up." Her mother has no idea what to do; she keeps pulling documents out her purse, not knowing which are necessary to register her daughter. Somehow the proper forms get signed, and almost instantly, a teacher comes to take the girl away, and the mother must surrender her: "She passes through the doors and I can still hear the loud sounds of her shoes. And even when the teacher turns me toward the classrooms and I hear what must be the singing and talking of all the children in the world, I can still hear my mother's footsteps above it all."

Critics of realist fiction would call this moment an example of sentimental, manipulative falseness, and they might not be wrong. All the details of the girl's sensory world—her barrettes, her new underwear and slip and Mary Janes—draw readers toward an image of a wide-eyed child swallowed by an unloving, indifferent vastness. But there's something else happening in that space, not as noticeable, but more important: the girl is learning to read the cues of the adults around her, the hierarchy of soft power that shuts her mother, but not her, out. What her mother sees as undifferentiated she is already learning to decode. The story does almost nothing to draw attention to this kind of structural insight (I would call that inattention a defect, though Jones would probably disagree), but it exists, regardless. This girl's eye has a life of its own.

In *The Poetics of Space*, speaking of the kinds of dwellings that appear in fairy tales, Gaston Bachelard writes, "One might say that these houses in miniature are false objects that possess a true psychological objectivity." Spaces in fiction, like houses in a bean or a shoe, are "false" spaces; they exist only provisionally, on the page, in the privacy of the reader's mind; but they are also public, meant to be inhabited, not one reader at a time, but by any reader all the time. They invite close attention, not least because, as Bachelard says, they say something about the real spaces readers inhabit. And it may be that empty spaces have the most to say. In a country shaped by colonization, enslavement, and racialized capitalism—practices of exclusion and exploitation very much alive in the early twenty-first century—few places remain empty by accident. Someone was removed; someone was prevented from entering; someone is here but out of sight. There are implicit and explicit barriers that govern the visible world, and these lines are themselves a design, or authorship, that deserve to be read. It's possible to lay a particular story atop a particular map and see the lines intersect: how the storyteller's imagination mirrors the visible world and—more often than not—mimics it. Hence the plural meaning of "White Flights." The map I want to follow tracks the white American imagination outward, away from people of color, into emptied spaces that seem designed to resist close inspection.

Maybe thinking of fiction this way is unbearable. I stand by it, in solidarity with the girl seeing things she isn't meant to see. Think of the space in this story as a network, or a prism: the girl, myself, the mother, the helpful and condescending ladies, Edward P. Jones, and you, whoever you are, reading these words. (I'm trying to do what the poet Erica Hunt suggests, in her essay "All about You": I want to place "you in a genealogy of the visible, the legible, trying to find a way into the 'I,' that Cartesian empire, and 'we' the possibility of being one of the tribe of humanity.") Inside the story, our faces turn toward one another, neither fully available nor exposed, nor private and alone. At that moment we are all seen. We have that in common.

# 2

There's a moment toward the end of Marilynne Robinson's *Housekeeping* when the young narrator, Ruth, whose mother has recently committed suicide, finds herself alone, exploring an abandoned homestead at the edge of a lake while her eccentric and unreliable aunt Sylvie has wandered off, perhaps never to be seen again. Ruth imagines the homesteaders who once lived there and the ghosts of children who died there, until gradually she begins to feel herself among them, more ghostly than real. "Loneliness is an absolute discovery," she says:

> When one looks from inside at a lighted window, one sees the image of oneself in a lighted room. . . . The deception is obvious, but flattering all the same. When one looks from the darkness into the light, however, one sees all the difference between here and there, this and that. Perhaps all unsheltered people are angry in their hearts, and would like to break the roof, spine, and ribs, and smash the windows and flood the floor and spindle the curtains and bloat the couch.

A few moments later she gives in to this feeling of abandonment and lies down on the grass: "Sylvie is nowhere, and sometime it will be dark. . . . Let them come unhouse me of this flesh, and pry this house apart."

It's a thrilling scene, especially phrased in Robinson's quasi-biblical English ("unhouse me of this flesh"); it feels like the announcement of a kind of secular scripture, as indeed, at the time, it kind of was. Like Alice Munro, Mary Gordon, Annie Dillard, Anne Tyler, Joyce Carol Oates, Alice Walker, and Toni Morrison, in *Housekeeping* Marilynne Robinson was trying to create a new language for representing a woman's interior life, with an unmistakable, if ambivalent, relationship to second-wave feminism. I was born in 1974, so to me this is the language of my mother's generation—something I didn't appreciate until I was an adult and had read enough of these writers, and understood enough of the cultural context, to be able to draw the connections between them and other artists and thinkers of the time.

And yet there is something radically different going on in *Housekeeping*—something that explains why this novel is much more widely read today, and seems to belong more to the present, than do the 1970s or early 1980s writings of most of the other authors I've just mentioned. Ruth is not only psychologically but literally alone, in a landscape she assumes is empty of other people. The novel's title is deeply, desperately ironic; she is "unsheltered" and "unhoused," and to her this is an absolute discovery, a metaphysical state. She has looked into the abyss, and rather than retreating, has become the abyss, has become abject and abysmal, as a defining experience.

In its evocation of radical isolation *Housekeeping* resembles the large number of American novels by white writers of the 1970s and beyond in which one person, or a small group of people, is silhouetted against a vast and unforgiving landscape. *Suttree*, *Blood Meridian*, and *All the Pretty Horses*; *The Shipping News* and "Brokeback Mountain"; *Outerbridge Reach*; *Legends of the Fall*; *A River Runs Through It*; *Cold Mountain*; *Plainsong*; *Jesus' Son*; *A Thousand Acres*—it's remarkable, to say the least, that in an era when the white American population clustered more and more around urban metropolitan zones, fleeing small towns and depopulating entire states—South Dakota, Iowa, Nebraska, Kansas—so much of the white American literary imagination became consumed with a need to escape populated areas and discover human solitude juxtaposed against what Americans think of, vaguely, as "nature."

What accounts for this turn, or return, to the natural world and isolation within a landscape, as a subject and setting for contemporary fiction? Robinson herself, directly and indirectly, has been trying to answer this question for years. In an essay about the origins of *Housekeeping*, "When I Was a Child I Read Books," she writes that the most important companions of her own childhood in Sandpoint and Coeur d'Alene, Idaho, were works of European history and classical literature. "Relevance was precisely not an issue for me," she says. "I think it was in fact peculiarly Western to feel no tie of particularity to any single past or history, to experience that much underrated thing called deracination, the meditative, free appreciation of whatever comes under one's eye."

The *OED* sources "deracination" in the French *déraciner*, meaning "to pluck or tear up by the roots, eradicate, exterminate"; secondarily, "uprooted from one's national or social environment." In a British context *déraciné* means "rootless" in the pejorative sense: a pretender, an arriviste, a fraud. But in Robinson's hands, it turns into an ideal. In modern culture, she writes, loneliness is seen as a pathology: "By some sad evolution . . . people who are less shaped and constrained by society are assumed to be disabled and dangerous." In another instance, she lingers on how the word "identity" has changed from Whitman's time to the present: "Rather than acknowledging the miraculous privilege of existence as a conscious being," she writes, "identity seems now to imply membership in a group, through ethnicity or affinity or religion or otherwise . . . and this is taken to be a good thing."

There are at least two ways of reading Robinson's skepticism about society, both informed by her embrace of Calvinism, and both applicable to American attitudes about nature more generally. The milder tradition argues, with Thoreau, that being alone in wild places awakens a person's ability to embrace society and other people as skeptical, autonomous, liberal democratic subjects. But it's just as easy to read into Robinson's generalities a validation of the other American attitude about nature, which can also be found in Thoreau: that the wilderness is a refuge against the inevitable tyranny of the state; that living in society is a perversion and a distortion of the individual's miraculous consciousness; that the true heroes are the loners and the outcasts. These are divisions in a debate that has raged for decades, among writers, philosophers, environmentalists, and ecologists; but by drawing attention to the word "deracination," Robinson illustrates an important way in which the very terms of the debate are fictive, even fantastic. Deracination, in her description, assumes that in certain states of being, like finding oneself in an extremely isolated or remote place, a person's racial identity falls away, and that person feels "no tie of particularity to any single past or history." It's simply not possible for that to happen, except through an act of imaginative self-blinding, to a white descendant of Europeans anywhere in the United States, and particularly not in the upper Plains or Rocky Mountain West. Robinson, like my father, was the grandchild of settlers who occupied lands taken by force. Sandpoint, Idaho, her hometown, was the summer fishing ground of Salish tribes, the Kalispel and Kootenai, who remained active in the area until at least 1930, thirteen years before she was born; the Kootenai Indian reservation is forty miles north of Sandpoint on US Highway 2. It couldn't have escaped Robinson's attention that she was growing up in an area inextricably defined by one particular history, that the emptiness she observed was largely man-made. It couldn't have escaped her attention, at some level, but in *Housekeeping* it does escape her language, or her ability to articulate experience. Or does it?

> Perhaps all unsheltered people are angry in their hearts, and would like to break the roof, spine, and ribs, and smash the windows and flood the floor and spindle the curtains and bloat the couch.

One memory of the West passed down through my family for generations comes from my great-great-grandmother on my mother's side, who as a young girl (so the story goes) survived an "Indian raid" on the settlement of Deer Lodge, Montana, where her father was a missionary. There was a small window in the door of her house, or cabin, and during the raid an Indian face appeared at the window, staring at her. That is the sum total of the memory. It reminds me of the scene in *Little House on the Prairie*—a source of cultural memory for untold millions of American children—where Laura Ingalls, whose family is living illegally in treaty territory in Kansas, sees Native Americans up close for the first and last time, when two warriors (perhaps Osage) come into her log cabin, demand food from her mother, and then leave:

> When Laura peeked out from behind the slab again, both Indians were looking straight at her. Her heart jumped into her throat and choked her with its pounding. Two black eyes glittered down into her eyes. The Indian did not move, not one muscle of his face moved. Only his eyes shone and sparkled at her. Laura didn't move, either. She didn't even breathe.
>
> The Indian made two short, harsh sounds in his throat. The other Indian made one sound, like "Hah!" Laura hid her eyes behind the slab again.

It seems specious, and disingenuous, to look for specific allusions in a passage that Marilynne Robinson obviously intends to be metaphorical, even metaphysical: a passage that she would say unashamedly is about the soul. But in a way that's precisely the point: the land had to be cleared, imaginatively emptied, before this soul-work could take place. In this sense the language of *Housekeeping* itself does the work of deracination, erasing one existence in order to present another one in the proper proportion, at the proper scale.

Because deracination is work: it doesn't happen by itself. Like so many of the things Americans think of as "natural" ("simple," "organic"), it has to be carefully contrived, protected, set apart, and paid for. Consider a more familiar, aspirational term, "colorblindness" (when used as a social metaphor, not a physical condition): colorblindness is something I have to impose on myself artificially, through my own efforts. It doesn't exist by itself; in fact it's impossible to achieve, except as a figure of speech. What it reveals, if it reveals anything, is a thwarted desire for an unachievable purity—purity of intention translated into purity of a visual field. And because it's unachievable, deracination is always anxious work, always looking over its own shoulder.

Robinson took a kind of twenty-four-year-long artistic fast after publishing *Housekeeping*; out of that silence came a trilogy of novels set in a tiny Iowa town in the 1950s, *Gilead*, *Home*, and *Lila*. If *Housekeeping* seems haunted by a seemingly empty landscape, these novels are framed by an actual history: Gilead was founded by abolitionists in the 1850s for the purpose of concealing runaway slaves and battling slave-state militias in Kansas. The narrator of *Gilead*, John Ames, an elderly Congregationalist minister, keenly remembers his grandfather, a visionary who rode with John Brown; he himself once handled his grandfather's bloody shirt and pistol. But in Gilead itself that history has long since disappeared. The town once had black residents, but they disappeared in the indistinct past, sometime after the town's only black church suffered a "small fire."

This absence of racial justice—as a source of spiritual energy, and as a present fact—gives *Gilead* and *Home* their intertwined dramatic structure. In *Gilead*, Jack, the son of John Ames's best friend, the Reverend Boughton, returns to town suddenly, and inexplicably, after leaving in disgrace twenty years before. In the novel's last few pages Jack reveals that during his time away he fell in love with, married, and had a son with a black woman, and he's returned to his hometown without them, because he's not sure they'll be safe, let alone happy, in Gilead. "I can't give you any assurances . . . one way or the other," John Ames says, when Jack asks him, directly, what the Reverend Boughton will say. "You'll have to let me reflect on it." A little later, when Jack says, "And it has been many years since there was a Negro church," John Ames again reflects. "Of course there wasn't much I could say to that."

The whole trilogy depends on how the reader interprets these pauses for reflection. Or, rather, whether the reader is meant to reflect on them at all. Gilead itself, very much like the fictional version of Sandpoint in *Housekeeping*, is a series of unpeopled vistas; even Ames's and Boughton's own congregations flicker on the margins, delivering casseroles to their doorsteps or dying in the space of a paragraph. The overwhelming pull of the narrative is toward moments of meditative stasis, an active helplessness in solitude. In *Home*, narrated in the third person from Jack's sister Glory's perspective, Jack lingers for weeks in his father's house without mentioning his wife or his child. When the three Boughtons watch coverage of police brutality against civil rights demonstrators in Alabama, Jack's father dismisses the demonstrators as lawbreakers and troublemakers, while Jack stays silent. Only after Jack has left Gilead in despair—again, in the final few pages of the novel—do his wife, Della, and their son, Robert, finally arrive, looking for him. They've driven into Iowa from Missouri and have to be back across the state line the same day; along the way are "sundown towns" that threaten violence against black people seen in public after dark. Robert gets out of the car just to "lay his hand on the trunk of the oak tree" in the front yard. It's a shattering moment, and in it, Glory feels her perspective shifted:

> Maybe this Robert will come back someday. Young men are rarely cautious. What of Jack will there be in him? And I will be almost old. . . . I will invite him onto the porch and he will reply with something civil and Southern, "Yes, ma'am, I might could," or whatever it is they say. And he will be very kind to me. . . . He will be curious about the place, though his curiosity will not override his good manners. He will talk to me a little while, too shy to tell me why he has come, and then he will thank me and leave.

A spatial reading of *Home* raises one obvious, overwhelming question: Why, even in the fantasy, the redeemed, transfigured version of Gilead, does Robert have to leave? Why can't Glory imagine him inheriting the house, which he has as much right to as any other grandchild of the family? Or, to put it another way: why does Glory recognize so intuitively that Robert is a figure of inspiration, even a message from God, but not actually a member of her human family, not someone she can address or engage directly? That cleaving together would make narrative closure impossible, at this point, but it might also collapse the separateness that makes revelation possible. "In every important way we are such secrets from one another," John Ames says in *Gilead*. "Those around us have also fallen heir to the same customs. . . . But all that really just allows us to coexist with the inviolable, untraversable, and utterly vast spaces between us."

Robinson repeated this point in a 2015 conversation with President Obama, published in the *New York Review of Books*: "I believe that people are images of God. . . . It's not any loyalty or tradition or anything else; it's being human that enlists the respect, the love of God being implied in it. . . . I think that we have created this incredibly inappropriate sort of in-group mentality when we really are from every end of the earth, just dealing with each other in good faith. And that's just a terrible darkening of the national outlook." Does this mean Glory has failed in her imagination by not recognizing Robert's full (godly) humanness, or has she actually maintained the necessary godly distance from her own nephew that allows her to practice good faith? It's hard not to feel Robinson's own ambivalence on this point. Gilead may be a fallen place, judged by the visions of Ames's grandfather, but it's a beautiful, necessary ruin: the only place, the only radically restrictive spatial poetics, where an encounter like this could happen. "These ugly facts complicate the beauty of 'Home,'" A. O. Scott wrote in his *New York Times* review, referring to Gilead's racial realities, "but the way Robinson embeds them in the novel is part of what makes it so beautiful. It is unsparing in its acknowledgment of sin and unstinting in its belief in the possibility of grace."

Deracination, then, is not exactly a matter of the facts; it's a matter of perspective. Fiction, at least in the way I'm advocating for it, is the art of perspective, the art of choosing what and what not (whom and whom not) to see. Without imagining it as a place to live, a white reader can take Gilead as a spiritual home. Because Robinson's theology is literally one of perspective—"the inviolable, untraversable, and utterly vast spaces between us"—her narrative has a moving, sacramental quality, which inserts a certain distance between two facts:

Iowa has a history of racial progressivism.

Gilead is a town where black people have disappeared.

This distance makes it possible almost to forget that nothing whatsoever has changed for Jack, Della, and Robert. To say that this is actually
a tragic story, and a depressing one, would be half-right, but somehow—
for many readers, if not for Robinson herself—the story always rights itself upward, in the direction of beauty and grace. Having kept the space
empty feels like its own achievement.

## 3

In a country that today is about as far from racially homogeneous as
it is possible to be, it's fascinating, and deeply telling, that the impossible desire for deracination still has such a deep hold on the white
American psyche. A friend of our family once told my wife, in complete seriousness, that she chose to raise her children in a virtually all-
white community in the Pacific Northwest—instead of the East Coast
metropolitan area where she grew up—because she felt they would be
less racist if they weren't surrounded by black people, and thus didn't
constantly feel a sense of what she called "racial tension."

Here is where the trope of deracination in American literature—
which goes back almost to the invention of race itself—and the fantastic ideal of colorblindness as a social practice may actually converge:
in real estate, which is to say in the spaces Americans buy, or rent, or
choose to occupy, or imagine themselves occupying. As any reader
of Marilynne Robinson, or any real estate agent, knows intimately, a
house is not just a house: it's an act of psychic positioning, a feedback
loop, in which visual surroundings condition the owner's inner landscape, and vice versa. For white Americans, in particular, the house,
or the home, preexists any sense of community, because the original
American home—the log cabin on the frontier, whether in Plymouth
or Sandpoint—was built before a village or town grew up around it.
This may explain why, in the absence of an actual frontier, American
home buyers seem always to seek more space: building larger houses
or enlarging existing ones; buying houses in new subdivisions instead
of existing communities; building in hazardous and fragile locations
with ocean or river or mountain views; and above all, creating and

maintaining enormous lawns. (In *Crabgrass Frontier*, his definitive study of the rise of American suburbia after World War II, Kenneth Jackson notes, "The United States has thus far been unique in four important respects . . . : affluent and middle-class Americans live in suburban areas that are far from their work places, in homes that they own, in the center of yards that by urban standards elsewhere are enormous.") To read these homes spatially, looking for invisible boundaries and fault lines, is to notice how much of the square footage is simply *empty*: rooms hardly used; atriums and "great rooms" with two or three stories of airspace; grass no one walks on. The boundaries of these homes express an acute desire for space as a buffer or barrier, but also space as a perspectival shift: the unusued space around me is my territory, my comfort zone, an extension of my personality, even my body. Its emptiness affirms me.

I lived in large and mostly empty homes as a child, and have never wanted to own one, but I experience another variety of this spatial desire intensely when I hear words like "Moab," "Denali," "Canyon," "Sierra," "Switchback." Even with my critical faculties fully intact, I can't enter an outdoor store, or look at an inspirational poster of a climber edging a crack on El Capitan, without feeling what I might call a frustrated virtuous lust for escape, a feeling that my true self is out there somewhere; as Biff puts it in *Death of a Salesman*, "Men built like we are should be working out in the open." This is a structure of feeling (as Raymond Williams would say) constructed partly out of my own experience—I've been camping, paddling, sailing, hiking since I was very young—but more powerfully, more ideologically, out of reading. All my life, it seems sometimes, I've been absorbing one story after another—from *My Side of the Mountain* to *Huck Finn* to *Lord Jim* to *The Snow Leopard* to *Housekeeping*—in which a person who looks like me defines him- or herself against a rocky crag, a pathless desert, a glacier, a remote Montana valley. It feels unquestionably like the necessary and natural scale of my own experience, against which my life should be measured. Jane Tompkins, writing about the iconography of the Western in American film, puts it this way:

The blankness of the plain implies—without ever stating—that this is a field where a certain kind of mastery is possible, where a person (of a certain kind) can remain alone and complete and in control of himself, while controlling the external world through physical strength and force of will. . . . The desert flatters the human figure by making it seem dominant and unique. . . . And the openness of the space means that domination can take place virtually through the act of opening one's eyes, through the act, even, of watching a representation on a screen.

In college, in the mid-1990s, still very much in the thrall of wilderness as a literary trope, I imagined myself living in a town that still had the feeling of the frontier, urbane but not urban, close to the mountains but still with the comforts of decent restaurants, bookstores, coffee, bars. In my case the fantasy town was Flagstaff, mostly because it was the one I'd actually visited, but it could have been Boulder, or Moab, or Bend, or Laramie, or Missoula, or the Portlands (Maine and Oregon), or Burlington, Vermont. To my mind this was the proper artistic order of things: I would publish my first book, get a job in an MFA program, build a cabin in the mountains nearby, grow a beard, and spend my free time meditating, fly-fishing, ice-climbing. It sounds like a caricature, and of course it was: but moreover it was prepackaged, not a vocation but an aspiration. A pattern of consumption, not a life so much as a lifestyle. I had conflated Gary Snyder's poetry with the inside of a Patagonia catalog and Jim Harrison's *Legends of the Fall* with *Outside*'s "Best Towns to Live In." And I wasn't alone. Wherever I went, the trails and the parking lots were full; the gear became more expensive and elaborate; and much of it seemed vaguely Buddhist inspired, with pseudo-Sanskrit names like "Prana" and "Dakine." Tibetan prayer flags and yoga studios sprouted up everywhere. My imagination, which I thought of entirely in idealistic, ecological, aesthetic terms, was literally being monetized under my feet.

I hadn't yet heard the term "the culture industry"; I had only a glancing understanding of what late capitalism was; but I could grasp, on an intimate level, what was happening: the impulse to escape, to pioneer, to be "outside," was being subsumed into a new economic order structured around—to use the cold sociological terms—individuation and consumer choice. As J. M. Bernstein puts it, paraphrasing Adorno:

"Life-styles," the culture industry's recycling of style in art, represent the transformation of an aesthetic category, which once possessed a moment of negativity, into a quality of commodity consumption. The expansion of the role of competing lifestyles, the permeation of these styles into the home . . . all these phenomena token a closing of the gap between the culture industry and everyday life itself, and a consequent aestheticization of social reality.

What does it means to call white flight—the white flight of the mind—an "aestheticization of social reality"? To begin with, it's a posture of avoidance or evasion: the desire not to have one's visual field constantly invaded by inconveniently different faces—relationships that are fraught, unfixed, capable of producing equal measures of helplessness and guilt. Via the fantasy of deracination, however, that avoidance turns into a desirable thing, a psychic good: because white people feel, so often, that in order to think and feel, in order to be their "true selves," they have to find themselves in a landscape that silhouettes them, that flatters their individuality by allowing them to meditate freely. In this sense the most troubling part of deracination as an imaginative practice is not even that it draws writers toward all-white environments but that it can happen, as it does in *Home*, even when the troubling face of a person of color is present. Guilt, helplessness, the longing for redemption, the presumption of racial benevolence marked as, or indistinguishable from, innocence—those things linger around the white subject like trace elements in the air, like our own private Idahos, and turn longings for justice and reconciliation into something foreshortened and already foreclosed.

Or, to put it another way: the particular genius of whiteness in this cultural moment is that it has become transportable; any space, imaginary or physical, present or past, can be deracinated, or, in the language of gentrification, "pioneered." These regions include Crown Heights, the Mission, Boyle Heights, South Austin, or U Street in Washington; or the inside of a Whole Foods, an artisanal bakery, a spinning studio, a coffee roaster, an art gallery. There's always a feeling about white flight—which could be better described as white movement, white space appropriation, or, as some critics call it, a new form of colonization—that it is a natural, inevitable, irresistible process, like the movement of the free market itself, which undergirds an equally irresistible pessimism about ever changing it. In 2012, when Lena Dunham was widely criticized for the all-white cast of *Girls*—a show set in rapidly gentrifying neighborhoods of Brooklyn—she responded that her choice of the main characters, four white liberal-arts-college-graduate women in their midtwenties, was an accident. "I really wrote the show from a gut-level place," she said, in an interview with NPR, "and each character was a piece of me or based on someone close to me. And only later did I realize that it was four white girls."

I think of this way of understanding the world—the fetishization of familiarity and comfort and instinct—as "proxemics," a term coined in an obscure book, *The Hidden Dimension*, by the American anthropologist Edward T. Hall in 1966. For Hall, the way people exist in space is a rich and almost entirely ignored form of communication; almost an art form in itself. Break down the perception of space into its sensory components, and you begin to see why it's so stressful for an American to sleep in a Japanese hotel room for the first time, or for a person from a small town in India to shop at Walmart: all our ways of locating ourselves, from the floor underfoot to a certain smell (or lack of any smell) to our perceptions of distance and depth, are disrupted at once. "Man's feeling about being properly oriented in space runs deep," Hall writes. "Such knowledge is ultimately linked to survival and sanity. . . . The difference between acting with reflex speed and having to stop to think in an emergency situation may mean the difference between life and death."

What's most troubling about proxemics—what haunts *The Hidden*

*Dimension*, even through the veil of Hall's distant, technocratic language—is precisely this juxtaposition of the subtlety, even invisibility, of space as an object of perception, and the automatic, seemingly autonomic, responses people have when their sense of it is violated. "Like everyone else," Hall writes, speaking of his research in the Middle East, "Arabs are unable to formulate specific rules for their informal behavior patterns. In fact, they often deny that there are any rules, and they are made anxious by suggestions that such is the case." This unconsciousness, he suggests, has to do with the relation between spatial stress and violence. Like all animals when threatened, humans move: aggressive species (or species that perceive aggression) require more space. It's a response—essentially a variety of the "fight or flight" reflex—so deeply behavioral, so hardwired, that it doesn't rise to the level of conscious choice. To use a contemporary term, proxemics is a form of implicit bias.

Notably, *The Hidden Dimension* almost never uses the word "white." When Hall refers to norms of white American behavior, he alternates between the terms "American" and "northern European." Hall's unnamed concept of American white proxemics is a familiar one: "Americans" require lots of space, around the body and the body-associated objects, like houses and cars. (On seeing American cars in Paris, he writes: "[They] look like sharks among minnows. In the United States, the same cars look normal because everything else is in scale. . . . The American behemoths give bulk to the ego and prevent overlapping of personal spheres inside the car so that each passenger is only marginally involved with the others.") When Hall turns to nonwhite Americans of the 1960s, however, the tone of his analysis shifts dramatically: rather than neutrally evaluate the proxemics of a nonwhite space—say, an urban Chinatown—he becomes a pathologist. Echoing the racial essentialism and condescension of the Moynihan Report, Hall takes a highly pessimistic stance on the future of American urban life—not because of pervasive discrimination or chronic underdevelopment, but because the city simply doesn't "fit" the proxemic needs of nonwhite residents:

The degree to which peoples are sensorially involved with each other, and how they use time, determine not only at what point they are crowded but the methods for relieving crowding as well. Puerto Ricans and Negroes have a much higher involvement ratio than New Englanders and Americans of German or Scandinavian stock. Highly involved people apparently require higher densities than less involved people. . . . It is fairly obvious that the American Negroes and people of Spanish culture who are flocking to our cities are being very seriously stressed. Not only are they in a set-ting that does not fit them, but they have passed the limits of their own tolerance to stress. The United States is faced with the fact that two of its most creative and sensitive peoples are being destroyed and like Samson could bring down the structure that houses us all.

"You can't shed culture," Hall argues, in the conclusion of *The Hidden Dimension*. Instead of desegregating cities, he says, city planners should allow for the existence of "ethnic enclaves," each with its own type of building, suited to the spatial norms of its residents: "Urban scale must be consistent with ethnic scale, since each ethnic group seems to have developed its own."

Why does this matter to the story of white flight I'm trying to tell? Hall had no discernible influence on 1960s urban planning—which in any case was just one iteration of a movement toward racial segrega-tion that began many years before—but his recasting of racist stereo-types in the sober language of social science helps explain it. Proxemics is a way of saying "this place *feels* right to me," which for most people is an inarticulate and presumably individual experience; Hall calls proxe-mics an expression of culture, but only in the delusional sense—so common among liberal intellectuals of his generation—that culture can be divorced from power. It's only invisible, or "natural," to the per-son least likely to experience discomfort, the person comfortable in space created for her benefit. To use proxemics as a form of reading, in the way I'm suggesting, is something like the opposite: to see spatial comfort as an expression of the subject's relation to power.

This essay has to stand in relation to an invisible larger project that would map the proxemics of whiteness—the literature of houses, landscapes, movement in space—against the parallel and sometimes overlapping proxemics of African/Latinx/Asian/Native American writing, in obvious locations (*Beloved, Ceremony, The House on Mango Street*) and less familiar ones, like Gloria Naylor's *Linden Hills* or David Treuer's *The Translation of Dr Apelles*. I'm starting with this part of the story because it only seems appropriate—necessary—to start with myself, that is, to start at home.

## 4

Like my mother, who vividly remembers, and repeats, the story of seeing National Guard troops on her own block in Adams Morgan in 1968, many white Americans of a certain age have a proxemic story about "the riots." I heard many of these stories growing up; they became for me a fundamental part of the white American narrative, even before the riots of my own time, in Los Angeles, Crown Heights, and elsewhere, in the early 1990s. These stories, not so much as I heard them but as I sensed them, listening for the underlying logic, are expulsion stories; they have a "before" and an "after." They mark the end of an era, which of course maps onto the general disillusionment of American culture in the late sixties, the idea of "the war coming home"; but they almost always position the teller, the observer, as an innocent, if not precisely a victim. As a helpless person who has no option but to flee.

In *Middlesex*, tracing a Greek family expelled from Turkey first to Detroit and then, after the riots, to Grosse Pointe, Jeffrey Eugenides captures this mood through the eyes of his intersex narrator, Callie, then a small child, watching her father's restaurant burning:

> As I look up at the canopy of elms, the sky is just beginning to grow light. Birds move among the branches, and squirrels, too. A kite is stuck up in one tree. Over a limb of another, someone's tennis shoes dangle with the laces knotted. Directly below these

sneakers, I see a street sign. It is full of bullet holes, but I manage to read it: Pingree. All of a sudden I recognize where I am. There is Value Meats! And New Yorker Clothes. I am so happy to see them that for a moment I don't register that both places are on fire. Letting the tanks get away, I ride up a driveway and stop behind a tree. I get off my bike and peek across the street at the diner. . . . At that moment . . . the figure that has been approaching the Zebra Room enters my field of vision. From thirty yards away I see him lift a bottle in his hand.

These are traumatic memories; they represent a collective trauma, passed on to me and millions of other white Americans too young to experience them. And part of the trauma is a crisis of self-knowledge: understanding that the racial stratification of the cities was inherently, structurally unjust; being trapped in a structure you can't defend. Callie, listening to her elders:

"No respect for private property whatsoever," cried Mr. Benz, who lived next door. And his wife Phyllis: "Where are they going to live if they burn down their own neighborhood?" Only Aunt Zo seemed to sympathize: "I don't know. If I was walking down the street and there was a mink coat just sitting there, I might take it." "Zoë!" Father Mike was shocked. "That's stealing!" "Oh, what isn't, when you come right down to it. This whole country's stolen."

For my generation, born after the riots of the 1960s, there was an isolated, but very significant, echo of this historical trauma during the Los Angeles riots after the Rodney King verdict in 1992: the televised beating of Reginald Denny, a white truck driver, who was pulled from his cab at the intersection of Florence and Normandie, struck with a brick, and beaten nearly to death by four black men. The attack was filmed by a news helicopter and broadcast on repeat, becoming the most dominant TV footage of the riot.

The proxemic nature of this image is crucial to the way the viewer understands it. Unlike Callie's street-level view of the Detroit riots, this is a shot taken from the air; neither the photographer nor the viewer has to be nearby, or even in Los Angeles, to witness it. There is no view of the surrounding neighborhood, or any sense of whether the incident is isolated or widely repeated. In every sense, it's a post-white-flight image—a satellite image, not in the sense of being taken from space but being taken from a satellite of the city, from the point of view of those who have already left.

When I saw this footage in 1992 I had just come from a multiracial rally protesting the King verdict, at the Baltimore Armory, off Mount Royal Avenue; I drove back to my house and turned on the news in my parents' bedroom. The event seemed momentarily to wipe out anything else. I cried, witnessing it—not as it happened, of course, but as a video loop, a short clip repeated over and over.

The story of Reginald Denny's beating is not, metonymically, the story of the LA riots; the story of the 1992 riots is not the story of the Watts riots in 1968; the story of riots is not the story of white flight. But in the white American imagination this chain of substitutions overwhelms the actual narrative at every turn. The actual narrative, to the extent I can compress it here, goes something like this: the "flight" in white flight, the dramatic movement of the white population out of cities and into suburbs and exurbs, and the economic hollowing-out of what came to be called the inner city, was not a spontaneous event, or largely even a matter of personal or specific community choice; it was the result of American urban planning and housing policies dating back to the end of the Civil War, when large numbers of black people became able for the first time—and only for a brief time—to choose where they lived. The image of African Americans moving in an unrestricted way, spreading across the landscape, determining their own business arrangements, personal relationships, and spatial distances from whites, was in a sense the guiding phobia of white American civic life from the late nineteenth to the mid-twentieth century; this phobia made its way into housing covenants, urban planning, and Federal Housing Administration policies, which demanded racial segregation throughout the country. After these explicitly racist policies were defeated, one after another, in the courts (resulting, most notably, in the passage of the Fair Housing Act in 1968), politicians, developers, lenders, and landlords evolved "unofficial" practices of discrimination, such as redlining, which achieved virtually the same effect. As Ta-Nehisi Coates puts it in a vivid description of the history of segregation in Chicago, white homeowners had very little choice in whether or not their neighborhoods could be preserved:

> In 1947, after a few black veterans moved into the Fernwood section of Chicago, three nights of rioting broke out; gangs of whites yanked blacks off streetcars and beat them. Two years later, when a union meeting attended by blacks in Englewood triggered rumors that a home was being "sold to niggers," blacks (and whites thought to be sympathetic to them) were beaten in the streets.

In 1951, thousands of whites in Cicero . . . attacked an apartment building that housed a single black family, throwing bricks and firebombs through the windows and setting the apartment on fire. A Cook County grand jury declined to charge the rioters—and instead indicted the family's NAACP attorney, the apartment's white owner, and the owner's attorney and rental agent, charging them with conspiracy to lower property values. Two years after that, whites picketed and planted explosives in South Deering . . . to force blacks out.

When terrorism ultimately failed, white homeowners simply fled the neighborhood. The traditional terminology, *white flight*, implies a kind of natural expression of preference. In fact, white flight was a triumph of social engineering, orchestrated by the shared racist presumptions of America's public and private sectors. For should any nonracist white families decide that integration might not be so bad as a matter of principle or practicality, they still had to contend with the hard facts of American housing policy: When the mid-20th-century white homeowner claimed that the presence of a Bill and Daisy Myers decreased his property value, he was not merely engaging in racist dogma—he was accurately observing the impact of federal policy on market prices.

In a sense, the consistent objective of racial segregation as a nationwide government policy and popular movement was to maintain the economic conditions Americans still largely inhabit today, which social scientists often describe as "invisible capital": the enormous interlocking network, or feedback loop, of social, cultural, and economic advantages that white people have possessed for generations, sometimes as a result of long-vanished laws and practices (like racially restrictive housing covenants) and sometimes as a result of present-day, pervasive, though technically illegal, discrimination in mortgages, housing, preferential hiring, and credit. Invisible capital stays invisible because segregation, for the most part, either keeps its consequences hidden or makes them seem inevitable. "The aim of the suburbs," writes Adrienne Brown, coeditor of the anthology *Race and Real Estate*, "was to make whiteness both a broader and less visible category, replacing racial language in its documents and decrees with the language of value and investment, better equipped to uphold the *idea* of racial segregation without its ugly rhetoric. . . . Whereas blackness in both the northern city or the southern town was subject to internal segregation . . . the project of suburbia was to expel and export blackness from its borders."

It's the very invisibility of invisible capital—making "whiteness both a broader and less visible category"—that makes spatial perceptions of race so difficult to articulate for white writers. To look at the story of white flight from the perspective of the real estate market means to see it as a proxemic matrix, where subtle or invisible forces overlap with visceral responses. It makes the political personal. Everyone, after all, has to live somewhere. To choose the most glaring example from my own life: when I was fourteen and entering high school, my family moved from Phoenix to Baltimore, and rented a house—a claustrophobic, ugly house, which I immediately hated—in Roland Park. My parents knew next to nothing about the cultural geography of north Baltimore; they chose a temporary location halfway between my mother's office (my father worked at home) and the private school my brother and I would attend. Roland Park, they were told, was a "good" neighborhood, and of course, it looked like one: the streets were lined with old oaks and maples; the large houses had manicured lawns, and were widely spaced; there was a tidy row of stores on Roland Avenue, a beautiful library, a brick elementary school.

None of this was by accident: Roland Park was a planned community, one of the first American suburbs (it was at that time outside the city limits) developed in the late nineteenth century and designed by Frederick Law Olmsted, the creator of Central Park. In other ways, too, as the veteran *Baltimore Sun* reporter Antero Pietila puts it in *Not in My Neighborhood: How Bigotry Shaped a Great American City*, Roland Park was the foundational suburb: "Because its development uniquely spanned the whole Progressive Era . . . and also coincided with the peak of the national interest in eugenics," he writes, "Roland Park gauged changes in the American upper crust's attitudes and behavior, including . . . shrinking social tolerance toward other races and religious groups." Edward Bouton, Roland Park's developer, a fervent believer in the Progressive ideals of urban reform—planned sanitation, improved schools, natural spaces, public libraries—was also an avowed white supremacist, who evicted black residents as the first homes were built, and by 1910 had established a written company policy barring "nonservant blacks from residency." He also used unwritten policies to exclude Jews and Catholics; as a result, in a city with a very large and prominent Jewish population, not a single Roland Park home belonged to a Jewish family for fifty years.

It goes without saying—as so many things in Roland Park go without saying—that when we moved in, in 1989, none of this history was visible. There's no historical marker on Roland Avenue attesting to the neighborhood's role in modeling the patterns of residential segregation that make up so much of America's spatial history. What was visible was the proxemics: the silent psychic imprint of a landscape designed, like Central Park, to express solidity and security and permanence, to feel it had always been this way. But it was also seedier, more ragged at the edges, than it had been two or three decades before. Many of the houses—my friends' houses—had sagging porches, flaking paint, indifferent or overgrown landscaping. Roland Park had never been intended to be an exclusively wealthy neighborhood; Bouton encouraged builders to offer many different house sizes and designs. As Baltimore had fallen into economic decline, housing prices had stagnated.

This is the "Roland Park" most people outside Baltimore know: not the actual neighborhood but the backdrop of Anne Tyler's novels. Tyler has lived in Roland Park since the late 1960s, and most of her books are set there, or in other nearby parts of Baltimore. In 2012 NPR ran a feature about the geography of "Anne Tyler's Baltimore," with an interactive map, in which all of the dots cluster together tightly around the city's northern perimeter. Which is not to say that Tyler writes effusively or at any great length about the visual landscape of the neighborhood, let alone about any of its most obvious features—the Roland Park Country Club, or the private schools that

line Roland Avenue and Charles Street. Tyler's Baltimore is dominated by interiors; her characters tend to be introverts, sometimes
to great extremes, and their feelings about the city itself tend to be
vague, passive, and self-effacing, subsumed by their personal quirks,
their imperfect marriages or divorces, their unhappy, deprived, or un-
pleasant childhoods.

In this sense Tyler is a deeply paradoxical writer: rooted in a place
that is so comfortable, unthreatening, and familiar that it becomes almost featureless, a state of psychic stability that needs no explicit expression. There's probably no better exponent of this view than Macon
Leary, the protagonist of *The Accidental Tourist* (played with terrifying inertness by William Hurt in the 1986 film), who writes guide-
books for American business travelers to help them experience as little
as possible overseas. Macon himself might be called an Accidental
Baltimorean: he has what he calls "geographic dyslexia," and keeps
"a stack of index cards giving detailed directions to the houses of his
friends." But what's most striking and characteristic about Macon is
his depressive visual imagination:

> He'd stand at the bedroom window looking over the neighborhood—
> black branches scrawled on a purple night sky, a glimmer of white
> clapboard here and there, occasionally a light. Macon always took
> comfort if he found a light. Someone else had trouble sleeping too,
> he assumed. He didn't like to consider any other possibility—a
> party, for instance, or a heart-to-heart talk with old friends.

What drives characters like these to abandon their sense of belonging,
to subsume their cultural or political agency, or even awareness or curiosity, while maintaining a sense of the most extreme self-assurance
that their world will never be significantly altered? The best way to answer this question is to use a wider lens, and consider the convulsions
that have gripped Baltimore in the five decades of Tyler's career—the
riots of the late 1960s; the economic collapse and emptying-out of entire sectors of the city; the bankruptcy of Bethlehem Steel, the city's
largest employer; the crack wars and soaring murder rates that have

persisted from the early 1990s to the present. Tyler's response to these events has been a silence so absolute that "silence" itself seems to be the wrong word. The proxemics of her work speaks for itself.

Several years after I moved to Baltimore, when I was volunteering at a food pantry off Greenmount Avenue, an impoverished neighborhood only a few miles from Roland Park, the pantry director—a black man named James, in his forties, who had lived in Baltimore his entire life other than his tours in Vietnam—told me, "When I was young, our name for Roland Park was Hang-a-nigger. My parents made sure I knew never to go up there, not for any reason."

I don't know the best way to describe this kind of geographic dyslexia. Should I call it "one person's depressive normalcy superimposed on a silent guarantee of violence"? Or a depressive normalcy that shrinks away from the violence that has always protected it? There is no historical record—or not one I was able to locate—of a black person being murdered for straying into Roland Park during the years of legally enforced segregation. Of course, there doesn't have to be. In the early twentieth century the *Baltimore Afro-American* routinely reported that the police were "shooing colored people out of neighborhoods where a majority of the residents are white"; the *Afro-American* also carried account after account of police killings of unarmed black men, a pattern echoed by the recent Justice Department report issued after the "riots" following the 2015 police killing of Freddie Gray. In 1930 one headline read, "Baptist Minister Says Brutality Surpasses Anything South Has Seen."

Here is a thought that has haunted me for years—years longer than I've been able to articulate it: how much of my own sensibility, the dimensions of my emotional life, have been formed between the two poles or valences of violence I've just described? On one side is the specter or spectacle of black violence that made cities in the 1960s and '70s "uninhabitable" by white people; on the other is the very real, if rarely visible, threat of state and communal violence—white violence—that kept people of color out of the places where I lived.

Sometimes it seems to me that this is the hidden dimension, the proxemic code, that reveals the whole spectrum of strange silences and absences in white American fiction since the 1970s—the fascination with empty landscapes and the fetishization of the West; the near-obsessive interest in claustrophobic families; the cultivation of a confined, limited, stilted form of emotional intimacy that has defined the careers of so many writers of the era. There is a feeling here of existing within a narrow band, even a razor's edge, of possibilities, but also, literally, places to exist: places where "we" can be happy, where we can thrive; but wherever that place is, it's haunted by the specter of a kind of inner vacancy. The house we expected to be full is empty. "My eyes were still closed," says the narrator of Raymond Carver's "Cathedral." "I was in my house. I knew that. But I didn't feel like I was inside anything." This is usually taken as a universalizing gesture; but what would it mean to say the opposite: that the space, more than the person, is speaking?

It's a commonplace to say that most white and nonwhite Americans "live in different worlds." It could be more accurate to say that they understand the same spaces, the same worlds, differently. Can anyone describe a more profound difference than the one that separates living in a neighborhood, never leaving it, owning a home in it, and refusing to ever set foot in that neighborhood, knowing that your face, your very presence, could get you injured or killed? "It is a peculiar sensation," W. E. B. Du Bois said, in the single sentence that perhaps more than any other defines African American life, even today: "this double-consciousness, this sense of always looking at one's self through the eyes of others, of measuring one's soul by the tape of a world that looks on in amused contempt and pity." If there is an opposite to double consciousness—single consciousness—what is its normality, its unpeculiarity?

There's a nightmarishly funny scene in Spike Jonze's *Being John Malkovich* where Malkovich himself learns of the existence of the wormhole—a rip in the space-time continuum—that allows other people to enter his brain. To the horror of the hapless busybody (played by John Cusack) who has discovered and exploited the wormhole, Malkovich insists on going through it himself, to see what his own brain looks like, as it were, from the inside of the inside. He emerges in a restaurant scene surrounded by duplicates of himself, saying, in their private conversations, a babble all around the room: "Malkovich, Malkovich! Malkovich, Malkovich, Malkovich."

This is only half a joke: the other half is a pressing question. It's easy to find reflections on what it means to belong to a culture obsessed with the self; much less easy to locate the voices describing a culture trapped by sameness. Instead of an answer, I hear silence. Not wanting to be there; not necessarily knowing where there is. Not wanting to be counted, or accountable. Here is where reading as I described it at the beginning of this essay—reading as spatial recognition, as an attempt at common space—breaks down. Macon Leary's "geographic dyslexia," his refusal to navigate Baltimore, is also a refusal to be seen or addressed as a social subject. To return to Erica Hunt's terms: there is no genealogy of the visible in *The Accidental Tourist*, no sense of "we" at all: the sheer largeness of the city, the public, the common, outside his door. The door itself—so vital and painful a spatial figure, in a story like "The First Day"—might as well not exist. The reader has to accept Leary as nothing more or less than how he appears to himself, as the sum of his eccentricities. To use a favorite phrase among Anne Tyler's characters—the denizens of neighborhoods like Roland Park, whom I've known, in one way or another, all my life—anything else would be more than he can manage.

# 6

Vacancy, though, cuts two ways. For a writer looking for a sense of certainty, belonging, rootedness, or depth, it's inherently frightening or upsetting; but for a more entrepreneurial spirit, comfortable within a margin of flux, it's an opportunity: a void that needs to be filled. Listen to the way Richard Ford describes his journey from Jackson, Mississippi, for Michigan State University as a teenager, determined—as he said quite explicitly in a 1996 *Paris Review* interview—to leave his southern identity behind: "I simply didn't understand some very fundamental things in Mississippi in the early sixties and fifties. . . . I couldn't piece it out, couldn't make racism make sense. . . . I was not brave enough or committed enough or selfless enough to stay in Mississippi during the civil-rights movement. . . . I wasn't enlightened. I was nothing, that's what I was. But I knew I was a little nothing—which helped."

What does it mean to say of oneself, "I was nothing"? When I think about this I see a long procession of picaresque heroes who rise from nothing—Oliver Twist, Kim, Huck Finn—or the nameless wandering heroes of gunfighter movies. But Ford's "nothing" is another matter entirely: it's a nothing born of a something, that is to say, born of racism, and the failure to respond in an "enlightened" way. To be nothing, in these terms, is not to be brave, committed, or selfless. Which is again not quite the same thing as saying "lazy," "uncommitted," or "selfish." Or "ignorant." Or "passive." To be nothing in this sense means to have vacated oneself in preparation to be something else. The defining feature of Ford's work is rootlessness, both in the subjective sense—I refuse to be defined by my family of origin, my hometown, my region—and in the broader, if not quite objective, sense: a resistance to the claims of any kind of history or consciousness of the past. To put it in the voice of Frank Bascombe, Ford's most celebrated character, a transplanted southerner who settles in New Jersey as a young family man and stays through three careers and two marriages into prostate-ridden old age: "My own history I think of as a postcard with changing scenes on one side but no particular or memorable messages on the back. . . . The stamp of our parents on us and of the past in general is, to my mind, overworked, since at some point we are whole and by ourselves on the earth, and there is nothing that can change that for better or worse, and so we might as well think about something more promising."

What makes Ford's work so appealing even to people who don't accept all the political implications of his logic—a quality he shares with Marilynne Robinson—is the hypnotic aspect of his prose, which always feels invested with a certain kind of moral certainty, even though he claims no certainty at all. When I first encountered Ford's work—I saw him give a reading when I was seventeen—I fell hard for this effect, not in the Bascombe novels, but in *Rock Springs*, a collection of stories set in Montana and Wyoming. Having absorbed a lot of

Hemingway already, I was sensitive to the paratactic effect of the neutral conjunction "and," as in the opening of *A Farewell to Arms* ("The trunks of the trees too were dusty and the leaves fell early that year and we saw the troops marching along the road and the dust rising and leaves, stirred by the breeze, falling"). In Ford's story "Optimists," a middle-aged man recounts in great detail the night when, at fourteen, he witnessed his father murder another man by punching him in the heart. After that night, he lived with his mother for two more years while his father was in prison, and then joined the army, leaving the wreckage of his unhappy family behind. "I was apart from all of it," he says. "And when you are the age I was then, and loose on the world and alone, you can get along better than at almost any other time, because it's a novelty, and you can act for what you want, and you think that being alone will not last forever."

Those five "ands," the elasticity of Ford's clauses, the simplicity of the words themselves ("you can act for what you want") suggested to me a profoundly spatial kind of wisdom, a reproduction of those vistas, so to speak, a Montana of the mind. And this effect is only doubled by the desolation of the narrator's outward speech, as when, at the end of the story, he meets his mother in a supermarket for the first time in fifteen years, and is all but incapable of accounting for himself:

> "I've been down in Rock Springs, on the coal boom," I said. "I'll probably go back down there."
>
> "And I guess you're married, too."
>
> "I was," I said. "But not right now." . . .
>
> "Do you ever see your dad?"
>
> "No," I said. "I never do." . . .
>
> "I wish we knew each other better, Frank," my mother said to me. She looked down, and I think she may have blushed. "We have our deep feelings, though, don't we? Both of us."
>
> "Yes," I said. "We do."
>
> "So. I'm going out now," my mother said. "Frank." She squeezed my wrist and walked away through the checkout and into the parking lot.

In a blurb on the back cover of the Vintage paperback edition, Joyce Carol Oates praises *Rock Springs* as "the very poetry of realism." I read "Optimists" over and over again in my late teens and early twenties, wondering when I would be able to write sentences that had that ringing echo. I thought of it as being a musical effect, like a certain kind of simple blues chord, that could only sound authentic with enormous effort and practice. But I was haunted by the word "realism"; I could never quite explain why it attached itself to writers who seemed determined to reveal so little of the actual world around them. When would I be able to expose that authentic emptiness/fullness that I felt sure was my own? The answer to this question, if it ever came, happened years later, when I stumbled across a passage in an essay on Ann Beattie by Jay Parini, in *The Columbia Companion to the Twentieth-Century American Short Story*: "Proponents of minimalism focused on the concept of space, which they regarded as a 'free' medium, unrelated to intention. Translating this concept to literature, critics pointed to the silences and absences in a story as the 'free' element. . . . By the deft use of silences and absences . . . the minimalist writer intensifies what is said."

One crucial detail is missing in this analogy: minimalist art, whether in its earliest form (Kazimir Malevich) or as a movement after World War II (Donald Judd, Robert Morris, Ad Reinhardt) is entirely abstract; whereas minimalist fiction, closely tied to realism, is understood to represent the world in some faithful, recognizable sense. Minimalist art turns the artist's materials and the use of space in the gallery into objects of "pure" contemplation, in the sense that any trace of the artist's personhood is removed; but minimalist fiction makes a larger, and less aesthetically consistent, claim: the space intended for contemplation is the world itself, only strategically erased or emptied—to emphasize the loneliness of the figure in the foreground.

What does it mean for actual space, observable space, to be treated as empty or "free"; and what does it mean to invite the reader to this kind of contemplation and call it "realism"? To begin with, borrowing the language of the minimalist artists, it draws all attention to the figure at the center and makes that figure the measure of all things.

Frank O'Connor, who sets out his theory of the short story in *The Lonely Voice*, calls this figure, paradoxically, the representative of a "submerged population"; but he's never quite able to explain how this theory applies to a writer like Hemingway, whose protagonists are heroically singular, not representative. Ford, like Hemingway, sees solitude and autonomy as something necessary and desirable.

Frank, the narrator of "Optimists," remains, in that supermarket parking lot, in a space where all other human faces—even his mother's face—have disappeared, unseen by anyone, because the presence of other minds, even his mother's mind, is somehow unbearable. This moment at the end of the story ("she turned away, finally, and left me there alone") is a perfect achievement of the human figure in vacant space, like an Edward Hopper painting, or a still from a classic film noir.

At the risk of belaboring the obvious: this is a kind of realism that is achieved by foregrounding one human figure and removing all the others—the others the viewer knows do exist. The city is not actually empty; the viewer is primed by the image to imagine it is. The social world has not collapsed; the viewer just wants to believe that it has. In this sense the logic of social erasure, the "free space" brought about by this particular use of perspective, is infectious: in the American cities of the 1950s, '60s, and '70s, it spread through the biological metaphor of "blight." Ford inserts himself into this landscape in a way very few other contemporary writers have tried: in *Independence Day*, he makes Frank Bascombe into a landlord who owns two properties in what he calls "the Negro trace," a black neighborhood in Haddam, New Jersey. He invested in this property, he says, partly to "stash money where it'd be hard to get at," but mostly for "the satisfaction of reinvesting in my community":

> I would, I felt, be the perfect modern landlord: a man of superior sympathies and sound investments, with something to donate from years of accumulated life led thoughtfully if not always at complete peace. Everybody on the street would be happy to see my car come cruising by, because they'd know I was probably

> stopping in to install a new faucet.... What I thought I had to offer was a deep appreciation for the sense of belonging and permanence the citizens of these streets might totally lack in Haddam (through no fault of their own), yet long for the way the rest of us long for paradise. . . . The residents of Haddam's black neighborhood, I concluded, had possibly never felt at home where they were either, even though they and their relatives might've been here a hundred years.

This is a fantasy, as even Bascombe seems to realize, and one with deep roots: it harks back to the Progressive values of the first suburbs, but also underwrites (in 1995) the permanence of housing segregation and the lack of black homeownership. The language of development, renewal, and ownership itself is a benevolent language, consistent with the interests of the owners. More to the point, it's a fantasy he describes to no one other than the reader. Who, in 1990s New Jersey, would understand what Bascombe meant by the phrase "Negro trace," an obscure southern colloquialism? Who would think it acceptable for him to call his tenants "Negroes," period? (Ford has used this term consistently in his fiction up to his most recent novel, 2012's *Canada*.)

The closest Ford has ever come to a full-on reckoning with race is a 1999 essay, "In the Same Boat," he was commissioned to write for the *New York Times Magazine*. The assignment—which in retrospect is so absurd it seems to have come out of a comic novel—was for Ford to travel down the Mississippi from Hannibal, Missouri, in a riverboat, with Stanley Crouch, whom Ford had never met. The riverboat trip barely happened, due to inclement weather, but Crouch and Ford, like any writers would, made the most of the opportunity to collect their checks, and produced essays designed to be published side by side in the magazine.

These essays are fascinating reading. Crouch writes at some length about how Hannibal has been overrun by Twain-themed tourist kitsch, and about his own ambivalent feelings about *The Adventures of Huckleberry Finn*; he mentions Ford only briefly, and generally ("Ford . . . the Southern writer"), when describing how natural it felt to be out on the river with "three white guys": "This camaraderie, this sense that we now consciously share a much broader vision of Americana, became ever clearer as we spoke of books, films, families, the landscape. When the boat's fuel line went haywire, I thought of all the times Americans had been brought together by problems. . . . An improvisational inclination underlies our national tale. Individually or collectively, we invent a way."

Ford, on the other hand, devotes nearly his entire essay to his own mostly silent uneasiness in Crouch's presence. He finds Crouch physically impressive and loquacious ("In his shiny yellow rain gear that profoundly deepens the baked-ebony matte of his skin and makes even more dramatic the beamy roundness of his head, Stanley is an untroubled fountain of words") but deeply unnerving in the way Crouch never hesitates to use the national "we," while all the time speaking of his own immersion in black culture and the black intellectual tradition. This pushes Ford into a defensive position: why, he wants to know, is Crouch entitled to speak from the "peculiar" position both of a racial subject and an American citizen? "I don't really know how to have a genuine conversation about race," he says:

> Most of what I currently think about race involves just the usual rotating miscellany of racial attitudes and reactions that are on most white people's minds—whites, that is, who aren't bigots. These include a self-conscious awareness that I wouldn't knowingly bar anybody from anything because of his race. . . . "White" and "black" are not really races to me, and I have no wish to make them be, or to make being white a consideration in knowing me. . . . Beyond that, I don't understand why anybody might think I would personally apologize for the abomination of slavery when I never caused it. . . . None of this is really anything terribly serious, I realize, and generally falls under the heading of nothing human ever being perfect.

"The usual rotating miscellany," he assures us, in the beginning: and in the end, "none of this is really anything terribly serious": that is, slavery, black culture, "black" and "white" as categories, the use of the word "n_____," the possibility of a black president. There's perhaps no better honest expression of default white attitudes toward race in the age of white flight and resegregation: for white people living in low-density suburbs or exurbs, which is to say most white Americans, to think about race is a choice, and not a very serious or meaningful one:

> Of course I know these views leave me vulnerable to the complaint that they're convenient views to hold if you're white, and how dare I act surprised that race features so prominently in what a black man might do or think in America; and that, yes, I can't know what it's like to be black. But my answer is that if I believe that racial problems are as much a spiritual and moral detriment to me as to any black American (and I do believe that), and that the legitimacy of experience is not allocated along racial lines, but rather that equality means equality for me, too, then I'm entitled to view race as a tiresome, irrelevant, nowhere issue that just keeps us all from playing the game we want to play—the game of life on a flat field.

The logic of the second sentence of this passage deserves to be unpacked and studied—not because it makes sense but because of the precise way it doesn't. There is a landscape and an aesthetic that correspond to Ford's thinking; it begins with the word "allocation." White and black Americans are damaged by racism, but if the damage is comparable, it's not the same; it's inherently different, because "I can't know what it's like to be black." The damage, therefore, is allocated, and the allocations have to be legitimate, separate, and equal for each individual. They are "entitlements," and Ford's particular entitlement is to see race as "tiresome, irrelevant, and nowhere," because it prevents us from playing "the game of life on a flat field."

And what is the game of life? It's the deadest of dead metaphors; Ford has borrowed it from a stock of received ideas, like the "level playing field," or indeed colorblindness itself, that mean less and less the more you inquire into them. What Ford really wants to stress, what stresses him, is the allocation of experience, its separateness and its legitimacy: the autonomy of his own imagination. Stanley Crouch, with his emphasis on the collective "we," has intruded on it. Crouch's mentor, Albert Murray, argues in *The Omni-Americans* that black people are central to the American experience, constitutive of that experience, because (among many other reasons) their suffering produced the greatest American cultural form, the blues. The idea that collective experience exists at all seems, to Ford, a kind of madness. "I'm sure that there are plenty of black Americans who don't know what it's like to be other black Americans," he writes, "and that black experience is no more uniform than white experience, and that therefore this particular citadel could be usefully abandoned. My own faith is a literary one, forged in the larger humanist dilemma, and it is this: while it's mostly impossible to know what it's like to be anybody but myself, I and all of us, by paying conscientious heed to the signifying details of one another's lives, might yet break the tautology of race, might imagine our way out of ignorance and do better toward one another, one by one."

If I apply a visual dimension to this thinking, a proxemic dimension, I come up with something larger than Ford's or Robinson's own aesthetic of fiction: it becomes an aesthetic ideology of white American life in the post-Reagan era, the era of voluntary, spatially expansive, emotive, intellectual, financial, educational self-segregation. Which could be summed up with the entrepreneurial phrase "Do better toward one another, one by one." "One by one" is not actually a serious idea, or intention, because as Ford admits, he's not capable of having a genuine conversation about race; it's a self-canceling thought, or a way of forestalling thought. "My failure to enact a crucial exchange with Stanley is obviously illustrative of my general failure to find fellowship with all my companions. What better chances I'll still have, I'm not sure. I will need to look for them."

To make an obvious observation: "fellowship" is not the same as "authorship." It may well be the opposite. Ford is admitting a human failure that may be, for him, the evidence of artistic success. Whatever he has done with Stanley Crouch, he has not failed the reader. His imagination—"our" imagination—survives by not imagining. But there is another, even more important, dimension to Ford's series of admissions in "In the Same Boat": it's both the diagnosis of a problem and the admission of his resistance to inquiring into a solution. "I believe," Ford says, "that racial problems are as much a moral and spiritual detriment to me as to any black American." It would be interesting just to end the essay with that thought.

## 7

When I went to Zuccotti Park in the fall of 2011 I felt, for the first time in my life, a collective American identity rooted in the fundamental historical facts of the past forty years: the reversal of the postwar social contract, the subjection of human existence to the profit motive. What mattered about the Occupy movement, of course, was not just the slogans but the physical space: the creation of what the radical social theorist Hakim Bey calls a "Temporary Autonomous Zone." It was a refutation of the social logic of privatization, but also a reflection of the specific madness of the 2008 housing crisis: how the great armature of federal government programs that created white housing ownership and invisible capital in the twentieth century by the end of that century had spawned a market that grew like a carcinoma, making homeownership—or even living in a home at all—unaffordable even for many in the white middle class.

I'm not sure that without Occupy I would ever have started thinking about the crisis of spatial anxiety and spatial meaning in American life. The "occupation" in Occupy, in the profoundest sense, was a proxemic act: it was an invasion of psychic space by way of physical space. To pitch a tent on Wall Street, in figurative terms—because the encampment was never allowed onto the actual street—was to ask: why does anyone live anywhere? "Housing is a human right," read one of the signs posted on the Zuccotti Park fence. As a socialist I had always believed this to be true. But what did it mean for it to be true of me? In one sense, this was a fictive question: I had never had to doubt, in my own life, that I would have a place to live. But in another sense, at that moment, it was not: I could imagine a circumstance in which my savings would be wiped out by a catastrophic health crisis or a stock market crash; where my job, at a public university, would be eliminated. I was vulnerable enough to imagine, for the first time, being vulnerable.

That was what Occupy meant, at least to me, in a slightly ridiculously overstated but also politically important way: for the first time in my adult life, since I'd left the world of anarchist collectives and punk rock, I felt the possibility, and the need, of not being alone.

Where did the particularly American fiction of the sovereign individual, the greatest proxemic illusion of the current era, come from? Largely, of course, from homeownership, which is to say from the government programs I've mentioned earlier: the Homestead Act, the Federal Housing Administration, Fannie Mae, the mortgage-interest tax deduction. These programs, like many successful government policies, have a way of becoming invisible over time. In a society so deeply rooted in doctrines of individual salvation and free will—the Calvinism Marilynne Robinson celebrates and defends—it's psychologically impossible, for many people, not to believe their successes and failures are their own doing, even when the evidence suggests otherwise. The spatial logic of suburban life supports it. You rake your own leaves and cut your own grass. But these metaphors have never been stable: the suburbs had hardly been built before writers like John Cheever and Richard Yates began to feel haunted by them. And in moments of great uncertainty—the moments of the past few decades of American life—those metaphors can collapse all at once, like a cascading power outage.

This is precisely the circumstance that begins the most famous self-identified "social novel" of the past twenty years, Jonathan Franzen's *The Corrections*: a novel constructed around a particular suburban house outside St. Louis, but which—at least in the beginning—seems to want to encompass every house in 1999, trembling on the verge of the millennium:

> Gust after gust of disorder. Trees restless, temperatures falling, the whole northern religion of things coming to an end. No children in the yards here. Shadows lengthened on yellowing zoysia.

Red oaks and pin oaks and swamp white oaks rained acorns on houses with no mortgage. Storm windows shuddered in the empty bedrooms.

*The Corrections* moves through a series of spaces—rooms, apartments, staterooms on cruise ships, restaurants, offices, corporate atria—that are all congested, cramped, overstuffed, unsatisfying. Alfred and Enid's three children, thoughtfully raised, ostensibly successful, have fled not only this particular suburb of St. Louis but also the entire model of domestic security and stability, thrift, modesty, and continuity it implies. The youngest child, Chip, is a former literature professor whose career collapsed after he had an affair with a student; the middle child, Denise, is a successful chef who can't help sleeping with the wrong people—in one case, her business partner's madly needy wife.

But the novel's most troubled landscape, in many ways, is the lavish house in Chestnut Hill where the eldest child of the family, Gary, is quietly losing his mind, surrounded by every tangible indicator of happiness: three healthy, active sons, a highly educated wife, Caroline, who doesn't need to work, and every consumer good any of them could possibly need, from a vast outdoor grill to his own personal darkroom to a finished basement that houses "the necrosis of clutter that sooner or later kills a living space: stereo boxes, geometric Styrofoam packing solids, outdated ski and beach gear in random drifts." Gary's life is a dream of free-market autonomy turned feverish and rancid: Caroline is petty, self-involved, a permissive and narcissistic parent; his eldest son is obsessed with surveillance cameras and wants to film everything in the house; and his own emotions, which he imagines as brain chemistry, refuse to cooperate. He fears nothing more than the approach of anhedonia, the inability to experience pleasure, which encroaches on every side: "a fungus spoiling the delight in luxury and joy in leisure which for so many years had fueled Gary's resistance to the poorthink of his parents."

In this way Gary is the anti–Frank Bascombe, the person for whom meditative space has become crippling and the illusion of rootlessness has only ensnared him further in a cycle of familial repression and return. For him—and for his siblings, and for his parents, caught in the novel's tightly layered negotiations over a single, catastrophic Christmas holiday—the sensible world is an echo chamber, where every detail, from weather to food to the content of an informational video, amplifies Franzen's sense of a world dissolving its own sense of proportion into something approaching pornography:

> A visionary in a warm-up jacket was lecturing to pretty college students. Behind the visionary, in a pixilated middle distance, were sterilizers and chromatography cartridges and tissue stains in weak solution, long-necked medicoscientific faucets, pinups of spread-eagled chromosomes, and diagrams of tuna-red brains sliced up like sashimi.

*The Corrections* is a deeply, avowedly self-knowing book, in at least two senses: there's Franzen's extraordinary confidence in the range of his references, the book's sheer thickness of turn-of-the-millennium cultural savvy, and then there's the way the book seems to arrive pretheorized, with a critical vocabulary already in place, a reflexive move Franzen borrows from Pynchon and DeLillo but most obviously from his friend and sometime rival David Foster Wallace. This is a writer, the reader is made to feel, who sees and gets everyone and everything, from the intricacies of restaurant management to feminist theory to the conspiratorial politics of Baltic states. It's such a lucid and ambitious performance, a synthesis of the arch tradition of postmodern satire with the padding of exposition and a familiar narrative arc, that it's difficult to see where the range of Franzen's references, the field of his vision, breaks off.

How do you create a wide-ranging novel, set primarily in cities on the East Coast in the 1990s, and create the illusion of a panorama that doesn't include people of color? This has to be done with surgical precision. Robin Passafarro, Denise's lover, was raised in Mount Airy, a racially integrated neighborhood, by leftist parents; guilty about her privileged existence, she quits her teaching job at a private school, and as an act of penance—to whom, exactly?—starts a gardening project in an impoverished neighborhood. But when Denise comes to visit her there, the neighborhood kids who work in the garden have vanished, and Robin is working alone, clearing the ruined earth:

> She whacked the rubble in the sieve to urge some dirt through. Caught in the mesh were fragments of brick and mortar, gobs of roofing tar, ailanthus limbs, petrified cat shit, Baccardi [*sic*] and Yuengling labels with backings of broken glass. . . .
> "This is basically a selfish project," Robin said. "I always wanted a big garden, and now the whole inner city's going back to farmland. But the kids who really need to be out working with their hands and learning what fresh food tastes like are the ones who aren't doing it. They're latchkey kids. They're getting high, they're having sex, or they're stuck in some classroom until six with a computer. But they're also at an age when it's still fun to play in the dirt." . . .
> "This is very admirable," Denise said.
> Robin, mistaking her tone, said, "Whatever."

The novel's echo chamber is never quite as loud as it is at this moment, when, in the midst of a devastated landscape ("Robin looked away, across the street, at a row of dead buildings with rusting sheet metal cornices"), a white liberal, a lifelong do-gooder, admits what the reader already knows: her altruism is merely another form of acquisitive play, and the people she claims to be helping, or working with, are figures of her imagination. What the reader sees is not their details—their faces, their voices—but the landscape (where they live) absent of them.

In this way *The Corrections* marks a kind of apotheosis of white flight, and deracination, as a historical process and an imaginative procedure: proceeding from the suburbs, and ending there, it captures a completist's view of American culture, an obsessive analytical interest in places, details, processes, that constitutes itself as if race is one among a thousand tiny details. "I miss the days when more novelists lived and worked in big cities," Franzen wrote in a much-read 1996

essay in *Harper's*. "I mourn the retreat into the Self and the decline
of the broad-canvas novel. . . . I like maximum diversity and contrast
packed into a single exciting experience. . . . I still like a novel that's
alive and multivalent like a city." But he's just as explicit about what
that multivalence can, and can't, include. "I have thought about it," he
said, as if stating the obvious, in an interview with *New York* magazine
in 2016, "but I don't have very many black friends. I have never been
in love with a black woman. . . . I write about characters, and I have to
love the character to write about the character. If you have not had direct firsthand experience of loving a category of person—a person of
a different race, a profoundly religious person . . . —I think it is very
hard to dare, or necessarily even want, to write fully from the inside
of a person."

When I read this interview I was reminded of J. M. Coetzee's
Jerusalem Prize speech, given in 1987, when South Africa was still
seven years away from the end of apartheid. Referring to one of the
apartheid regime's earliest laws, the forbidding of sexual relations between whites and nonwhites, Coetzee says:

> At the heart of the unfreedom of the hereditary masters of South
> Africa is a failure of love. To be blunt: their love is not enough
> today and has not been enough since they arrived on the conti-
> nent; furthermore, their talk, their excessive talk, about how they
> love South Africa has consistently been directed toward *the land*,
> that is, toward what is least likely to respond to love: mountains
> and deserts, birds and animals and flowers.
>
>    If one fails to see the relevance of this talk about love, one
> can replace the word *love* with the word *fraternity*. The veiled un-
> freedom of the white man in South Africa has always made itself
> felt most keenly when, stepping down for a moment from his lonely
> throne, giving in to a wholly human and understandable yearning
> for fraternity with the people among whom he lives, he has dis-
> covered with a shock that fraternity by itself is not to be had, no
> matter how compellingly felt the impulse on both sides. Fraternity
> ineluctably comes in a package with liberty and equality.

When I first encountered this speech, sometime in the early 2000s, before I had started to write directly about race in America, I wondered in a speculative way about what it meant for a culture to have failed at love artistically by not having enough of it. I had recently read Nadine Gordimer's *The Conservationist*, and I could recognize intuitively what Coetzee meant about South Africa in Gordimer's protagonist: a white gentleman farmer in the Eastern Cape who lives alone, hopelessly alienated not only from his farmworkers but from the Boer families nearby, the Indian shopkeepers in the closest town, and his own estranged family; I could see a sickening extension of this failure in *Disgrace*, where Coetzee seems to pull apart the hopes of post-apartheid reconciliation strand by strand. I knew the parallel was there, deeply seated in my own American life, but I couldn't locate it; it seemed too large to be contained in any one expression.

After all, what was enforced in South Africa during the apartheid regime by law and explicit violence was sustained in the United States, by a less visible system: the threat of violence, but also a sense of voluntary, subjective, emotional isolation. Franzen says it is hard to "necessarily even want, to write fully from the inside of a person" you haven't personally loved. The phrase "necessarily even" sits inside the infinitive and shades all of white American life. Is it even necessary? Is it necessary to go there, to take it on? It is not. The world is full, overfull, overflowing, even without people of color: even the weather always seems to reflect and magnify the characters' emotions. There is no sense of a deficit.

But there is also very little sense of love. Which might be the best way of answering the question of where love goes in a society committed to enforcing inequity not as an explicit matter of law but as a passive aftereffect of consumer preference, proxemics, individual choice. In *The Corrections*, anxiety takes the place of Ford's pastoral complacency, or Robinson's spiritual austerity: it fills up the space one might otherwise expect to be filled with other people. It becomes very difficult, in a claustrophobic environment like this, to feel love of any kind without also feeling that it comes attached to a set of vulnerabilities, a kind of custom-fitted anxiety: and one of those vulnerabilities, the most self-reinforcing one, implies that to love one thing is to choose not to love another. Unstable historical and economic moments are like that: they force privileged, well-intentioned people to make compromise after compromise, and crowd into smaller and smaller spaces, to limit their moral horizons to spaces they can control, and, ideally, purify. But these compromises don't appear as compromises; they appear as opportunities. To reject race as subject matter, as Franzen does, is not even really, in his eyes, a choice; it's a way of pursuing his artistic imperative. The choice not to care about race is thus transmuted into a necessity, the same way, in a late capitalist world, subjects come to see so many of their priorities as necessities.

This is the part of the story of white flight that most fully, and literally, inhabits my own body: in the armature I carry around with me, the defensive mechanisms I use to preserve my sense of health, safety, sanity. Because, in the end, in this mode of life, the world always reduces to me. This is why, as a writer, I can't disavow *The Corrections*. Its world is my world; its realism, as much as I hate to say it, is (or was) my realism. But realism doesn't have to remain a static, passive technique—that is, a vehicle for spatial pessimism, for accepting and reifying the world as it is. As the art critic Dushko Petrovich once wrote, realism doesn't have to remain a window; it can also be a door. It can enclose a space or rupture it.

And the rupture doesn't have to be particularly remarkable to matter. Michael Chabon's *Telegraph Avenue*, like *The Corrections*, is unapologetically conventional in its ambitions, another sprawling, upper-middle-class family comedy of manners; only in this case there are two families, one black and one white, who have evolved into a single intimate unit: the husbands jointly own a record store in Oakland, the wives run a midwifery practice in Berkeley. Chabon's narrator moves from one character to another with remarkable evenness and an almost excessive sympathy, as if to assure the reader that everyone shares the same comic flaws, and that this border between cities—an area Chabon calls "Brokeland"—is a shabby utopia. The result is a novel with very little dramatic tension: the crises these couples face (the record store threatened by a new mall down the block; a malpractice lawsuit; the appearance of an unknown son) barely ripple the placid surface, in a demonstration of early-Obama-era good feeling. (Obama himself makes a brief appearance, at a rally in support of his senatorial campaign.) Even when he imagines losing everything, Nat, the white partner in the record store, clings to his own sense of blamelessness:

> For years his life had balanced like the world of legend on the backs of great elephants, which stood on the back of a giant turtle; the elephants were his partnership with Archy, and Aviva's with Gwen, and the turtle was his belief that real and ordinary friendship between black people and white people was possible.... There was no tragic misunderstanding, rooted in centuries of slavery and injustice. No one was lobbing vile epithets. . . . It just turned out that a tower of elephants and turtles was no way to try to hold up a world.

*Telegraph Avenue* can be infuriatingly easy on its characters, and on the economic and racial realities of the East Bay; it needs to be juxtaposed with Ryan Coogler's film *Fruitvale Station*, which depicts, in loving and terrifying detail, the last day in the life of Oscar Grant, a young black man murdered in an Oakland BART station by police on New Year's Eve, 2008. But I still think of Chabon's novel as a worthwhile gesture. In a brief essay in the *New York Times Magazine* shortly after the book was published, Chabon linked *Telegraph Avenue* to his childhood home on a block of mostly black families in Columbia, Maryland, one of a tiny number of planned, intentionally integrated communities built in the 1960s and '70s. After he left Columbia to go to college, Chabon wrote, black people gradually receded from his life; only when he witnessed the celebrations after O. J. Simpson was acquitted in 1995 did he realize "the sudden, bitter awareness . . . of my own blindness, of the apartheid of consciousness under whose laws I had gradually come to live." The novel, he wrote, was a self-conscious attempt to regain the utopian relatedness of his childhood, within the confines of a record store: "For the first time in years, flipping through the bins, inhaling the time-heavy perfume of moldering LPs, I was where I had wanted to be all along."

An apartheid of consciousness can't be undone without self-conscious effort. It will never happen naturally, now or in some theoretically resolved future. The question for the novel is: what kind of self-consciousness is required? Utopias, or dystopias, are one vein, satire is another, but for all its failures, I'm always drawn, almost perversely, back to realism as an act of reading: that is, seeing the spaces Americans actually occupy now, as they are—fraught with contradictions, failed hopes, crossed messages. Here's one small example: a scene in Ben Lerner's quasi-novel *10:04*, where the narrator, also named Ben, also a white writer in his early thirties, is describing his ambivalent relationship to the Park Slope Food Co-op, the quintessential safe space for white liberal Brooklyn values in the year 2012. "Although I insulted it constantly," Ben says, "I didn't think the co-op was morally trivial. I liked having the money I spent on food and household goods to go to an institution that made labor shared and visible and that you could usually trust to carry products that weren't the issue of openly evil conglomerates." In exchange for reduced prices, co-op members have to work a monthly four-hour shift in the store; on one such occasion, Ben is sorting dried mango in the basement storage room, listening to another member explain why she pulled her son out of a public school first grade to attend a private one:

> "It just wasn't the right learning environment for Lucas. The teachers really tried and we believe in public education, but a lot of the other kids were just out of control."
>
> The man working on bagging chamomile tea immediately beside her felt obliged to say, "Right."
>
> "Obviously it's not the kids' fault. A lot of them are coming from homes—" The woman who was helping me bag mangoes, Noor, with whom I was friendly, tensed up a little in expectation of an offensive predicate.
>
> "—well, they're drinking soda and eating junk food all the time. Of course they can't concentrate."
>
> "Right," the man said, maybe relieved her sentence hadn't taken a turn for the worse.
>
> "They're on some kind of chemical high. Their food is full of

who knows what hormones. They can't be expected to learn or re-spect other kids who are trying to learn."

This is a variation of the same sentiment, even the same vocabulary, embedded in Robin Passafarro's self-effacing description of her urban gardening project; it's easy to imagine Franzen writing this scene, making it his version of the contemporary city. But it isn't his city: someone else is listening. The proxemics of the scene flow in more than one direction. The reader knows nothing about Noor other than her name, which suggests a Middle Eastern origin, and her tension. How does her tension suggest itself? The narrative doesn't say, which is to say, in a casual elision, it passes the moment over to the reader's imagination.

This is a tiny moment, so tiny it might easily pass unnoticed. The contemporary term for what the woman is doing is a "microaggres-sion," which is to say, causing offense by acting and speaking normally and not paying attention to who is listening. Microaggressions, as anyone who has read Claudia Rankine's *Citizen* knows, cause an acute sense of spatial stress. One person's experience of comfort becomes another's agony. Microaggressions, that is, lead to micro-observations: realism on a very minute scale, where every choice—to describe, not to describe, how to describe—becomes fraught. In this moment, Lerner performs a silent and almost imperceptible trick of inclusion, turn-ing to the reader, and saying, effectively, "You know what I'm talking about."

In the wake of the Brexit vote and during the run-up to Trump's election, a graphic (designed by a French artist named Maeril) began circulating widely on social media describing "what to do if you are witnessing Islamophobic harassment." The graphic, showing an (ap-parently) white woman, a Muslim woman in a hijab and long dress, and her harasser, an angry white man, demonstrates an exercise in what might be called proxemic substitution: to disarm the (verbal) at-tacker, the white bystander stands or sits next to the Muslim woman, and engages her in conversation, speaking over the man's voice while ignoring him completely. "Keep eye contact with them and don't ac-knowledge the attacker's presence," the guide says.

This guide was written & illustrated by Maeril | @itsmaeril - Translated in English for The Middle Eastern Feminist

There is a complex proxemic imperative at work here, which is to say, also, a complicated form of public address, of invoking the implied reader. I don't know how it feels to be inside the body of a person of color, Lerner's narrator is saying, but that doesn't mean I'm blind; that doesn't require me to relinquish all my powers of observation. It is possible to be something other than passively white; which means, in a social space, a public space, it is possible to take cues from nonwhite people. This too is a form of artistic observation. But where does it lead? In the case of this scene, and narrator, it leads to the following observation, when Ben says,

> It was the kind of exchange, although *exchange* isn't really the word, with which I'd grown familiar, a new biopolitical vocabulary for expressing racial and class anxiety: instead of claiming brown and black people were biologically inferior, you claimed they were—

for reasons you sympathized with, reasons that weren't really their fault—compromised by the food and drink they ingested; all those artificial dyes had darkened them on the inside.

In his mid-1970s lectures at the Collège de France, Michel Foucault described biopolitics as the point in the nineteenth century when state power first became able, through technological means, to control every aspect of an individual's existence: "Covering the whole surface that lies between the organic and the biological," he wrote, "between body and population. We are, then, in a power that has taken control of both the body and life or that has, if you like, taken control of life in general—with the body as one pole and the population as the other." American racial politics, as Lerner implies, has always been biopolitical: concerned with the most basic physical processes, reproduction, movement, residence, consumption, self-presentation. Only the vocabulary, the logic of exclusion, is new.

It's easy to see descriptions of biopolitics, and even the word itself, as the most fatalistic of all turns the cultural Left has taken in the last two decades. No matter how we try to overcome our divisions, this line of thought goes, racial hierarchies, as long as they serve the interests of power, will always reassert themselves. Lerner, to say the least, is not immune to this fatalism. In *10:04*, he details, at length, his resistance to one particular vision of American inclusivity: Walt Whitman's poetry. "Because he wants to stand for everyone," the fictive Ben writes, "because he wants to be less a historical person than a marker for democratic personhood, [Whitman] can't really write a memoir full of a life's particularities. . . . He has to be nobody in particular in order to be a democratic everyman, has to empty himself out so that his poetry can be a textual commons for the future into which he projects himself." In his essay *The Hatred of Poetry*, Lerner takes this argument even further:

What makes Walt Whitman so powerful and powerfully embarrassing . . . is that he is explicit about the contradictions inherent in the effort to "inhabit all." This is also what makes it so silly to imply Whitman's poetic ideal was ever accomplished in the past and that we've since declined—because of identity politics—into avoidable fractiousness. "I am the poet of slaves, and of the masters of slaves," Whitman wrote in his journal, indicating the impossible desire to both recognize and suspend difference within his poems.

This is a problem for the all-encompassing "I" of the lyric poem; it's a problem for Whitman just as it is for Langston Hughes, in "I, too, sing America." But in fiction, which is not such a totalizing art form, simultaneously recognizing and suspending difference isn't impossible. Or even, necessarily, all that difficult. After all, those of us who live racially multivalent lives (more and more of us, all the time) do it ourselves, in practice, in life. If biopower can find new vocabularies for exclusion, fiction can find new vocabularies for inclusion: new implied readers, new forms of address. It takes nothing more or less than putting our powers of proxemic observation ahead of our capacity for wishful thinking.


8

On October 6, 2014, seven weeks after Michael Brown was killed in Ferguson, a group of Black Lives Matter protestors gathered outside the St. Louis Cardinals' National League playoff game at Busch Stadium. While they chanted "Justice for Mike Brown," groups of fans in the crowd chanted back, "Let's go, Darren!" One member of the crowd wore a handwritten sign taped to the back of his shirt: "I am Darren Wilson." "We're the ones who gave all y'all the freedom that you have," a young woman shouted at them. An older white man shouted, "If they were working, we wouldn't have this problem." Another fan gave the protestors a Nazi salute.

In the week after Trump's election, two years later, I remembered the YouTube video I'd seen of this incident and what I'd found, at the time, to be so disturbing about it. First, the response was not only radical but preprogrammed and reflexive: it wasn't just "Blue Lives Matter" but "Let's go, Darren"; not just "get a job" but "Heil Hitler."

Second, these people were shouting horrible, execrable, violent things, unchallenged, in public. Hundreds of other people could hear them, and did nothing. This was a safe space for racism. And why, in that year that the Black Lives Matter movement took hold—the first year of our present state of emergency—did stadiums, and not malls, movie theaters, airports, or any other public gathering places, become the first notable venues where white Americans felt entitled, or provoked, to shout vile names at black people, threaten them with murder, applaud murderous police officers?

If you know anything about the geography of major American cities, especially in the East and Midwest, it takes only a minute to understand why. Stadiums, particularly baseball stadiums, are pure expressions of the absurd logic of white flight and the metropolitan disasters white flight has created: they are constructed in cities for financial, practical, and historical reasons, but the fans who attend their games—overwhelmingly white fans—come from the suburbs, exurbs, and rural areas surrounding the cities, sometimes from hundreds of miles away. In their daily lives, these white fans may never, or almost never, encounter people of color, particularly not African Americans; therefore it was likely that these were people encountering the angry and aggrieved faces of black people for the first time, probably the first time in their lives. Feeling targeted, and singled out, by what felt like an accident of geography and timing, they lashed out in response: the boundaries of acceptable social behavior collapsed, as Edward T. Hall could have predicted. "When aggressiveness increases," he wrote, invoking his own understanding of biopolitics, "animals need more space. If no more space is available . . . a chain reaction is started."

In this same moment, the first weeks of November 2016, I began thinking about a building I hadn't seen in a long time: Michigan Central Station, in Detroit, which stands not far from the riverfront and Tigers Stadium and the International Bridge. Once among the busiest train stations in the country, it was abandoned in the 1980s, and now sits on more than forty acres of fenced-off land. It's literally a shell: the windows are missing, long since blown out by winter storms, so that from the right angle, or nearly any angle, you can look straight through to daylight on the other side.

Seven years ago, around the time my father was diagnosed with an incurable form of cancer, I discovered that YouTube and Netflix were a treasure trove of film noir movies from the 1940s and '50s, and I began watching them whenever I had a free moment: *The Stranger, Call Northside 777, He Walked By Night, Central Station, The Naked City, The Woman in the Window, Scarlet Street.* I could watch these movies over and over again, but rarely all the way through: what I wanted to see was the people in the buildings, their ordinary interactions, conversations, movements. The urban world of film noir, for all its associations with cynicism and decay—and the shadow it threw over postwar perceptions of the city—was a functioning world, a living organism. I could watch Edward G. Robinson pour himself coffee from a silver urn, or Jimmy Stewart place a telephone call, with an almost hypnotic sense of relief. What I wanted, I realized, after a while, was a memory, an imprint, of my father's world. He was born in 1934 and traveled to college by train, three days from South Dakota to New Haven, in 1952. It's likely that his trains connected at Central Station in Detroit. The building where he worked when I was a young child, the Department of Agriculture, was built, like Central Station, in the thirties, when public buildings were supposed to exude heaviness and permanence and a grand scale. What I was seeing in these movies, I realized, was a city that actually worked: where the mail came twice a day, an operator answered when you picked up the phone, people rode streetcars to work, the subway station restrooms were open. These were the details, weirdly, where my mind rested. It would be easy to call it nostalgia, but I wasn't caught up with the double-breasted suits and the pipes and hats and women's gloves; it was the sheer normalcy of a kind of urban life, unspoken social codes, proxemic conventions, that I had never seen.

I would never say that city life of the 1940s and '50s was an ideal world or even an admirable one. What fascinated me, in those years after my father's death, was how unimaginable it felt to me, how completely lost and unrecoverable, if it ever really existed: the idea of a city actually open to the public. What do I mean by the public? To recall Erica Hunt's phrasing: "You in a genealogy of the visible, the legible, trying to find a way into the 'I,' that Cartesian empire, and 'we' the possibility of being one of the tribe of humanity." Maybe the simplest way of stating it is this: a place where everyone's needs are recognized. And, if possible, cared for.

It came to me, in those first few weeks after Trump's election, that what Central Station needs to be is a slightly improved version of what it already is: in its scale, its symmetry, its grounds, a monument. The Flight Memorial.[2] "There were 1,600,000 white people in Detroit after the war," Detroit's former mayor Coleman Young wrote in his memoirs, "and 1,400,000 of them left." When children, or tourists, visit monuments, their first response is almost always, simply: why? This is a question that should be allowed to hang over us. Why aban-

---

2. Given the pace of redevelopment and gentrification in Detroit, it's not surprising that in June 2018 Ford announced it would acquire and restore Central Station as a shopping destination and office complex devoted to innovative concepts in "the future of transportation." Whether this plan will succeed where many past plans have failed is uncertain. As of now, the station remains untouched.

don and waste the great public works of the midcentury city, and the unachieved ideals of citizenship and the social that went along with them? Because the aesthetic of white flight, in the end, is just that: not so much a search for purity as an extravagance of waste. The absolute discovery of loneliness, as Robinson puts it, comes at an absolute cost: to be fully committed to it, in a mysterious way, means to relinquish the possibility of self-knowledge. When you refuse to allow for the presence of others, you lose the ability to be seen by them. At that point, a social bond, a human bond, is severed. This is a form of imaginative violence Americans practice so routinely that it has become, in the biopolitical sense, second nature, or just nature.

A monument or memorial, of course, does cultural work that fiction is never required to do: it exists in public, in open view, and is designed, required, to be artistically uncomplicated. A monument has to have obvious meaning. You have to be able to take it all in at once, visually, physically—to enter and leave in the space of half an hour. But that doesn't mean there's no relation between the two.

What would it mean to accept that America's great and possibly catastrophic failure is its failure to imagine what it means to live together? A culture so accomplished at breaking and abandoning things, by definition, lacks an intuitive grasp of repair, reparation, reconciliation. But literature works according to its own eccentric logic. And maybe the most eccentric, unacceptable imaginative projection is a vision of an imperfectly reconciled world, the alternate realities already here but unseen. Leave the monument open so that people can walk through it and see what lies on the other side.

# Parts of Us Not Made at Home

Forever is a long time.

Charles W. Chesnutt, "What Is a White Man?"

All American literature is multicultural.

Ishmael Reed, Kathryn Trueblood, and Shawn Wong,
*The Before Columbus Foundation Fiction Anthology*

# 1

For decades—no one knows exactly how long—my grandfather kept a portrait of his mother, the only image that remained of her, in the back of his bedroom closet, facing the wall. When we discovered it after he died, in 1998, no one, not even my step-grandmother, knew it was there.

The portrait showed a woman with an impatient expression and very striking features: dark hair and prominent dark eyebrows, set a little higher in the oval of the face than you might expect. It reminded me a little of the famous self-portraits I'd seen of Frida Kahlo. It also reminded me of myself. This woman, Amy—Amelia—Brazil, my great-grandmother, resembled me more closely than either of my parents.

As I understand it—to the degree I will ever understand it—my grandfather spent his adult life resenting Amy and resisting her influence; though when she died in 1963, he didn't refuse his inheritance, which gave him disposable income he'd never achieved himself.

His father had died when he was in his twenties, and Amy went on to marry three more times, each husband wealthier than the last. My mother remembers her as a grande dame among the influential families of Piedmont—the genteel town set high on a hill in the middle of Oakland—who took her out for fancy dinners at Trader Vic's and paid for trips to Europe my grandparents couldn't afford.

There's another way of telling this story: Amy Brazil was not white. Nor was she, as I'd usually heard, Portuguese: her parents were immigrants from Flores, an island in the Azores, a volcanic archipelago in the middle of the Atlantic. (Technically an autonomous region of Portugal, the Azores lie almost nine hundred miles west of the Iberian Peninsula and northwest of Morocco.) Like islanders in many parts of the world, Azoreans complicate continental racial logic; they are descended from Christian or Jewish Portuguese colonists, North Africans, sub-Saharan African slaves, immigrants from other parts of Europe, or all of the above. I never met Amy, but I did once meet her brother, my great-great-uncle George Bartholemew Brazil, who lived alone (he never married or had children) in a large Victorian house in Oakland, near Fruitvale Station. It was the house his own father had built in 1906. His skin was a medium, lustrous brown, and he had blue eyes. I would never have recognized him as a relative without being told.

Amy Brazil, the face in the frame so much like my face, became white by powdering her skin. Every day, all day. Through artificial means, that is, she passed. She found herself to be unacceptable and chose to do something about it. She reinvented herself. If I had to guess, I would say that was what my grandfather hated most about her. Through marriage, she passed, and passed down whiteness to her only child, my grandfather, and through him to me.

This is not a story but the marker of an absence of one. It's unexceptional. There's a teleological quality about it: *this is how we became who we inarguably are.* Azoreans who emigrated in the late nineteenth and early twentieth centuries took advantage of their unclassifiable racial appearance, and the geographic uncertainty of their origins, to perform what Matthew Frye Jacobson, in *Whiteness of a Different Color,* calls the special "alchemy of race" available to southern Europeans: they became white through conscious acts of differentiation, assimilation, and erasure. George Brazil's maternal grandfather, who came from Flores to Boston in 1861 and immediately enlisted in the Union navy, changed his name to "Patterson," the name of the captain of his ship. This was a matter of survival in an era when scientific racism, Social Darwinism, and political nativism all agreed on the inherent inferiority of "swarthy" or "Mediterranean" Europeans, alongside Jews and Slavs.

For years I thought about writing a story about Amy Brazil. She seemed like an obvious subject, my own great-grandmother, a "dramatic" person given to grand gestures. But I could never fix her in view. A face in a painting, in this case, was not enough; a few pieces of heavy jewelry, some Chinese export furniture she'd acquired on cruises—she loved chinoiserie—and the smell of the Jean Patou perfume Eau de Joy, which, my mother told me, she used to sprinkle on her clothes instead of taking them to the cleaners. These are the details; somebody else should use them. I tried to imagine her meeting my great-grandfather, the serious and doomed young doctor, who'd grown a beard to appear older to his patients but nothing came. Maybe most family stories work this way. Most actual lives are not as remarkable as writers want them to be. I was looking for the drama of her passing, among other things, but found none, because it was successful: she remade herself. That was the end of her story.

Racial classification is a reductive process: any way of simplifying the world, making it artificial, involves first taking things away. Severing connections and bonds: practicing symbolic, as well as actual, violence. One of the results of this symbolic violence is to make interesting lives, layered histories, and complex identifications disappear. In other words: by flattening life, racism makes it feel boring, exhausting, embarrassing. This is what happened to me, when I tried to write the story of my great-grandparents: I stopped because I was afraid it would be pointless. I had nothing to build on and nothing to go on.

Is it possible to describe the shape, the limits, the dimensions of this state of boredom? I sometimes think if I could do that I could unlock, with my own kryptonite, the secret power of whiteness over American life. At the college in central New Jersey where I've taught for twelve years, I often find myself sitting face-to-face with a student telling me, explicitly or implicitly, *I don't know what to write about*. It's a statement that rotates silently around the truism *write what you know*. This sentence presents not only an epistemological—what does it mean to know? what kind of knowledge presents itself to be written?—but an ontological trap. Who is the self, what is the place, where is the point of origin that I am supposed to know? What does the "what" in "what you know" consist of? Due to the demographics of suburban New Jersey, the student in front of me most often identifies as white and has an Italian surname. She was an American success story until she entered my creative writing class. Predictability, for her, has always been an asset.

And I've always wanted to say: like you, in the summers, or anytime I'm in the sun for extended periods, I turn a rich, coppery brown, darker than anyone else in my family. I have always been secretly proud of my ability to tan.

What does it mean, or does it mean, to be the great-grandchild of a woman who passed? For most of my life I would have said: nothing. To have known, or not known, this detail makes almost no difference in my life. What does it mean in the present?

"Regretting the absence of meaning itself has meaning," Jean-Luc Nancy writes in *Being Singular Plural*. Not because we need to chase after some absolute, hidden truth; because, as he puts it, "We do not 'have' meaning anymore, because we ourselves are meaning—entirely, without reserve, infinitely, with no meaning other than 'us.'" Interracial life always seems to be sending its regrets and not showing up. I want to bring it out into the open. Not only as a subject for writing—which it has been, in an American context, at least since William Wells Brown published *Clotel, or The President's Daughter* in 1853—but as its own distinct subjectivity. What would it mean, what does it mean, to write from a point of view that is not divided but intrinsically plural?

2

"I went to the territory to renew my supply of stories," says the narrator, speaking of California, in James Alan McPherson's 1978 short story "Elbow Room": "There were no new ones in the East at the time I left. . . . And the caste curtains were drawn, resegregating all imaginations. . . . If I had approached a stranger and said, 'Friend, I need your part of the story in order to complete my sense of self,' I would have caused him to shudder, tremble, perhaps denounce me as an assailant."

Paul Frost and Virginia Valentine are an interracial couple in San Francisco: he's white, from a small town in Kansas, a pacifist completing alternative service in a mental hospital in Oakland; she's black, from Tennessee, a just-returned Peace Corps volunteer—"a country raconteur with a stock of stories flavored by international experience. Telling them, she spoke with her whole presence in very complicated ways." The narrator, a black man, otherwise unnamed and unidentified, knows them personally, and watches them with a keen, hungry, even obsessive interest. Like a nineteenth-century narrator—like George Eliot, say—he wants to see them whole, the first time, as "characters," not in the casual sense we use the word today, but as graven images, physiognomy crossed with moral constitution and temporal destiny:

> I know that when I looked I saw dead Indians living in his eyes.
> But I also saw a wholesome glow in their directness. They seemed
> in earnest need of answers to honest questions always on the verge
> of being asked. . . . And yet at times, watching Virginia's eyes soften
> as they moved over his face, I could read in them the recognition
> of extraordinary spiritual forces, quietly commanded, but so self-
> assured as to be unafraid of advertising themselves. I am sure he
> was unaware of his innocence. And perhaps this is why Virginia's
> eyes pleaded, when he openly approached a soul-crushed stranger,
> *Don't hurt my baby! Don't hurt my baby!*, even while her voice laughed,
> teased, or growled.

Who would be possessed to write this way, about this subject, in 1978? In a sense, "possessed" is precisely the word, because the story is a manuscript, battled over by the narrator and his editor, who keeps inserting combative notes and queries, and who claims to have cut and shaped the words before us: *In order to save this narration, editor felt compelled to clarify slightly, not to censor but to impose at least the illusion of order. This was an effort toward preserving a certain morality of technique.* Later, as a "point of information," the editor asks the narrator the following:

> *What has form to do with caste restrictions?*
> Everything.
> *You are saying you want to be white?*
> A narrator needs as much access to the world as the advocates of that mythology.
> *You are ashamed then of being black?*
> Only of not being nimble enough to dodge other people's straitjackets.
> *Are you not too much obsessed here with integration?*
> I was cursed with a healthy imagination.

The story does feel, from the beginning, under the weight of a curse—which it resists, at first gleefully, then sadly, then not at all. Sitting in Paul and Virginia's kitchen, shortly after their wedding, the narrator listens to them talking about Paul's parents in Kansas—who have refused to accept the marriage, who have never even spoken to Virginia over the phone. "While there is still time," the narrator says to Paul, in the disembodied, oracular voice he uses throughout, "you must force the reality of your wife into your father's mind and run toward whatever cover it provides. . . . You have enlisted in a psychological war." Paul gets angry and orders him to leave, but later, after a traumatic encounter, calls him back:

> "What's a nigger?" he asked me on the telephone. "I mean, what does it *really* mean to you?"

I said, "A descendant of Proteus, an expression of the highest form of freedom."

Who is actually telling the story, and whose story is it to tell? It's painful, almost excruciating, to draw this question out of life and into the realm of what the editor calls the "morality of technique." But that pain is what "Elbow Room" exacts on me. By what power, what authorization, do I allow myself to make fictions out of human lives, or lifelike fictions? A narrator, the narrator tells us, has to be cursed with a healthy imagination. When Virginia gets pregnant, and Paul's father refuses to see the baby, she confesses to the narrator that she feels her hopes for the future ebbing away: "Wouldn't it of been something," she says, "to be a nigger that could relate to white and black and everything else in the world out of a self as big as the world is?" The narrator, too, is losing hope; the baby may be black or white, but will never rise above those categories: "black and blind," he says, "or passing for white and self-blinded. Those are the only choices." He abandons his search for new stories and decides to move back east; when he says good-bye, Paul calls after him: "At *least* I tried! At *least* I'm *fighting*! And I know what a *nigger* is, too. It's what you are when you begin thinking of yourself as a work of art!"

The short story collection *Elbow Room* was the end of McPherson's career as a fiction writer. He was thirty-four when it was published; thirty-five when it won the Pulitzer Prize. In his essay "On Becoming an American Writer," originally published in 1979, McPherson wrote that *Elbow Room* came out of a feeling of overwhelming despair he felt in the seventies, in spite of his own achievements: admitted to Harvard Law, published in the *Atlantic*, hired to teach at the University of Virginia. "I have benefited from all the contracts," he wrote. "I have exhausted all the contracts." Quoting from Albion W. Tourgee's doomed defense of the Fourteenth Amendment in *Plessy v. Ferguson* in 1896, he described the radicalism of the view that "each United States citizen would . . . be on at least conversant terms with all its diversity, carry the mainstream of the culture inside himself":

This was the model I was aiming for in my book of stories. It can be achieved with or without intermarriage, but it will cost a great many mistakes and a lot of pain. It is, finally, a product of culture and not of race. And achieving it will require that one be conscious of America's culture and the complexity of all its people. . . . Such a perspective would provide a minefield of delicious ironies.

It's hard to think of a writer as nuanced, thoughtful, and humble as McPherson as an extremist of any kind, but "Elbow Room" is among the most radical works of American fiction published in the postwar era: a confession of its own impossibility, which is also America's impossibility. It's a kind of artistic suicide note left outside the minefield. The story wants to recuperate the word "n____" as a statement of artistic freedom, and it does, within the domain of the text. But outside it? In the culture at large? Silence is the answer. The taboo is broken, but at the cost of becoming an isolated incident. There's something almost Rilkean about "Elbow Room"'s extravagant self-annihilation: to be the cup that shattered as it rang. You could compare it to Hofmannsthal's "Lord Chandos Letter," a seminal text of German fin de siècle modernism, in which the twenty-six-year-old author effectively ended his career in poetry, declaring in the voice of the fictional Chandos that his imagination, once seized with cosmic visions, has now abandoned language altogether. But Hofmannsthal—a prodigy, raised in the most cultivated circumstances, rapturously acclaimed since his teenage years—was speaking of a personal, purely internal, breakdown; McPherson is describing to us a fantasy of a national aesthetic that pours through his fingers like sand. *Friend, I need your part of the story in order to complete my sense of self.* The story never arrives; the self never arrives.

Interracial American literature—to the extent that such a thing exists—is full of these silences, blind alleys, dead ends. It could almost be called a tradition of silences, cut through with frantic attempts to speak, extreme, hyperbolic statements, outbreaks of cursing and shoving. It never comes to rest. It mourns an impossible dream. Interracial texts tend to be singular and unrepeatable, self-erasing and/or self-canceling. As such, they can be vehicles for rage: most famously, and most indelibly, in the play *Dutchman*, the last text Amiri Baraka produced as LeRoi Jones, before abandoning his own interracial family, his name, and Greenwich Village for Harlem in 1965:

> CLAY: And I'm the great would-be poet. Yes. That's right! Poet. Some kind of bastard literature . . . all it needs is a simple knife thrust. Just let me bleed you, you loud whore, and one poem vanished. A whole people of neurotics, struggling to keep from being sane. And the only thing that would cure the neurosis would be your murder. Simple as that. I mean if I murdered you, other white people would begin to understand me. You understand? No I guess not. If Bessie Smith had killed some white people she wouldn't have needed that music.

The choice is always between love and death: or to see love as a form of death, or death as an expression of love. Writing, in these conditions, is murky, neurotic, impossible; only violence is clarity, and it's going to happen any minute, if not right now.

In my mind "Elbow Room" is always matched with another story, also set in San Francisco, also rooted in the seventies, which could be its sequel: Gina Berriault's "Lonesome Roads." A black man sees a white woman on a playground bench, watching her daughter play, and greets her. Twelve years before, they were lovers; they haven't seen each other since. The story is narrated from his close point of view. He feels solid and self-assured, no longer the "skinny, agitated" kid he once was. To him, she seems scattered and exhausted. They fall into a cryptic, telegraphic conversation, like ex-lovers everywhere. "I guess every joy brings a burden along with it," she says. "You don't realize that so much until you've got kids":

> "You never used to talk that way," he said. "When you were always deploring burdens there wasn't any compensation that came along with them."
>
> "But I still deplore them," she said.

"That's good," he said drolly. "That's good. And are you still on the right track? About how to get rid of burdens? Though the way I heard it, that track collapsed."

She was not cornered, he saw. "What we learned from that," she said, "is there are more answers than one."

"Lonesome Roads" is so carefully and exquisitely composed, so faithful to every shade of nuance in the scene, that it takes on enormous metonymic weight. It has that quality of short stories in which the last scene of a long dramatic arc becomes the only necessary scene (Fitzgerald's "Babylon Revisited" is one defining example). But interracial love has to survive beyond the aesthetic force of understatement—or, for that matter, overstatement. Read "Lonesome Roads" through the filter of *Dutchman* and you get a composite American memory of rage, betrayal, bitterness, disillusionment, and abandonment; and what this aesthetic memory composes, in no uncertain terms, is a message of impossibility, that interracial love is a journey that always speeds off a cliff. This is the afterlife of the narrative of the tragic mulatto, still doing damage in the present.[3]

This morning I was standing in my son's first grade classroom at drop-off time and contemplating the faces of the children in the room. Asa is multiracial, and so, by my count, are at least a third of his classmates. In most cases I have no way of knowing, by looking at them, what their ethnic origins are. They are *noticeably* indeterminate, unlocatable, by normative American racial standards. In some cases I know some version of an origin story—the kind that you hear in one or two sentences on the playground—but mostly I'm happy not to ask. These children are not tragic figures; not isolated; also not intrinsically remarkable or interesting; not carriers of some torch of utopian promise. They are "the future" only in the obvious sense that they

---

3. I use the term "mulatto" (which some people experience as a racial slur) only when it's historically appropriate, as in the phrase "tragic mulatto," or when it applies to my Portuguese-speaking Azorean family, who used the word in its original linguistic context (see page 201).

will be alive after you and I, the people reading this, are dead. They are one version of the ordinary present. This is a subset of a subset of the population, a public school in the West Village of Manhattan, but the demographics of the United States are shifting toward the composition of this class. A major study from the Pew Foundation found 17% of new marriages, roughly one in six, were identifiably interracial as of 2015; 14% of the population polled in 2015 disapproved of intermarriage, compared to 63% in 1990.

Is it possible to locate an aesthetic in this classroom, let alone, or attached to, a politics? For someone my age the reflexive answer would include a passing reference to United Colors of Benetton's advertisements and/or Whitney Houston's "The Greatest Love of All" ("I believe that children are the future / teach them well and let them lead the way"). Which is to say, in shorthand, no. Or, it's been done: it was done by the ad agency McCann-Erickson with the "I'd Like to Teach the World to Sing" TV spot for Coca-Cola in 1970, a moment savagely re-created by Matthew Weiner as the climax of *Mad Men*. These images of a multiracial peace, all the colors of the rainbow, have been around as long as I have and are a staple cliché of two different eras: the 1970s and the late 2000s, particularly 2008, the year it seemed, for a brief moment, that a postracial future had actually arrived. Anne Anlin Cheng calls these images "pathological euphoria." Another term for them, used by Lee Edelman and others, is "reproductive futurism": a politics that believes that children are both the inspiration and the solution.

I get that. I imagine that anyone who has ever been in an interracial relationship imagines love is the answer and then eventually (if the relationship lasts) realizes it isn't. There's a reason superimposing romantic and reproductive love over politics makes intuitive sense: the rhetoric of love assumes that love works, love is forever, when other kinds of bonds are severed. It requires a kind of emotional maturity entirely absent from American political life to grapple with the necessity of different kinds of love, concern, or care. On the simplest level, there's the idea of Christian love itself, which has to be broken down into three separate terms: eros, philos, agape. Martin Luther King took great pains to separate agape from eros, a position best summarized by Cornel West's famous line, "Justice is what love looks like in public." But the rhetoric of the 1960s and '70s made this distinction socially and politically impossible. The result, Jeff Chang writes, is the central paradox of the "'post-racial' moment": "While our images depict a nation moving toward desegregation, our indices reveal growing resegregation and inequity."

In a sense what this conversation hinges on, what the question of interracial life has always hinged on, is the nature of the simple word "freedom," by which I mean nothing more or less than the promise made to my generation, before we were old enough to understand what promises were: free to be you and me. Freedom to do what, exactly? Free to *be* what, exactly? Those of us born in the 1970s have been the test market, the focus group, for freedom, for the most part as an incoherent disorganizing force that, in the guise of the free market, has always taken more than it gives. For my generation, interracial marriage, if it expresses anything, primarily expresses freedom through a private and individualized concept of citizenship as consumption: *this is my choice.* Out of many friends my own age and younger in interracial marriages and relationships, I can't name one (including myself) who would say that idealism, or political commitment, brought them together, or that their relationship is meant to be a "statement." That would be embarrassingly retro, recalling our parents' era, before "multiculturalism" and "diversity" became neoliberal buzzwords, a corporate Fruitopia.

I'm writing this essay for Mina and Asa, in memory of George and Amy Brazil, and also for myself: because I think embarrassed silence around pluralism and hybridity—the fact of hybridity, in my own body, or my children's bodies—is as dangerous as euphoria. It leads back to a kind of cynicism that only affirms the power of privatized citizenship, and it deflects the possibility of another kind of freedom, which *is* out there, at least in the fictive world of a story like "Elbow Room": a freedom that dodges all straitjackets.

American writers keep telling the story of the tragic mulatto because they can't believe, against all available evidence, that sometimes love really can triumph over death. In a climate like the present, it's hard to affirm that belief, or for that matter, affirm much of anything. But that's what the imagination is for.

## 3

There's another foundational novel within this narrative I haven't mentioned, because I'm incapable of writing about it with much of a degree of critical distance. Until recently it was almost forgotten; now, as part of the larger revival of interest in Baldwin's work, it may finally be recognized as a necessary and central postwar American novel, as important as *On The Road* or *Invisible Man* or *Herzog* or *The Crying of Lot 49*. I first read *Another Country* when I was in graduate school in Michigan, and I remember the night I finished it: I said out loud, to Sonya, lying next to me in bed, "I will never be able to write a novel like this." It felt like a confession of failure. She said, sensibly, also probably half-asleep, "No one expects you to."

What was I thinking, at that moment? Which is to say, why would I project my white, heterosexual male self, born in 1974, onto a novel published by a gay black man in 1962? I could easily and fatuously call that state of mind "negative capability," in the sense Keats intended— refusing to connect the dots, or warp poetics into a theory, the way he despised Coleridge for turning from "Kublai Khan" to German ideal- ist philosophy. But negative capability is an evocative and renewable concept that has led many lives since 1817; most recently, the phi- losopher and political theorist Roberto Unger has made it a central point of argument in his work. Negative capability, for him, is an ac- tive psychological state, in which the political subject simply refuses to respect the limitations of the present—that is, false necessity. It means, in his words, "to seize on deviant, subsidiary, or repressed ele- ments in present or remembered experience and to push them toward a dominant position, all the while changing them in the course of this extension."

Unger, in his own way, is an unrepentant optimist, while refusing to hold on to any rigid predictions or narratives about history; his most recent book is *The Religion of the Future*. *Another Country* (published in

1962) also practices, in its own way—with the force of biblical prophecy turned to secular ends—the religion of the future. It shifts from extreme darkness into one displaced version of hope. Very briefly—because this is a book that has to be read, not summarized—it has three movements. In the first, Rufus, a struggling black musician who has just left a doomed and abusive relationship with a white woman, wanders the streets of New York, descending into a depressive spiral, and finally jumps off the George Washington Bridge. The novel reorganizes itself around the reverberations of Rufus's death; what was a descent into the underground from a single consciousness becomes a collective aftermath. In this desperate circumstance, Rufus's best friend, Vivaldo—who is white—and Rufus's sister, Ida, fall into and then out of love. Entangled in their relationship is Eric, Rufus's former lover, who, like Baldwin, fled sexual repression to find love in Paris; Yves, Eric's current lover; and Richard and Cass, a young white couple who were close to Rufus and are undone by his death.

*Another Country* is narrated in a loose, accumulative, naturalistic style that treats Rufus's death as a catastrophe but not a tragedy; the emphasis is on the state of mourning as a state of possibility, the most radical openness. Unlike nearly every other interracial couple in American literature up to that point, Ida and Vivaldo don't *always* live in a state of fear, secrecy, or denial. At moments, in little flashes, they get to act the way we imagine couples act, rather than as vehicles for history:

> "Love me," he said. "I want you to love me."
> She caught one of his hands as it moved along her belly.
> "You think I'm one of those just-love-to-love girls."
> "Baby," he said, "I sure hope so; we're going to be great, let me tell you. We haven't even started yet." His voice had dropped to a whisper and their two hands knotted together in a teasing tug of war.

When I teach *Another Country*, I'm always surprised at how my students recoil, just a little, from Baldwin's frank bodily descriptions. For them the most unthinkable part of the novel is another kind of crossing: not Ida's relationship with Vivaldo but what happens to Vivaldo after Ida abandons him: he goes to Eric for companionship and support, and winds up sleeping with him. He "seemed to have fallen through a great hole in time," Baldwin writes of Vivaldo, the morning after, "back to his innocence, he felt clear, washed, and empty, waiting to be filled. . . . He felt fantastically protected, liberated, by the knowledge that, no matter where, once the clawing day descended, he felt compelled to go . . . there was a man in the world who loved him."

In the 1991 law review article that first defined the term "intersectionality," Kimberlé Crenshaw wrote that when people think intersectionally, they may find it "easier . . . to summon the courage to challenge groups that are after all, in one sense, 'home' to us, in the name of the parts of us that are not made at home." It may seem like a strange and pointless exercise to look backward from legal scholarship in the era of Anita Hill and Clarence Thomas to a novel written before the passage of the Voting Rights Act, but that is *Another Country*'s problem: it represents a form of life that wouldn't find a public name for itself for thirty years. To be bisexually and interracially romantic, even in Greenwich Village, was to feel like a minority that might literally fit in a closet. "There were not enough of us," Audre Lorde writes in *Zami: A New Spelling of My Name*, speaking of the tiny group of black lesbians she knew in the Village in Baldwin's era: "We tried to build a community of sorts where we could, at the very least, survive within a world we correctly perceived to be hostile to us; we talked endlessly about how best to create that mutual support which twenty years later was being discussed in the women's movement as a brand-new concept."

There's something about intersectional thinking that involves not only silences but actual leaps in time—temporal fractures, inconsistencies, dislocations, aporias. If interracial love feels, as it so often does, like a utopian state of impossibility, in which all our defenses and preconceptions are cast aside, and I, the lover, take shelter with you, the beloved, in our private refuge—the apartment, the bedroom, the tolerant community, the bar, even the no-questions-asked hotel—that utopian moment and its possibilities become detached from ordinary chronology or historical necessity.

One artistic response to this situation has been to move inter-racial love into the realm of science fiction, fantasy, or fabulism. But it's necessary to recall that these utopian moments did not just happen as private encounters or between exemplary couples: in the 1970s, particularly, they happened in public. Jim Jones, founder of the People's Church, was, among many other things, a radical advocate of inter-racial love and justice, and the church itself was an integrated utopian community. Many of Jones's most fervent devotees and assistants—including many of Jonestown's residents—were black people. The most heartbreaking and haunting photographs taken in Jonestown aren't the famous ones capturing the aftermath of the mass suicide, but the portraits of ordinary children at play:

I was born in 1974, at the peak of the era of alternative communities, and my childhood and young adulthood were marked, if only in small ways, by the failures, in a few cases even the horrors, of movements like Jonestown. I've had friends or friends of friends who grew up in Synanon or the Weather Underground or the Catholic Worker movement, in womanist communes, Sri Chinmoy centers, psychoanalytic theater cults, or EST. These are some of the most remarkable people I know; they tend to be extraordinarily self-reliant and committed to their work, as artists, activists, teachers, environmentalists, scholars. But they're also marked (in some cases, actively traumatized) by their disordered childhoods, their unreliable or wildly irresponsible parents, and by the sheer amount of failure and disappearance and cultural amnesia they—we—witnessed as the seventies gave way to the eighties.

There's probably no better record of this period, in interracial terms, than Danzy Senna's novel *Caucasia*, published in 1998—a largely autobiographical account of two biracial sisters, one light-skinned and capable of passing, the other unequivocally black, who experience a sudden and traumatic separation when their parents flee Boston, in separate directions, in 1976. (Senna is the daughter of the poet Fanny Howe and the writer and activist Carl Senna, who divorced in the same period after a turbulent and violent marriage.) Birdie, the light-skinned child, escapes to New Hampshire with her white mother, who believes the FBI are pursuing her for her marginal involvement with a violent revolutionary group. Her father, a black anthropologist, takes her sister, Cole, to Brazil, imagining it to be a multiracial paradise. After six unhappy years passing as white—her mother insists they assume the identities of a Jewish mother and daughter, Sheila and Jesse Goldman—Birdie, now a teenager, runs away, and finally discovers her father and Cole living in Oakland, where biracial children are unremarkable.

*Caucasia* is a lucid and absorbing novel, explicit and literal in the way it attends to the details of its historical moment; but it's also a deeply conservative book—instinctively conservative rather than disillusioned, because Birdie and Cole were too young to have illusions in the first place. It's a novel about being the victim of your parents' idealism, selfishness, and naïveté—an experience many children born in the 1970s can relate to—but unlike, say, Michel Houellebecq's *The Elementary Particles*, published in France the same year, it doesn't advance any argument about where the theories of that era went wrong.

In a quintessentially Anglo-American move, it defaults to the position that theories always fail in practice, and theoreticians fail to see the actual world in front of them, which is all that matters. "You are an overintellectualized creep," Birdie tells her father, when she finds him in Oakland, now working on a book about biracial children as the "canaries in the coal mine" of American racial relations, before she leaves to reunite with her sister.

The logic of *Caucasia*, which I recognize as the logic of my own adulthood, is that stability matters, the nuclear family matters, and children matter above all. When you've grown up seeing the effects of neglectful or oblivious parenting everywhere you look, it's hard to argue with this position. It's also hard to overstate how perfectly it dovetails with the more general cultural shift of the Reagan revolution, which defined my childhood, toward a more individuated and austere view of life defined by the ineluctable forces of the market. In the mid to late 1990s it was difficult not to feel that the 1960s and '70s were an impossibly distant and slightly ridiculous epoch, an aberration, in contrast with the more linear, streamlined, pragmatic, interconnected present, where no one any longer needed to belong to a "movement." From this vantage point it was easy to look back in a way that rendered the political as inevitably personal. It was a way of displacing my generation's failure of political agency by focusing on the past utopian moment as the source of that failure— again, conservative or wounded or traumatized, debilitated rather than disillusioned.

If I had been thinking clearly the night I finished *Another Country*, I would have thought about my friends, and about Jonestown, *Jungle Fever*, *Caucasia*, "Elbow Room," *Dutchman*, and *Guess Who's Coming to Dinner*. That is to say, I would have thought about all the ways interracial life has changed, become more possible, and yet, as a kind of politics, debilitated, unable to speak for itself. I would have felt closed in by these closed texts—which is, after all, what they are: texts in which the interracial relationship implodes, culminates, and ends the story. But I wasn't thinking that way; I was thinking irresponsibly, transhistorically, which is one version of the artist's prerogative. At the end of *Another Country*, as if to demonstrate his indifference to the grim and typical closure of the black/white plot, Baldwin shifts the point of view to Yves, arriving in New York for the first time:

> The hostesses stood there, smiling and saying good-bye. The sun was bright on their faces, and on the faces of the disembarking passengers; they seemed, as they turned and disappeared, to be stepping into a new and healing light. . . . The hostess with whom he had flirted was nearest the door. "*Au revoir,*" she said, with the bright and generous and mocking smile possessed by so many of his countrywomen. He suddenly realized that he would never see her again. It had not occurred to him, until this moment, that he could possibly have left behind him anything which he might, one day, long for and need, with all his heart. . . . And he wanted to say, *Vous êtes très jolie,* but it was too late, he had hit the light, the sun glared at him, and everything wavered in the heat. He started down the extraordinary steps. When he hit the ground, a voice above him said, "*Bonjour, mon gar. Soyez le bienvenue.*" He looked up. Eric leaned on the rail of the observation deck, grinning, wearing an open white shirt and khaki trousers.

There are many more and less charitable ways of reading this scene, which comes perilously close to being too glamorous for its own good—you can imagine it as a vintage airline poster or Louis Vuitton ad. (Although it's wise to remember, as my great-grandmother might have said, there are more purposes to glamorous than unglamorous people care to imagine.) Baldwin ends the novel with the line, still in Yves's POV: "He strode through the barriers, more high-hearted than he had ever been as a child, into that city which the people from heaven had made their home." This too is a transformative fiction, a resistance to the limitations of the present, which Unger would argue is the political subject's prerogative as well:

> The central difficulty in our understanding of ourselves and of society is that we cannot mark out the limits of the possible. The

possible . . . is not a well-defined, closed set of transmutations within which actual historical experience has developed as a subset. The possible is just what we can do next, getting there from here. However, so long as we make a living connection between our ideas about how we got here and our ideas about how we can get to the next place, we do not need to stare at what exists and to represent that stare as insight. We can imagine what exists as the resting place and the starting point that it always really is.

## 4

I'm trying to think of a way to draw a line to represent my racial history, my relation to whiteness, as Amy Brazil's great-grandchild—that is, as a descendant of multiracial people, one of whom chose, deliberately, to become white—and as a father of multiracial children. One way to do it, representing whiteness as normal, neutral, and central, would be to start with a curve upward to a straight horizontal line (whiteness as the horizon line, but also the flatline of the ECG) and then a curve downward, representing my children, one of whose skin is darker than Amy Brazil's ever was. Physiologically, in a map of melanin content, the line would go in reverse: I would be the bottom of the trough.

These are lines that call themselves into question, that have no business being lines at all. In *Tristram Shandy*, with great pretend precision, the narrator stops us at the end of the fifth book to assure us that each preceding book, though it seems to be filled with nothing but digressions that interrupt and postpone his own story, has gone on "in a tolerable straight line":

## CHAPTER XL

I AM now beginning to get fairly into my work; and by the help of a vegetable diet, with a few of the cold seeds, I make no doubt but I shall be able to go on with my uncle Toby's story, and my own, in a tolerable straight line. Now,

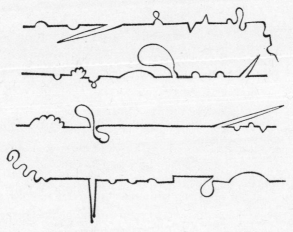

These were the four lines I moved in through my first, second, third, and fourth volumes.—In the fifth volume I have been very good,—the precise line I have described in it being this:

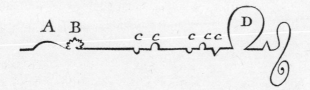

In "The Law of Genre" Derrida says any line that claims to separate or categorize, that creates "a law of 'do' or 'do not,'" actually bends to include both opposites at once, a figure he calls an "invagination."

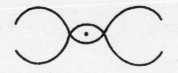

These squiggles, these lines that fold back on themselves and refuse to arrive, or stay straight, aren't whimsical or fantastic: they're a necessary tool when I try to hold in my mind the separate legalities, the concept of the legal itself, which created the United States as it is today. In *Interracialism* Werner Sollors puts it this way: "Could the question of what is American about American culture be answered with 'prohibiting black-white heterosexual couples from forming families and withholding legitimacy from their descendants'?" What Sollors means, less elliptically, is this: Legally, in the explicit sense, marriage between white and black Americans was only permitted throughout the United States by *Loving v. Virginia* in 1967. Legally, in the implicit sense, the sense of what is allowed and never prosecuted, coercive interracial sex and reproduction—the culture of rape within the culture of enslavement—was so widespread in the nineteenth century that most of the surviving population of African descent, after emancipation, was also of European descent.

This is a point of horror and laughter, where serious analysis has to stop because it can no longer be called "serious," where the word "legal" itself stops making sense. I'm thinking about the courtroom scene in the film version of *To Kill a Mockingbird* where Gregory Peck as Atticus Finch, the craggy features of his face embodying the Acropolis, solemnly informs the jury that Tom Robinson is on trial because a white woman lusted after him, never pointing out that virtually every person sitting above in the gallery (and probably more than a few of the white people in the good seats) is descended from a black woman and the white man who raped her. To think interracially in this moment, to grasp the actual racial composition of the room, and its history, you would have to make the moment into something more like *The Discreet Charm of the Bourgeoisie* or *Monty Python's Meaning of Life.* There is no way of reproducing *To Kill a Mockingbird* that is both realist and accurate. You have to try, but just barely, to keep a straight face, as Charles W. Chesnutt does, responding to white arguments about the supposed dangers of miscegenation in his 1899 essay "What Is a White Man?":

It is a fact that at present, in the United States, a colored man or woman whose complexion is white or nearly white is presumed, in the absence of any knowledge of his or her antecedents, to be the offspring of a union not sanctified by law. . . . This presumption of illegitimacy was once, perhaps, true of the majority of such persons; but the times have changed. More than half of the colored people of the United States are of mixed blood; they marry and are given in marriage, and they beget children of complexions similar to their own. Whether or not, therefore, [antimiscegenation] laws which stamp these children as illegitimate, and which by indirection establish a lower standard of morality for a large part of the population . . . are wise laws; and whether or not the purity of the white race could not be as well preserved by the exercise of virtue, and the operation of those natural laws which are so often quoted by Southern writers as the justification of all sorts of Southern "policies"—are questions which the good citizen may at least turn over in his mind occasionally, pending the settlement of other complications which have grown out of the presence of the Negro on this continent.

The regime of racial purity and separation, which Americans still inhabit, is a kind of fantasy or science fiction built on the implicit knowledge that impurity exists somewhere else. Hence the tired language, everywhere in the interracial symbolic order, of "light" and "shadows," which only reiterates the Platonic fantasy that there is a pure source from which all misunderstandings emanate, instead of ironies and double entendres, misprisions and blurred lines and squiggles. As Hortense Spillers puts it in her epochal essay "Mama's Baby, Papa's Maybe," names Americans conventionally call each other (even the simplest, in her case, "Black Woman at the Podium") are "embedded in bizarre axiological ground[;] they demonstrate a sort of telegraphic coding; they are markers so loaded with mythical prepossession that there is no easy way for the agents buried beneath them to come clean." The easiest way to understand this is to observe elementary-age

American children trying to work out, in their own minds, what racial descriptions mean: not literally a reference to color ("black people aren't actually *black*; white people are actually sort of pink") but somehow related to color; not necessarily indicative of family relationships but obviously conditioned by one's relatives; rooted in history, although the historical terms are different. It's a semantic and psychological puzzle they often find impossible to explain, even if they know clearly, echoing the adults around them, who fits in which category.

I have a close friend, a woman my age, who teaches fourth grade in Montpelier, Vermont. She is married to a white-appearing husband and has white-appearing children. Her father is African American; her mother is white; she herself is racially ambiguous, but in Vermont, where she's lived most of her life, she reads as white nearly all the time. For years she kept one of the artist Adrian Piper's business cards taped to the wall in her kitchen:

> **Dear Friend,**
> I am black.
> I am sure you did not realize this when you made/laughed at/agreed with that racist remark. In the past, I have attempted to alert white people to my racial identity in advance. Unfortunately, this invariably causes them to react to me as pushy, manipulative, or socially inappropriate. Therefore, my policy is to assume that white people do not make these remarks, even when they believe there are no black people present, and to distribute this card when they do.
> I regret any discomfort my presence is causing you, just as I am sure you regret the discomfort your racism is causing me.

This card threads a careful, circuitous, absurd line between the practical and the actual: in actuality, there are black people (people who consider themselves black) who do not appear so, and white people (people who identify as white) who might in some other circumstance identify differently, but in everyday life, those distinctions often don't register. This is the absurdity of a visual hierarchical system that is not actually visual, the catachresis of using "white" and "black" as terms that do not always (or even often) signify what they describe, or describe what they signify. No one has radar good enough to cut through this fog of mystification.

But there is a problem with the card's logic: how does the person handing them out know that her friend, the person addressed, is in fact white? Laughing at a racist joke, by itself, is as inaccurate a racial marker as visual representation. To follow the (il)logic of racial self-representation you have to draw or write a chiasmus, like Derrida's invagination:

Unknown am I, as you are unknown.

or, better yet,

_____ am I, as you are _____

Piper's card is a closed system where the speaker, the card giver, is the only misunderstood one. It teaches the reader something, but maybe not enough. The truism for this state of being is "Race doesn't exist, but racism does." Follow the logic of that sentence all the way through: white people are indeterminate; the line that demarcates "white" and "black" (or "white" and "nonwhite") is indeterminate; there is no way of naming "legal," "normal," or "correct" in a racialized world without invoking its opposite, which cancels it out; in a situation where one person is making another person suffer, neither person enjoys more absolute racial "standing" than the other. Power and violence can and do exist without a firm metaphysical footing; systematic violence doesn't always occur as an extension of a preexisting system. This is borne out by historical evidence from many instances of genocide, including the campaigns of lynching and popular terrorism in the American South under Jim Crow; but it's oddly missing from most theories of mass violence, from Arendt to Foucault to Agamben to Elaine Scarry, all of whom refer violence back to a monolithic construction of the State.

The open system of interracial life has to operate by a different il-logic that does not reproduce the structural violence of the categories but defies them. Which might be to say something as simple as Albert Murray's statement: "The United States is in actuality not a nation of black people and white people. It is a nation of multicolored people":

There are white Americans so to speak and black Americans. But any fool can see that the white people are not really white, and that black people are not black. They are all interrelated one way or another. . . . The people of the United States are being misled by misinformation to insist on *exaggerating* their ethnic differences.

In *The Omni-Americans: Some Alternatives to the Folklore of White Supremacy*, published in 1970, Murray set out to create a theory for a culture he called mulatto at the root, "patently and irrevocably composite." Reading the introduction, even now, nearly fifty years later, is a dis-orienting experience. In this counternarrative Murray insists slavery was the ground for a new conception of American freedom, and that the enslaved person who has escaped—or revolted—is the represen-tative American, the omni-American. The practice of improvisatory freedom in black culture is the essence of American culture itself:

The fugitive slave . . . was culturally speaking certainly an American, and a magnificent one at that. His basic urge to escape was, of course, only human—as was his willingness to risk the odds; but the tactics he employed as well as the objectives he was seeking were *American* not African. . . . As for the tactics of the fugitive slaves, the Underground Railroad was not only an innovation, it was also an *extension* of the American quest for democracy brought to its highest level of epic heroism.

Murray is sometimes described as a conservative and a chauvinist, a bitterly exclusive and self-contradicting critic. He obsessed over European novelists, particularly Thomas Mann, while refusing to acknowledge that European music theory had anything to do with jazz—putting him at odds with virtually all jazz performed after 1958. (His one moment of cultural recognition came when he was widely criticized for the restrictive original repertory of Jazz at Lincoln Center, which he helped found with Wynton Marsalis.) He's all these things, and also a vitally eccentric and resistant cultural theorist precisely in the way he undoes American origin myths by redescribing them. Calling Nat Turner "a magnificent forefather enshrined in the National Pantheon beside the greatest heroes of the Republic" is an act of ironic subversion with deadly serious intent, not unlike Kara Walker's use of the portrait/silhouette to reinscribe the memory of slavery in the imagery of the masters. Against the Emersonian narrative of self-reliance and communion with nature Murray snaps back that *actual* American art, rooted in black performance culture, is all about stylization, artifice, parody, and play, an argument that turns up again and again in cultural criticism of the 1980s and 1990s (Henry Louis Gates's *The Signifying Monkey*, Eric Lott's *Love and Theft*, Jeff Chang's *Can't Stop Won't Stop*). Hemingway, Murray says, was a paradigmatic writer of the blues in prose:

> The simple, direct, concrete declarative statements that are so characteristic of [his] essentially coordinate prose style create a descriptive and narrative pace and precision, the affirmative effect of which is actually comparable to that created by the steady but infinitely elastic and inclusive 4/4 rhythm of the now classic Kansas City blues score. . . . [His] fiction . . . by the very nature of its emotional authenticity, its stylized precision, its flesh-and-blood concreteness, and the somehow relaxed intensity of its immediacy, qualifies not only as the blues but as classic Kansas City blues.

If I drew a line through Murray's narrative it would vibrate like a string on a double bass. Play, he says, is what art actually means, and has to remain at the center of our thinking:

I am so glad that we say, "You are going to *play* music." You don't *engineer* it or *work* at it. The word "play" has lost its true meaning. As I am using it here, I want it to be the full meaning of the word . . . as it resides at the very center of all culture. . . . Play in the sense of competition or contest; play in the sense of chance-taking or gambling; play in the sense of make-believe; play also in the sense of vertigo, or getting high, or inducing exhilaration; play also in the direction of simple amusement or entertainment—as in children's games; and play in the direction of gratuitous difficulty—as in increasing the number of jacks one catches or the height or distance one jumps, or decreasing the time one runs a given course; gratuitous difficulty also in the sense of wordplay; or play in the sense of sound—as in a Bach fugue. . . .

Another device for blues idiom statement is the "break," which is a disruption of the normal cadence of a piece of music. The "break" is a device which is used quite often and always has to do with the framework in which improvisation takes place. . . . The break is an extremely important device both from the structural point of view and from its implications. It is precisely this disjuncture which is the moment of truth. It is on the break that you "do your thing." . . .

   This kind of improvisation is applicable to educational methods, to scientific method, to inventions. Your knowledge of chordal structure and progression is your knowledge of the experience data of mankind. . . . That is what you "riff" on or improvise on.

No other writer has made the case for elasticity, improvisation, and relaxation as a theory of culture and also as a cultural gift, in the sense of Marcel Mauss and Lewis Hyde—a "property," in this case a practice, open to whoever wants to undertake it, outside the false necessity of ownership, payment, and debt. Which is exactly the nature of the black American artistic practices—jazz, the blues, graffiti, hip hop—now practiced almost everywhere on earth: hip hop in Catalan, Khmer, and Urdu; graffiti in Paris, Seoul, and Durban. Murray is explicit about his point of origin: the call for the nation to reinvent itself as a common culture, a "National Thing." White and black Americans, he says, in one of his most-quoted epigrams, are more like one another than they are like anyone else in the world.

There's an obvious problem, however, with allying hybridity and improvisation so closely to the nation-state and those born within it: a border is the most rigid and inflexible and unimaginative kind of boundary. In *The Amalgamation Waltz*, the performance theorist Tavia Nyong'o quotes Stanley Crouch, Murray's closest ally and protégé, proclaiming in 2006 that Barack Obama is African American but only pretending to be *black*, because his African heritage comes from the wrong part of the continent (East, not West) and doesn't include ancestors who were "plantation slaves." If you think of culture as national heritage, as a reproductive right—one Americans receive by being born American—then, Nyong'o says, you ultimately reproduce a new racialized hierarchy in place of an old one. Mixed-race populations have coexisted with violent racial power structures in many parts of the world—South Africa, Brazil, Malaysia, the Caribbean— and there is nothing *intrinsically* free or liberated about having a plural identity, much less claiming a Creole or hybrid culture as a point of origin, if that identity forms part of an oppressive or exploitative hierarchy supported by the state.

Which may be one reason why Baldwin decided, in defiance of the national narrative, to switch points of view at the end of *Another Country*. To follow the illogic of interracial thinking, in defiance of the law, embracing the plurality of what already exists, means, for Nyong'o, a kind of renunciation of meaning: our questions will never be resolved in the same terms we ask them. Interracial life—that is, children born to parents of different "races," however the divisions are assigned— is not new or intrinsically meaningful. What *is* meaningful is the refusal to pretend that the law or the power structure is real, the refusal to pretend that a racialized system can ever be anything other than a state of invalidity, hypothesis, and flux.

Randall Kennedy begins his book *Interracial Intimacies* with the story of Jacqueline Henley, born in New Orleans in 1950, whose birth mother, a white woman, died when she was two. Jacqueline's skin color was dark enough to raise questions about whether her father was white, but light enough to make it difficult to "prove" she was black (or, actually, biracial—though at the time that word could never be used in a legal proceeding). Given up for adoption by her white aunt, Jacqueline could not be placed with a black family because she had been registered as "white" on her birth certificate, and Louisiana law strictly prohibited cross-racial adoptions. A black couple, the Greens, sued the state to force her birth certificate to be changed, taking the case as far as the state's court of appeals, which refused to do so, stating that "the registration of a birthright must be given as much sanctity in the law as the registration of a property right." When Jacqueline Henley's case was featured in *Jet* magazine, another black couple, from Chicago, succeeded in adopting her through another legal technicality: out-of-state adoptions were not bound by the same restrictions of "birthright."

Jacqueline Henley, according to Randall Kennedy, was raised by a middle-class black family in integrated neighborhoods, attended Fisk University, became an ophthalmologist, and later in life returned to New Orleans, but never attempted to discover the "true secret" of her father's identity or her actual racial heritage. There's something triumphant about that refusal to pretend that racial logic moves in a straight line, even if refusing leaves the mystery unsolved, the story untold. As if to say, brutality is actually our common origin, brutality and incoherence, and that we were formed by it but will not re-form it; we will study it but not become it. A genealogy is not just a story but a performance, as Tavia Nyong'o would say. If we have to tell it we also have to undo it and its false necessity. To know a pattern is not to be forced to repeat it.

## 5

It may be that the fantasy of racial genealogy—the sins of the father—imposes a bind on the form of the interracial narrative that is almost impossible to escape. The fact of reproduction (which somehow always turns into the scandal of reproduction) becomes a single meaning that cancels out all others, and this meaning is transposed onto what Peter Brooks calls the narrative's "textual erotics": the tension between desire for an object and denial of that object, which forms what is usually called "plot." The plot of an interracial novel, in this sense, can never *not* be about the consequences of sex reproducing racial difference. This is obviously true of Thomas Dixon Jr.'s 1912 antimiscegenation novel, *The Sins of the Father*, in which a quadroon servant (that is, a woman with one black grandparent) seduces a white pro-segregation politician; the child she bears (that is, an octoroon) is sent to an orphanage. Decades later, the politician's son falls in love with her, not realizing they are half siblings; when the politician discovers her true identity, he kills his son and himself, purifying the family bloodline by ending it. But the same bind is present in *The Human Stain* and *The Time of Our Singing*, two major novels on interracial themes published almost simultaneously by major white writers, Philip Roth and Richard Powers, in 2000 and 2003, respectively.

Which is not to say these novels are superficially alike in any other way. *The Human Stain* is a campus novel set in the late 1990s; narrated by Nathan Zuckerman, it's very much of a piece with the rhetorical frames and devices of Roth's novelistic project. *The Time of Our Singing* is a self-contained twentieth-century epic, which begins with Marian Anderson's 1939 recital at the Lincoln Memorial and ends with the Los Angeles riots of 1992. Stylistically, Roth's second-self performance as Zuckerman is the same recognizable shtick, or genius, he maintained for three decades, before turning to the mordant seriousness of his last novels; whereas Powers is unwaveringly earnest and faithful to his source material: not only the racial history of postwar America but all of twentieth-century theoretical physics and the canon of classical European vocal music from Palestrina to Boulez.

These are novels that demand to be read and taken seriously; they perform the heteromasculine project of realist novelistic seriousness most American critics and cultural journalists still take for granted. It's very difficult, at least for me, to absorb them that way, for one simple reason: they both repeat and extend and encode the story of the tragic mulatto into the logic of the narrative, as if it's impossible to imagine the story any other way, when in fact, as in all tragedies, the architecture of the downfall is itself artificial and a species of camp.

Jonah Strom, the pivotal figure in *The Time of Our Singing*, is the eldest child of a white German émigré physicist and a black American singer, who fell in love instantly when they met at the Anderson concert in 1939. Fearful of the social stigmas surrounding interracial couples and biracial children, Jonah's parents raised him and his two siblings almost entirely at home. Their house was in Harlem (the father is a theoretical physicist at Columbia), but their world centered on classical music, and while all three children become musical prodigies, Jonah seems destined for world-class fame. He and his brother, Joseph, the novel's narrator, attend a vocal music academy and then Juilliard, where they remain almost entirely isolated within a world of European music and musicianship. Jonah, in particular, is incapable of referring to his own blackness without irony; he sees himself as a transcendent figure, and is devastated at the beginning of his professional career when reviewers refer to him as "the most promising Negro singer of his generation." Inevitably, though, he's tormented by subconscious guilt and longing for some connection with blackness, which Powers stages in an operatic historical repetition. By coincidence, Jonah happens to be performing in Los Angeles during the Watts riot, in 1965, and again, twenty-seven years later, during the Rodney King riots in 1992. Both times he insists on venturing out of his hotel room to witness the violence, the first time with Joseph in the driver's seat:

> Straight through our windshield, down the street, a mass condensed, drifting from block to block, stopping cars by force and stoning them, the only alternative to justice.... The laws of physics bent the air around us. It was like watching a flock of starlings twist and blot the sun.... Jonah was hypnotized by the movement, thrilled.

The second time—at the end of a lifetime of disappointments, bitterness, and isolation, including a decades-long estrangement from
his brother—Jonah dies alone. It's a virtuosic, symphonic ending, as
unrelenting as the prose itself, which rushes by with amphetaminic
breathlessness, piling up metaphors and derivations of metaphors, as if
determined to exhaust the subject by exhausting the reader. There are
some astonishingly powerful set pieces in *The Time of Our Singing*—as
when Joseph and Jonah's mother dies in an unexplained house fire
while they're away at school, and they're called to perform together
at her funeral, in front of a mixed crowd of friends and family they
hardly know:

> The piano in that rented room played damp and wayward. My
> brother's voice was wrecked with refusal. He'd chosen a song he
> could no longer sing, one pitched up a childhood above his highest
> note.... He wanted to do that Mahler he and Mama had once au-
> ditioned together. "Wer hat dies Liedlein erdacht?" Who thought
> up this little song? This was the way he wanted to remember her....
> We took it down an octave, and except for that jarring dissonance—
> the innocent words sung in his exiled range—we got through it.
> The mourners must have found this tribute inexplicable. What did
> this darling girl in her mountain house have to do with the matter-
> of-fact, irreverent black woman from Philadelphia, burned alive
> before the age of forty? But the girl in the song was Mama. Who
> could declare how her sons saw her?

But this novel, which has so many words for its ostensible subject, has
nothing to say about its most potent undercurrent: Joseph and Jonah
are incapable of loving anyone but one another. Neither of them is capable of sustaining a relationship or having children; only their sister,
Ruth, who rejects her white father and marries a black revolutionary, has a child. The brothers are quintessentially cursed, rendered
sterile, emasculated even, not for shock value, not as a parable or allegory, but because the plot rushes toward it and seems to demand it.

There's a quality of helplessness in these novels that deserves more attention, because it signals something that may be so basic to the form of prose fiction that writers and critics hardly ever attend to it. Textual erotics, Peter Brooks says, drawing on Freud's *Beyond the Pleasure Principle*, follow the structure of two drives: desire and death. The story needs to overcome all obstacles to reach the desired end, but in a sense the desired end is always *the* end: the story wants to finish or consume itself. Even novels that strongly resist the conventions of the form so often have a moment of helplessness, of "giving in," that allows the story a gesture of resolution and closure. That helplessness is a gesture of necessity; is it false necessity, and does it represent a signaling of the art form's innate conservatism, its desire to fold back the hypotheticals of the narrative into the so-called real world?

Roth's Zuckerman novels, read in this way, are all about helplessness and inevitability: the implacable and unacceptable rage of male vitality, the unstoppable self-assertion of the phallus against the confines of female envy and resentment. In the psychodrama of his work, his sexual conservatism and anxious overassertion of heterosexuality make him into a radical truth teller, a despised oracle. The downfall of Coleman Silk, the light-skinned African American at the center of *The Human Stain*, lies in his energetic male self-assertiveness, his quintessentially American individualism, which leads him to break away from his black family after his father's death, while he's still a teenager. In one feverish passage, where Silk has finally told his mother he's disowning her, Roth binds race, genealogy, the mother (what he calls "the all-but-pathological phenomenon of mother love"), and America into a single continuum:

> He was murdering her. You don't have to murder your father. The world will do that for you. . . . Who there is to murder is the mother, and that's what he saw he was doing to her, the boy who'd been loved as he'd been loved by this woman. Murdering her on behalf of his exhilarating notion of freedom! It would have been much easier without her. But only through this test can he be the man he has chosen to be, unalterably separated from what he was handed

at birth, free to struggle at being free like any human would wish to be free. To get that from life, the alternate destiny, on one's own terms, he must do what must be done. Don't most people want to walk out of the fucking lives they've been handed?

The rest of *The Human Stain*, in which Silk loses his professorship at a small liberal arts college in a firestorm after he makes an unconscious racist remark, has the strange effect of absorbing the dynamics of a Sophoclean tragedy into the realist texture of campus life in 1998. Silk's two deaths—the death of his career, a racist remark made by an actually black man, and his actual death, when he is killed by his lover's ex-husband, who hates him for being a Jew—are classically symmetrical, and aren't literally believable; but the novel, with all the weight of realist necessity behind it, treats them as actual events to be matched against Bill Clinton's own insufficient masculinity.

This is one way of understanding how a conservative art form works: you superimpose a static formal system onto the present and treat it as if it's a live antagonism, a preordained "clash of values," or civilizations, as if the antagonism preexisted you. In this way Roth is less a realist and more a fantasist of the present. But *The Human Stain* is useful in the way it demonstrates, radically, how writers reinvent the myth of the tragic mulatto by referring to it as a form of necessity and inevitability—without necessarily intending to. And how the form of the novel itself—the pressure of closure and the return to "the real"—may encourage fiction writers to embrace a politics of necessity they don't actually want.

# 6

I'm tempted to make a sweeping statement: the problem of interracial literature in the United States, like the problem of interracial life, has to do with an almost religious belief in the separation of subject and object, or content and form. As if interracial, or interrelated, life can be an object for our disinterested contemplation, rather than something Americans all participate in (in addition to participating in other kinds of life). As if "interracial literature" means only literature *about* relationships or people who are identifiably mixed, as opposed to literature that senses itself as coming from an interracial source, defined in the broadest terms. Which is to say, in public discussions about race and literature, American writers and critics are still mired in the idea that literature is representation rather than embodiment, engagement, or performance. What undoes a novel like *The Time of Our Singing* ultimately is its need to *say something* about interracial life rather than being or enacting the interracial, either as a hypothesis or a given.

Or, to put it in another way: the question returns to what to do with the parts of ourselves not made at home.

This is not an argument for an aesthetic of endless accumulation or absorption (or, to use the much more loaded and misunderstood term, "appropriation") but the opposite. Advocates for appropriation want to imagine the artistic consciousness as an unbounded space where anything is possible; I'm more interested in the question (to paraphrase Judith Butler) of how to work the trap one is inevitably in. When I ask, as I want to ask by telling the story of my Azorean ancestors, where race resides in my family memory, or in my bodily memory and associations, in my childhood associations or traumas, in my own trajectory of desires and attractions, I'm performing a double inquiry. The first question is one of construction, as in constructing a narrative: *How did I arrive in this place I find myself?* The second: *What do I do with where I am?*

These are not meant to be "serious questions" in the sense that I can answer them right away in some definite, categorical sense. The answer has to mirror the impossibility of the singular with its implied plural. There's no more joyful demonstration of this principle, more absolute in its belief in indeterminacy, than Zora Neale Hurston's classic "How It Feels to Be Colored Me":

> Up to my thirteenth year I lived in the little Negro town of Eatonville, Florida. It is exclusively a colored town. The only white people I knew passed through the town going to or coming from

Orlando. The native whites rode dusty horses, the Northern tourists chugged down the sandy village road in automobiles. . . .

But changes came in the family when I was thirteen, and I was sent to school in Jacksonville. I left Eatonville, the town of the oleanders, a Zora. When I disembarked from the river-boat at Jacksonville, she was no more. It seemed that I had suffered a sea change. I was not Zora of Orange County any more, I was now a little colored girl. I found it out in certain ways. In my heart as well as in the mirror, I became a fast brown—warranted not to rub nor run.

But I am not tragically colored. There is no great sorrow dammed up in my soul, nor lurking behind my eyes. I do not mind at all. I do not belong to the sobbing school of Negrohood who hold that nature somehow has given them a lowdown dirty deal and whose feelings are all but about it. Even in the helter-skelter skirmish that is my life, I have seen that the world is to the strong regardless of a little pigmentation more [or] less. No, I do not weep at the world—I am too busy sharpening my oyster knife. . . .

The position of my white neighbor is much more difficult. No brown specter pulls up a chair beside me when I sit down to eat. No dark ghost thrusts its leg against mine in bed. The game of keeping what one has is never so exciting as the game of getting.

I do not always feel colored. Even now I often achieve the unconscious Zora of Eatonville before the Hegira. I feel most colored when I am thrown against a sharp white background.

It may be that what Hurston wanted to practice, and wanted us—Americans, that is, as she imagines herself to be ("I am merely a fragment of the Great Soul that surges within the boundaries")—to practice is a kind of racial self-estrangement, or "enstrangement," the term coined by Vladimir Shklovsky and usually translated as "defamiliarization." To render ourselves as strange beings, beginning with the thickness of the language itself. This is a distinctive and rare quality for a novel. I remember feeling it the first time I read the early pages of Jonathan Lethem's *The Fortress of Solitude*:

> It was entirely possible that one song could destroy your life. Yes, musical doom could fall on a lone human form and crush it like a bug. The song, *that song*, was sent from somewhere else to find you, to pick the scab of your whole existence. The song was your personal shitty fate, manifest as a throb of pop floating out of radios everywhere. . . . Your days reduced to a montage cut to its cowbell beat, inexorable doubled bass line and raunch vocal, a sort of chanted sneer, surrounded by groans of pleasure. . . . The singer might as well have held a gun to your head. How it could have been allowed to happen, how it could have been allowed on the *radio*? That song ought to be illegal. It wasn't racist—you'll never sort that one out, don't even start—so much as anti-*you*. . . .
>
> September 7, 1976, the week Dylan Ebdus began seventh grade in the main building on Court Street and Butler, Wild Cherry's "Play That Funky Music" was the top song on the rhythm and blues charts. Fourteen days later it topped *Billboard*'s pop charts. Your misery's anthem, number-one song in the nation.

The first section of the novel tells the story of Dylan Ebdus's childhood in Carroll Gardens—a white child of bohemian parents in Brooklyn neighborhoods that were then overwhelmingly black—in unflinching detail. Dylan is ostracized, and bullied, but finds his closest ally is another alien child in the neighborhood: the biracial Mingus Rude, being raised by his black father, a washed-up R&B star, after his mother has disappeared. The relationship between Dylan and Mingus is tender and awkward and filled with homoerotic subterfuge, as well as a shared obsession with the secret powers of superheroes. It's such an intimate and perfectly achieved portrait that I always feel shocked and disappointed over again when the novel breaks off, in midstream, and moves forward twenty years: Dylan is now a music critic, obsessed with 1970s R&B, and Mingus is in prison. When Dylan visits him, he finds no trace of their bond left: "I met his rheumy eyes and . . . could no more ask [him] who he'd become . . . than I could imagine how to confess myself to him."

Maybe put it this way: the most radical interracial art is a practice of personal freedom and idiosyncrasy against the grain of unfreedom, which is not terrified by the condition of terror (or, if terrified, not immobilized)—but not oblivious to or separate from it either. It can multiply but not necessarily reproduce. And it is not invested in the logic of tragedy. These texts often feel as if they exist out of time, like all interracial art, but it's important not to treat them that way. They need to be recuperated with a sense of finding the real necessity of life in the present.

Theresa Hak Kyung Cha was born in Korea and moved to San Francisco when she was thirteen, in 1964; as a student at a convent high school and UC Berkeley she studied classical languages, avant-garde performance, and film theory, and had already embarked on a career as a performance and visual artist when she wrote her only novel, *Dictee*, in the early 1980s. The week after it was published, in 1982, she was raped and murdered by a security guard at the Puck Building in lower Manhattan.

*Dictee* takes its structure from the nine Muses of classical Greek thought—Clio, History; Calliope, Epic Poetry; and so on—and incorporates, within this loose and evocative framework, the inner world of a woman born during the Korean War, whose parents and relatives lived most of their lives under the terror of Japanese occupation, who has learned to speak English and French fluently in addition to Korean, and has been catechized as a Catholic but is no longer faithful. As a performance artist, Cha is interested in enacting her experience directly with the audience rather than narrating it *for* the audience; the text shifts from French grammar exercises to passages of personal history to slogans and pronouncements:

From A Far
What nationality
or what kindred and relation
what blood relation

what blood ties of blood
what ancestry
what race generation
what house clan tribe stock strain
what lineage extraction
what breed sect gender denomination caste
what stray ejection misplaced
Tertium Quid neither one thing nor the other
Tombe des nues de naturalized
what transplant to dispel upon

This is not a text to follow in a linear order, or even a text that can be "fully" interpreted (though it helps to read French, Latin, and Sino-Korean characters); it traces a genealogy of a kind, through Cha's mother, who was an independence fighter against Japan, and Yu Guan Soon, a legendary figure in the Korean resistance to colonial Japanese rule who died in 1920, but *Dictee* cannot be nationalized. In her artist's statements and interviews, Cha often spoke of "the dream of the audience": interracial writing, or plural writing, is in the business of that kind of dreaming, or dreaming the audience into being—as Cha did herself.

But the self-conscious difficulty of *Dictee* is not the only kind of radicalism I mean: I'm also talking about a text that can exist in plain sight, widely recognized but not fully appreciated. Anna Deveare Smith's documentary plays *Fires in the Mirror* and *Twilight: Los Angeles, 1992* are canonical American performances, broadcast on PBS and the recipient of a long stream of awards; her acceptance in the mainstream has insulated her from critique, for the most part, but also made her work seem far more superficial than it actually is. Deveare herself is African American but racially ambiguous, both in her light skin color and distinctive facial features, and her appearance is the unstated subtext of her presence in these plays, in which she slips, chameleonlike, into dozens of personas, drawn from her own interviews. The hyper-realism of her affect is always just on the edge of caricature; but somehow the potential offense is canceled out by the multiplicity of perspectives itself. Deveare comes across as a racial comedian who is an equal opportunity offender, and there's no way this performance could work without the presence of her own interracial, intermediating self. Her body reads as a figure of acceptable contradiction.

It's interesting to look at examples of interracial art that find success, or acceptance, and ask what they actually mean, rather than just assigning them a generic notion of "progress." How can I learn from them? What do they actually pass down, what kind of insight into my own otherness, my self-displacement? This is what I return to when I ask the question: what did I want, exactly, from *Another Country*? The answer has to be, in an exact and absurd sense, I wanted a different kind of "father." I wanted to come from a different source. The trajectory of that desire is unacceptable, but it doesn't go away when ignored. I chose to make art out of it.

## 7

My great-great-uncle, George Bartholemew Brazil, of the medium-brown skin and blue eyes, is sitting at a table in his house in Oakland—his father's house, built half before and half after the great earthquake of 1906—with my grandparents, speaking into a cassette recorder in 1985. His immediate family is gone. Why did he never marry? He belonged for a time to the Christian Brothers, a Catholic organization for laymen that trained teachers for parochial schools; he was a teacher, then worked overseas for the Red Cross during and after World War II. Much of his life is still opaque to me. Early in life, he says, he trained as a singer; he learned to find the point of maximum projection in his throat. Even in high school he was a star singer. He performed in an operetta, a Gilbert and Sullivan production; he can't remember which one. It made him hugely popular. This was in 1917, 1918. My phone rang and rang, he says. People wanted me to go horseback riding with them in the hills. Do you remember how there used to be stables up in Piedmont? All of them had their horses there. They wanted me to come to all the parties. This went on for years. But I never went, he says. I was shy. You understand that I had dark skin. Maybe I brought it on myself. But I never went.

The word "mulatto" is Iberian—Spanish and Portuguese—from the Andalusian Arabic *muwallad*, referring to "the adopted ones," non-Muslims raised as Muslims. Another way of translating it is "other than by birth." Once they learned English my great-great-grandparents apparently never spoke Portuguese again. Writing, though, is the practice of freeing ourselves from the language, or nonlanguage, of parents and families, often in order to understand them. George is dead and it doesn't matter what I call him. But it still matters to say the word. Why be afraid of it? Mulatto. Tertium quid.

I have the feeling there is more to be told about his life, more than is necessarily true or even necessary. I want him to be loved, to have been loved.

Say he was, and give the feeling a name: Ahmed. (I'm slipping here into fiction, my first language.) They met in Milan in 1947 in a customs office. George was arranging a permit to ship crates of powdered milk to refugee camps near Trieste and Ahmed was paying a bribe, a large bribe, for an export stamp for an olive-pitting machine he needed for his factory in Tunis. Ahmed did not speak English (though he spoke quite good Italian) and George did not speak Arabic, but, fortunately, he was nearly fluent in French. They shared a rented room for two weeks just off the Piazza Soave. They listened to Ella Fitzgerald on Ahmed's portable record player.

Ahmed said to George one day, you know you don't have to go back there. Come live in Tunis. You can get an apartment for almost nothing. Ahmed was married and had three children; George said, you mean you want a mistress. Ahmed got up, not bothering to cover himself, and began to run a bath. George felt angry and shouted over the sound of the water running, I'll do it, but I have to return to San Francisco to finish my contract, so you'll have to come fetch me first.

I don't even know where San Francisco is, said Ahmed.

But he promised he would come. After he returned home to Tunis they wrote fervent letters and telegrams for months. George's assignment ended and he embarked for home, a three-week voyage, and when he got back to Oakland a letter was waiting from Tunis saying that Ahmed had booked his passage already, but only one way; on the way back they would fly. Buy the airplane tickets for us, he said, I'll wire you the money. The money came. He bought the tickets. It was the most money he had ever spent in one place, handing over one hundred-dollar bill after another, straight out of the yellow Western Union envelope. After that he carried the tickets with him, in his jacket pocket, wherever he went. San Francisco to Denver; Denver to Chicago; Chicago to New York; New York to Paris; Paris to Tunis. He was carrying them when he drove to the pier the day Ahmed's ship would arrive.

He had wanted to bring Ahmed a bouquet, but, conscious of the looks they would receive, bought him a bottle of champagne instead, in a plain brown paper bag. And pinned a single yellow carnation to his lapel. When he arrived at the terminal the passengers were just beginning to disembark; he pressed forward into the crowd until he was standing just a few feet from the customs desk. He waited there for two and a half hours, until only the steerage passengers were left. Why would Ahmed have traveled in steerage, or was he delayed on board? The crowd had dispersed; the redcaps had disappeared. They would have to manage somehow with the luggage. He stayed there another forty minutes, until the purser came down with the ship's manifest to get stamped. Was there an Ahmed Louby on board? he asked. The name Ahmed Louby was written by hand at the very bottom, in Italian, passage booked from Milan, failed to appear at embarkation.

I'm watching George now from my present and his future. He's driving, alone, in a blue Packard, which he borrowed for the occasion from his cousin Billy Almeida, across the bridge to Oakland. What is he seeing, in his misery? Is he seeing me? I have this feeling he isn't. I want to know what he *is* seeing. I want to see it too: that place we will all live when the curtain of dread is lifted.

What Is the Point of This Way of Dying

A White Blues

Racism seems to Mark a kind of weird masochism. A way to
make us feel utterly and pointlessly alone.

David Foster Wallace, "Westward the Course
of Empire Takes Its Way"

## 1

I saw *Harold and Maude* for the first time at summer camp, in the summer of 1988, when I was thirteen. It was, unapologetically, nerd camp:
the Center for Talented Youth, on the campus of Scripps College, a
mission-style villa in the mountains outside Los Angeles, with foun-
tains, lots of wrought iron, improbably green lawns, cool, echoing tiled
rooms. All these details matter in some way. My camp friends were
the artsy ones, with goth or punk affiliations; Shoshana, Rachel, Sean,
Gabby. They were all two or three years older, sneaked cigarettes,
quoted Wilde, and dispensed all kinds of worldly knowledge; they
said this movie, above all others, would change my life.

In the first scene—filmed in such low light that at first it's difficult
to distinguish one object from another—a young man in a three-piece
suit, filmed almost entirely from the shoulders down, moves around a
richly appointed room, lighting candles and incense, putting a record
on the hi-fi (Cat Stevens, "Don't Be Shy"), writing a note on a side
table, pinning it to his lapel, finally climbing onto a chair and kicking
it away, leaving his shoes swinging in midair.

This is a faked suicide: a moment later, and then over and over in the first third of the movie, his face appears in the pose of pretend death. Harold Chasen is a fatherless only child of an obscenely wealthy family; he's dropped out of prep school and lives with his mother in a mansion near Big Sur. All this takes place in 1971. To draw attention to himself, to pass the time, to channel his otherwise unfocused rage and despair, he stages his own death. In one of these scenes, he imitates a Vietnamese monk's self-immolation, using a dummy and a disappearing trick; when he reappears, unharmed, and fully dressed, in front of his mother's fury, he looks at the camera and smiles.

He knows the viewers are with him. Who is he? An absurdly large puffy Windsor knot that only makes him look more childlike, a boy in a man's suit, with a boy's overgrown bowl haircut and slight dimples. He's acting. Everything in his life is a performance, between quotation marks, "as if." Except for one ambiguous feature: his face is extremely white, several tones lighter than his mother's skin. One word for it would be *pallid*. Deathly, or proto-goth.

Is Harold's extreme whiteness part of his performance, or is it the condition of his life? The goths I knew as a teenager—those who used that term and those who embraced the symbolism without it—used makeup but also stayed out of the sun, using their bodies as little as possible. I think they knew that belonging to a subculture was a way of making wishful thinking look permanent, as if their hearts really were on their sleeves. To be goth, to wear death drag, is a way of making ordinary life look unbearably dull and cloying and lamely theatrical by comparison. Reverend Moody, in Hawthorne's "The Minister's Black Veil," was in some ways the first goth; on his deathbed he accused everyone in the town of secretly wearing the same black veil.

In her review of *Harold and Maude*, Pauline Kael found the Cat Stevens lyrics that fill nearly every interstice in the movie unforgivable; she called them "mush-minded." Out of context, they might be; as part of the movie, they create the tension between performance and feeling that feels unbearable and is meant to be unbearable:

Don't be shy—just let your feelings roll on by
Don't wear fear—or nobody will know you're there

Only when Harold, the performance artist with an audience of one—the way all adolescent artists-to-be grasp the nightmare that their parents may be their only audience—meets an actual artist, Maude, who calls him on his pretensions, does his facade break down, and he begins to grasp the dimensions of his actual sadness. Then, with Maude's help, he begins to make art again.

This is a radical simplification of the movie—leaving out for the moment the part about Harold and Maude's love affair, her age, her background—but it's true to what I saw, at age thirteen, in surroundings very much like the film I was watching; I saw a movie that was trying to teach me, personally, how to live. That was what was so electrifying about it.

I lacked a language for explaining Harold's transformation until I read Peter Sloterdijk's *Critique of Cynical Reason*, which dwells at great length on the difference between cynicism and what he calls "kynicism." Cynicism, in the sense the term is used today, is what Sloterdijk calls a form of coping, of "enlightened false consciousness":

Psychologically, present-day cynics can be understood as borderline melancholics, who can keep their symptoms of depression under control and can remain more or less able to work. Indeed, this is the essential point in modern cynicism: the ability of its bearers to work—in spite of anything that might happen, and especially, after anything that might happen. . . . For cynics are not dumb, and every now and then they see the nothingness to which everything leads. Their psychic . . . apparatus has become elastic enough to incorporate as a survival factor a permanent doubt about their own activities. They know what they are doing, but they do it because, in the short run, the force of circumstances and the instinct for self-preservation are speaking the same language, and they are telling them that it has to be so. . . . Cynicism . . . is that modernized, unhappy consciousness, on which enlightenment has labored both successfully and in vain. . . . Well-off and miserable at the same time, this consciousness no longer feels affected by any critique of ideology; its falseness is already reflexively buffered.

Kynicism is an older, stranger, and far more radical way of life: it begins with Diogenes of Sinope, who lived in a dry cistern near the market-place in Athens and identified himself with dogs; "kynic" is derived from *kynikos*, "dog-like." "Other dogs," Diogenes said, "bite only their enemies, whereas I bite also my friends in order to save them." He called himself *cosmopolites*, "a citizen of the world," and carried a lantern through the marketplace at midday, saying he was searching for an honest man. Once, Alexander the Great came to visit Diogenes while he was lying in the sun, perhaps getting a tan. "Stand out of my light," Diogenes said. When invited to a wealthy man's house and cautioned not to spit anywhere—the kynics were famous for relieving themselves wherever and whenever—he spat in the owner's face, saying, "I can find no meaner receptacle."[4]

Maude, a Holocaust survivor who lives in an abandoned railroad car, steals cars and defaces statues for fun, and practices every art form she can manage, is a quintessential kynic; Harold, a cynic to the core, is appalled and frightened by her. "I don't know if that's *right*," he says peevishly, when she explains her philosophy of car theft. But slowly, indefatigably, Maude breaks down his defenses; the movie is entirely on her side. Diogenes, Sloterdijk writes, "could be taken . . . as the original father of the idea of self-help . . . he was a self-helper by distancing himself from and being ironic about needs for whose satisfaction most people pay with their freedom." *Harold and Maude*'s version of self-help partly involves turning his talent for pranks as performance art on authority figures other than his mother, including his uncle, a high-ranking army officer, and a police officer who tries to arrest them, in what is possibly the funniest chase scene in film history.

But *Harold and Maude*'s most radical self-help lies elsewhere. Cynics,

---

4. I've taken the title of this essay from an episode in the ongoing struggle (as Sloterdijk describes it) between kynicism and cynicism. The Roman writer and cynic Lucian once described the death of Peregrinus, a kynic and convert to Christianity who self-immolated at the Olympic Games in 185 CE: "If . . . he is so firmly determined to die," Lucian wrote, "why does it have to be by fire and with a pomp fit for a tragedy? What is the point of *this* way of dying when he could have chosen a thousand other ways?"

by definition, are unable to cry; Harold desperately needs to. Once he's had sex with Maude, and smoked a hookah, he can: his face screws up, becomes ugly, disfigured, ordinary, as he weeps, telling Maude the story he inevitably has to tell, of feeling isolated after his father's death, estranged from his mother, her pretensions and insecurities.

The ordinariness of this moment—how embarrassing it is, how hard to watch—deserves close attention. The entire film has led up to this experience of catharsis, which could have happened in any therapist's office, or in the arms of any lover or friend; but Harold is *so* traumatized, so isolated, such an "advanced case," that it takes extreme measures to lead him out. And the extreme measures are just beginning: shortly after this scene, Maude announces she's taken an overdose on the night of her eightieth birthday. After she dies, Harold drives his car off Big Sur, but jumps out at the last moment, and strolls away across the bluff, playing a banjo Maude has given him.

Where does he go? This is an unfair but necessary question. The end of *Harold and Maude* holds cynicism and kynicism in a perfect balance. It's Harold's greatest and (presumably) final performance, the last trick he will ever play on us, but also, of course, much more than a trick: this time the grief and the anguish are real. In Freudian terms, he *may* have broken through the cycle of melancholy and finally become able to mourn—depending on what he does next. What kind of artist will he be, and where will he go? What song will he sing?

If the problem of closed endings is one of false necessity—bringing the narrative back to the limitations of the so-called real world—the problem of open endings, in late capitalist culture, is that they are always subject to cynical recirculation: they can always become objectless gestures, "meaning" nothing but themselves. In 1998 Wes Anderson made an objectless, sanitized version of *Harold and Maude* called *Rushmore*, in which Harold is Max Fischer (played by Jason Schwartzman), a scholarship student given to bizarre, theatrical antics—as well as actual theater—at his prep school, and Maude is Rosemary (played by Olivia Williams), a beautiful thirty-something elementary school teacher. In this setting, the love affair never actually happens, and neither does the attempted suicide; Max Fischer's face never addresses the screen, and never breaks down into abysmal, ugly, ordinary grief. The surface and the pretense are perfectly consistent.

This is not to say that Anderson's characters—now duplicated, with slight variations, in the many movies he's made since, including *The Royal Tenenbaums, The Life Aquatic with Steve Zissou, The Darjeeling Limited*—have no emotions at all. They do. Their emotions are perfectly proportional to the closed, hermetic, purposely artificial worlds they inhabit; their strongest feelings come at moments when those worlds are threatened. They tend to be immensely wealthy, extremely fragile, highly naive, and very, very pale.

In an American context I don't think the question of cynicism can ever be unbound from the fact of white supremacy. Anderson's career demonstrates this, maybe better than any other artist of his generation in any field. Using Bill Murray's decaying face, he's created an index of white melancholy, both bland and inert, detached, literally self-effacing. Not surprisingly, he's stuck there: in a cycle of productivity that is itself a performance, the way Harold, in his mother's house, was always looking for another variation, a new entertainment, as an alternative to actually dying.

## 2

As a teenager, and even more intensely in my twenties, I didn't know what to do with my body. I mean this literally: I didn't know how to stand, how to carry myself, how to walk, what pose to adopt. Because it seemed to me that everyone had to have a pose. I remember, at eleven or twelve years old, trying to teach myself how to walk with a purposeful slouch, like Judd Nelson in *The Breakfast Club*. It didn't take. I had a much more charismatic, attractive older brother. I couldn't play sports. I had no real interest in violence. I couldn't skate. What I wanted, of course, and couldn't have, was coolness in any way signaled by the obvious strains of eighties youth culture. So I went where the music was so loud it didn't matter who you were as long as you were listening to it.

Punk was unambiguous and cheap, from the outside: it was the price of a pair of surplus store combat boots, an Agnostic Front T-shirt, and accessories from the hardware store. From the inside it was a burgeoning mess of related sub-subcultures under one odd umbrella; the one I attached to most strongly hardly had a name, other than the derisive term "emo." A band could be called emo if it used melodies in the major scale, or if its lyrics sounded vulnerable or moody; emo could be political or romantic; at that time, in the late 1980s, the term still mostly circulated around a legendary (and defunct) band from DC, Rites of Spring, whose fans openly wept and threw flowers at the stage. Over the next few years emo turned into a hugely appealing, and later marketable, aesthetic, centered on the image of a white man in a state of emotional and physical abandonment, with overtones of extreme sadness and a kind of explosive violence, in which the audience takes part.

There's a story that to me perfectly encapsulates emo's place in the broader culture of the era, recounted by Andy Greenwald in *Nothing Feels Good: Punk Rock, Teenagers, and Emo.* Jeremy Enigk, the singer of

Sunny Day Real Estate, probably the most significant emo band of the 1990s, briefly shared a label—Sub Pop—with Nirvana. When his A&R rep invited him to see Nirvana play, Enigk stood in the back and watched, with obvious disinterest, then left halfway through. To an outsider, this would make no sense; who wouldn't want to watch one of the greatest rock bands of all time, even out of curiosity? But the sensibility of emo was grunge's polar opposite, and Enigk's indifference to Nirvana—a band no one, at the time, was allowed to be indifferent about—in my mind stands out as a powerful, even kynical, refusal of the omnipresent and increasingly commercial cynicism of the time.

I drifted away from emo in my late teens and early twenties, at a time when the most exciting new bands, such as Antioch Arrow and Clikatat Ikatowi, were no longer playing songs as such, just minute-long explosions of noise and shrieking—that is, when the music had become objectless, the content of the ritual had become the ritual itself. (This was around the same time that "emo," the erstatz, highly produced, pop-inflected version promoted by bands like Dashboard Confessional, Fall Out Boy, and My Chemical Romance, was starting to hit MTV.) But I missed it. I missed it with a certain kind of muscle memory. I think there's a way in which emo was the one cultural form that made perfect and immediate sense to me, that collapsed subject and object. Emo presents the subject, the speaker, and the audience as intrinsically damaged, but the damage isn't a source of withdrawal or implosion or suicide; instead it becomes a kind of dance. "Where did all you shattered people come from?" the singer of Sideshow repeats over and over on the album *Lip Read Confusion* in 1995. "Where'd you come from? Where'd you *come* from?"

In this way—and I don't make this statement lightly—emo is the truest, most moving version I know of white blues, or, one could even say, whiteness blues. This is not meant as an endorsement. Like so many cultural forms that assembled around whiteness in the post–civil rights era, it deals in a kind of prosthetized emotion and is easy to ridicule. Its ridiculousness is part of the point: emo is inherently damaged, incomplete, inauthentic, in search of something it can't find. But it's *trying*. It cares enough to try, not to remain inert. It wants to break through, and find an object.

In *Ugly Feelings* Sianne Ngai describes "animatedness," being moved by an emotion, one of the "most basic ways in which affect becomes publicly visible." But there is a paradox present in animatedness, which to me is the crux and the mystery of emo: "On the one hand," she writes, "the state of being 'animated' implies the most general of all affective conditions . . . but also a feeling that implies being 'moved' by a particular feeling, as when one is said to be animated by happiness or anger":

> Animatedness thus seems to have both an unintentional and intentional form. In a strange way, it seems at once a zero-degree feeling and a complex meta-feeling, which not only takes other feelings as its object, but takes only other *intentional* feelings as its object. For we can speak of someone's being "animated" by a passion like anger, but not by an objectless mood like nostalgia or depression. . . . Animatedness bears a semantic proximity to "agitation," a term which is likewise used to . . . designate feeling prior to its articulation into a more complex passion, but that also underlies the contemporary meaning of the political agitator or activist.

Animatedness, Ngai goes on to say, can also be passive; a person can be animated by an outside force, the way a puppet is, or a clay figure in a claymation movie. It can be objectified. In an American context, certain figures are expected to be animated, and others not: the most stereotypically animated of all are African Americans and Latin Americans, who are assumed to be, depending on the circumstances, loud, rhythmically sophisticated, seductive, obnoxious, gracefully athletic, menacing, and violent. The white body is still, upright, self-contained, stiff, unemotional; black and brown bodies are fluid, move horizontally as well as vertically, liable to break out dancing or fighting or shouting at any moment. (José Muñoz, in his essay "Feeling Brown, Feeling Down," notes dryly that "it is not so much that the

Latina/o affect performance is so excessive, but that the affective performance of normative whiteness is minimalist to the point of emotional impoverishment.")

At the risk of overreading, or overreaching: to me emo has always been about the white body trying to escape itself. Which is to say, but also not to say, the white body dreaming of becoming brown or black—exactly the stylized, stereotypical version of excessive, "animated" brown or black movement that Ngai and Muñoz describe. The white emo performer wants to swing dance, or sing the blues, but can't: this connection became explicit in the 1990s and 2000s with emo bands like Swing Kids, whose singer chanted "3-2-5-0, 1-2-5 go!" at the beginning of one song, as if he was incapable of counting time, and Indian Summer, who layered clips from Bessie Smith and other black blues and jazz singers into their songs, building from whispered phrases and bits of guitar melody—where the singer was still audible in the background—to full-volume distorted chords and hoarse, mostly indecipherable screaming. (A key feature of later emo, and screamo, is that the lyrics are delivered with great force but for the most part can't actually be heard, unless a lyric sheet is provided.)

In this way emo in performance is a convulsive ritual that is both, as Ngai says, zero and meta, both self-aware and self-abnegating or self-vacating. Rites of Spring, by most descriptions the first emo band, summed up this quality in the song "Patience": "I can't sing this song without wondering / why these skies won't fall." This feeling of inherent brokenness or frustration brings it to the edge of a religious state, a state of prayer, and not surprisingly, in the 1990s, it tipped over in some cases to actual devotional music. One of my closest friends in high school, a devoted emo fan and preternaturally talented graffiti artist, converted to Krishna Consciousness (the Hare Krishnas), joining a wave of musicians and fans that saw emo as an expression of bhakti ecstasy, best exemplified by the band Shelter; other prominent emo musicians, including Enigk, had conversion experiences and began incorporating Christian symbolism into their lyrics. But this overt religiosity lasted only for a short period; when it was over, "emo" had become something else—a social fad, a meme, a hairstyle, a commercial affect with only traces of the unacceptable intensity of the music itself.

When I hear the rhetorical question "How are white people damaged by racism?," I always feel a certain astonishment, responding to the assumption that white people are in fact not damaged. I have always known white people to be damaged. Being damaged was the guiding principle of the culture I grew up in. Unarticulated, undefined trauma was in a way the connecting thread between the music I grew up listening to and the fiction I began reading in my late teens and early twenties. By talking about the trauma of whiteness, which is I guess what I'm doing, I'm just trying to answer a rhetorical question in the way that seems most obvious. "Trouble," Cat Stevens sings, as Harold is about to drive over the cliff, "oh trouble move away / I have seen your face / and it's too much for me today."

## 3

I had my own version of Jeremy Enigk's moment when Dave Eggers came to visit the University of Michigan, promoting *A Heartbreaking Work of Staggering Genius*, while I was a graduate student. The event was held in a ballroom-like space on campus, with Eggers on a stage in the front; in the back were several tables occupied by local literacy and antipoverty organizations he had invited to attend to raise money. There were at least a thousand people in the room, and the atmosphere was charged. Eggers invited several members of the audience onstage to sing "More Than a Feeling" during a crucial part of the passage he was reading. I left after about twenty minutes.

What was I doing, what kind of a gesture was I making (to myself, since of course no one else was watching)? I was extremely jealous, on one hand; on paper, Eggers was doing something I had always wanted to do, performing generational defiance and cleverness combined with a kind of altruistic (not political) morality. It genuinely felt like a new way of making art. But on the other hand it felt utterly safe and risk free; it was postmodernism with the edges sanded off. There was a coziness about it that repelled me. Not the smugness—I would have been happy to be smug, if I knew what I was being smug *about*. The truth was I had an inherent inner sense that I would just never be that particular kind of cool. ("I generally feel very alive and emancipated when I choose to walk out of something," Maggie Nelson writes in *The Art of Cruelty*: "Walking out reminds you that while submission can at times be a pleasure, a risk worth taking, you don't have to manufacture consent whenever or wherever it is nominally in demand.")

Coolness, as an affect, has no patience for dialogue, engagement, or listening. Quite the opposite: like a joke, you either get it or you don't. In the 1940s, at the scene of the actual birth of the cool, Charlie Parker and his inner circle wrote melodies over popular changes so complex and so fast other musicians couldn't bullshit their way through them, and thus ended the tradition of the open jam (and, indirectly, the swing era itself). Coolness was the indigenous American avant-garde. This was the pose the Beats carried through the fifties, that Godard and Truffaut turned into the New Wave, and then became so generalized, so nebulous, that by the time I was born it was a universal grammar of American youth culture.

These cultural forms—coolness, the hipster, and emo, the white blues—have a history and a prehistory derived from African American culture; they are black cultural forms turned white. In this way they follow the long trajectory of conscious and unconscious appropriation Kevin Young traces in *The Grey Album*: "In the face of alienation and anomie the mask, modern and often racial, becomes necessary," Young writes. "This is why the dominant mode of the modernist era is the *persona* . . . not just T. S. Eliot's blackface or Ezra Pound's love of Noh drama . . . but also the Janus mask of the blues, which laughs and cries at the same time." If emo wore the racial mask Ngai calls "animatedness," the white hipster was all about the gathered-in, self-enclosed, inscrutable, stylized mask of 1940s and '50s cool. Sonic Youth called it the Kool Thing. The debt of 1990s hipsters to black culture was never so obvious as it was among the Beats; advertising the debt itself would have been considered uncool. This was an era of second- and thirdhand semiotics. The words "It's a Black thing, you wouldn't understand" were everywhere in the early 1990s, and it was understood that there was an insuperable boundary—an explicit reference or analogy—we would never cross. But we (meaning "we," white teenagers and post-teenagers) were paying attention to everything happening in black culture, and, in our own way, absorbing it and indirectly addressing and invoking it.

Or to put it another way: in the years I was most devoted to emo I spent at least half my listening hours with hip hop; I absorbed everything from Ice Cube to Arrested Development, from the Geto Boys to Das EFX to Warren G to Poor Righteous Teachers. After seeing *Do the Right Thing* at thirteen, I'd started reading *The Source* and buying bootlegged tapes sold on streetcorners all over Baltimore. I was doing this without trying to understand it. I had no close black friends in high school; but I lived in Baltimore and had a full life as a volunteer and activist, surrounded by black culture, uneasily attached to it. It was just a condition of life. I couldn't write graffiti, not even a decent tag (though many of my white friends could); I couldn't DJ, let alone spit rhymes (though I had white friends who would become immersed in hip hop); but there was no way of differentiating my life, or writing, from these things, either.

Another way of understanding objectless art forms is to say that "objectlessness" is just a performance; the actual object exists, but is hidden, occult. Cynicism, Sloterdijk says, even when it appears to revel in its own uselessness, is addressing itself to power, showcasing its own inoculation. I think about this quandary when I remember the argument Thomas Frank made in his 1995 *Baffler* essay, "Why Johnny Can't Dissent," which popularized the phrase "commodification of dissent." In the 1990s, Frank observed, the countercultural language and attitudes of the postwar era were being recaptured and branded as corporate slogans ("The Revolution Will Be Televised"):

This imperative of endless difference is today the genius at the heart of American capitalism, an eternal fleeing from the "sameness" that satiates our thirst for the New with such achievements of civilization as the infinite brands of identical cola, the myriad colors and irrepressible variety of the cigarette rack at 7-Eleven.

In the two decades since, liberal and leftist critics of so-called identity politics have often argued that activism for racial justice (and writing that focuses or centers on race) plays into this capitalist "imperative of endless difference." American capitalism, according to this argument, *wants* to see itself as diverse, multicultural, even "postracial," identified with models of black and brown success (Obama, Jay-Z, Jennifer Lopez, Lin-Manuel Miranda), while the actual mechanics of the market remain as exploitative as ever.

When I encounter this line of thinking—now resurgent, as of this writing, after the 2016 election—I'm always amazed by the tissue-thin simplicity of its evidence, as if racialized desire and fantasy (and the images of nonwhite celebrities) haven't been American commodities all along. Proponents of "class, not race" (Walter Benn Michaels, Mark Lilla, most recently the editors of the socialist magazine *Jacobin*) insist that because the rise of neoliberal scarcity economics has been accompanied by advances in civil rights and political status for nonwhite and LGBTQ Americans, one must be to blame for the other; and the only solution is a return to leftist cultural politics that ignores "the illusion of difference." Who are they addressing? Clearly not those who have been harmed, or are most likely to be harmed, by the overt and covert violence of racism or homophobia; and probably not the vast majority of poor people, who tend to be quite aware of themselves as racial and gendered subjects. The people I knew in the 1990s who read and appreciated "Why Johnny Can't Dissent" were, overwhelmingly, people like Thomas Frank, which is to say white people like me; they understood it to be a cynical argument for the futility of protest and explicitly political art such, and responded accordingly.

## 4

This is the theory I'm working on: a cultural performance, a song, a novel, a play, a film, an exhibition is always addressed, in part, to someone not explicitly in the room. There is always, as Theresa Hak Kyung Cha said, the audience, and then the dream of the audience. This is not the same as tired arguments over artistic "intent," because address is rarely formalized and hardly ever made conscious and explicit. Nor does it ever leave out the self. When I write this, I'm asking you, whoever you are, to tell me what to do. But I can't hear you, so I can't hear your answer; what I'm hearing is the echo of my own imagination. To be clear, in writing this, I have to listen to that echo and incorporate it, somehow, without mistaking it for something else.

## 5

David Foster Wallace wanted us to know we are loved. This isn't hyperbole; it's the last sentence of "Westward the Course of Empire Takes Its Way": "You are loved." Instead of conspiring with the reader—which he believed was always actually condescending to the reader—he wanted to break metafiction's frame of permanent irony (what Friedrich Schlegel once called "permanent parabasis") and restore to it an aesthetic of emotional directness and intimacy apart from realism. This was the project he laid out, in no uncertain terms, in "Westward" (which rewrites and savagely satirizes John Barth's metafiction masterpiece "Lost in the Funhouse") and in "E Unibus Pluram: Television and U.S. Fiction," a manifesto he began writing in the late 1980s and finally published in complete form in 1993.

The pervasive cynicism Wallace detected in himself and other writers his age (he was born in 1962, which makes him either a Shadow Boomer or Gen X, depending on whom you ask) came from two sources: the doctrines of postmodern fiction, as defined by Barth, Gaddis, Pynchon, Barthelme, and DeLillo; and TV, which made postmodern narrative technique popular, fun, and inescapable. "Pop-conscious postmodern fiction," Wallace writes in "E Unibus Pluram," "has . . . made a real attempt to transfigure a world of and for appearance, mass appeal, and television; . . . on the other hand, televisual culture has somehow evolved to a point where it seems invulnerable to any such transfiguring assault." The tools of pop postmodernism, "irony, poker-faced silence, and fear of ridicule," are effective but also "agents of a great despair and stasis in U.S. culture." He ends the essay with what in retrospect may be the saddest passage he ever wrote, both an apologia and a call to arms:

It's entirely possible that my plangent noises about the impossibility of rebelling against an aura that promotes and vitiates all
rebellion say more about my residency inside that aura, my own
lack of vision, than they do about any exhaustion of U.S. fiction's
possibilities. The next real literary "rebels" in this country might
well emerge as some weird bunch of *anti*-rebels, born oglers who
dare somehow to back away from ironic watching, who have the
childish gall actually to endorse and instantiate single-entendre
principles. Who treat of plain old untrendy human troubles and
emotions in U.S. life with reverence and conviction. Who eschew
self-consciousness and hip fatigue. These anti-rebels would be
outdated, of course, before they even started. . . . Real rebels, as
far as I can see, risk disapproval. . . . The new rebels might be artists willing to risk the yawn, the rolled eyes, the cool smile, the
nudged ribs, the parody of gifted ironists, the "Oh how *banal*." To
risk accusations of sentimentality, melodrama. Of overcredulity.
Of softness.

In the decade since Wallace's suicide, this story—the literary history
of postirony—has been told and retold, with a small core of protagonists (and a few antagonists): how in the mid-1990s Wallace, Jonathan
Franzen, George Saunders, Ben Marcus, and Rick Moody, plus Dave
Eggers on the West Coast, invented post-postmodern fiction, a new
literature of feeling. "The thing on the table was emotional fiction,"
Saunders said in an interview with the *New York Times Magazine* in
2013, describing conversations with this group twenty years before.
"How do we make it? How do we get there? Is there something yet to
be discovered? These were about the possibly contrasting desire to:
(1) write stories that had some sort of moral heft and/or were not just
technical exercises or cerebral games; while (2) not being cheesy or
sentimental or reactionary."

Did it work? Did it happen? According to most sources it did.
Saunders is one of the most beloved American writers today, and
Wallace is celebrated as a kind of secular saint, not just an artist but a
paragon of fearsome difficulty in the service of kindness and humility,

as exemplified in his famous 2004 speech to the graduates of Kenyon College, "This Is Water": "If you've really learned how to . . . pay attention . . . it will actually be within your power to experience a crowded, loud, slow, consumer-hell-type situation as not only meaningful but sacred, on fire with the same force that lit the stars."

I always find myself thinking and writing about him from a point of unfeeling admiration. Which is also to say that I take him at his word, as he put it in "E Unibus Pluram," that his work is not actually fully successful because he is not only resident inside the aura but, being inside it, was incapable of fully naming it or understanding it. This is how I understand his way of describing the possibilities of American fiction, particularly the tension between postmodern skepticism and "single-entendre values," without mentioning the American writers most actively engaged with those questions in the late 1980s and early 1990s: John Edgar Wideman, Ishmael Reed, Toni Morrison, Tony Kushner. Or even Trey Ellis: a black writer exactly Wallace's age, whose first novel, *Platitudes*, published by Vintage Contemporaries in 1988 to some acclaim, shares so many of his obsessions that reading it now is like seeing a convex-mirror image of *The Broom of the System*:

> Donald says he's got dibs on the Wang, but Andy says, Homo you don't, and just sits at the terminal, turns it on just to bug Donald, because Andy really likes the DEC VeeDeeTee better. Earle sits next to Andy on the right, like he always does, and Janey walks in, her books over her chest, and sits right in front of Andy, like *she* always does. . . .
>
> Janey's already confused—she's more the artsy type—and raises her hand like a Nazi and says, Commander Considine, Commander Considine, but he just keeps on saying junk about making sure that the FOR isn't too big or else the NEXT loop might become infinite, which is obvious, and now Janey's arm is tired and hooked over her head like her hairband and she's waving at the Commander from over her other ear and breathing real loud on purpose, and every time she waves, her chest stretches her sundress, and Earle wouldn't be surprised if her boobs one day just

pop right through the fabric like sinus medicine capsules pop
through that foil backing.

Wallace was unquestionably—he would have admitted it, I'm guess-
ing, if anyone asked—writing within a sphere of literary white masculinity that assumed to itself a kind of autonomous, generalized, even
infinite irony about everything, including itself, and also assumed itself to be terminal and fatal. From this vantage point, which often
crosses over into a kind of spiritual vocation, it's easy to see how works
by writers of color, or women, fall into a category called concerns-
that-are-reflexively-dealt-with-by-other-means. In other words: race,
and racism, as social phenomena, line the periphery of his consciousness but aren't integral to his art. From this perspective, to describe
his work in racialized terms would be credulous and beside the point,
a category mistake. Imaginative autonomy, the default perspective of
white writing as I've described it earlier in this book, was to Wallace
an absolute value, related to the nature of the universe itself: "Who on
earth's entitled to declaim about light-sources too far out to get to?"
he wrote in 1989 in *Signifying Rappers*, one of the very few times he addressed the subject directly. "The night sky's spray of light is there, at
a distance, for anyone to see and invoke. The heavens, that best chiaroscuro, are color-blind. Not so culture, race in the U.S. present."

There's an important, if obvious, observation to be made here, not
about race necessarily, but about Wallace's own project as he articulated it, as a turning away from postmodern cynicism toward a posture of belief for its own sake: Wallace was not interested in political
paranoia, or the project of political satire, but in a kind of cosmic
innocence, wonder, naïveté, that subsumed politics; his own liberal
politics were self-consciously bland and held at a distance, out of
his disinclination to participate in the symbolic logic of the spectacle, as he illustrated with his brief, almost whimsical essay about
September 11, "The View from Mrs. Thompson's." If I had to describe his work in the terms and categories he himself used, I would
say something like this (not an original observation): Wallace took
the "systems novel," a term the critic Tom LeClair used to describe

novels like *Giles Goat-Boy*, *Gravity's Rainbow*, and *Ratner's Star*, and made a system out of his own selfhood, the particularities of his own experience. This scene of experiencing self-as-universe occurs in so many places in his fiction it's hard to choose just one, but try this passage from *Brief Interviews with Hideous Men*:

> I all too quickly, as an adolescent, trying merely to masturbate in private, found out that my single fantasy of unknown seduction outside time required that the very world's entire population itself must be frozen by the single hand's gesture, all of the world's timepieces and activities, from the activities of yam farming in Nigeria to those of affluent Westerners purchasing blue jeans and Rock and Roll, on, on . . .

The gesture at the heart of Wallace's work—particularly, and maybe necessarily, so, in light of his lifelong struggles with self-destructive emotions and impulses—was to make his ironizing self feel like a relaxed, expansive, endlessly interesting vantage point. His most characteristic pieces orient the self-system outward, in a blaze of generosity, humor, or good feeling. He seemed to believe, like Forster, that much human misery resulted from simple failures of connection, communication, understanding, as in the pivotal moment of *Infinite Jest*, where James Incandenza reveals he's recorded his lethal film, *The Entertainment*, not out of a maniacal desire to kill the audience but because he's never been able to find a way to communicate with his son Hal.

But peripheries are uneasy places, even if they firmly stay peripheries. The oddest passage of *Infinite Jest*—a book that is willfully odd at every turn—occurs early on, in the voice of a black woman, Clenette, about the abuse suffered by her friend Wardine. The entire segment is only about a thousand words, and doesn't connect to any other aspect of the novel; it reads like a parody of a first-person narrative of inner-city life:

> But I know Reginald tell. Reginald say he gone die before Wardine momma beat Wardine again. He say he take his self up to Roy Tony

and say him to not mess with Wardine or breathe by her mattress at night. He say he take his self on down to the playground at the Brighton Projects where Roy Tony do business and he go to Roy Tony man to man and he make Roy Tony make it all right.

According to his editors and Wallace himself, the original manuscript of *Infinite Jest* was nearly twice as long as the published book. Enormous, book-length sections were cut; why did this passage, not in any way part of the extant narrative, stay in? The idiom is stereotyped, exaggerated Ebonics; and Wallace had strong, distinctly racialized feelings about "correct" or Standard Written English, which he explained in detail in a *Harper's* essay, "Authority and American Usage," in 2000. This essay is notably different—harsher, more strident, and, in some ways, more cynical—than Wallace's earlier nonfiction. In it, he labels himself unreservedly a SNOOT ("Sprachgefühl Necessitates Our Ongoing Tendance"), a term left over from his childhood, a prescriptivist who believes in upholding SWE not because of its innate superiority but because of the pragmatic necessity of maintaining a single communicative language for a democratic culture. In one of the essay's many tangents, he rehearses a speech he's given to African American students who, in his view, haven't learned, or don't want to learn, SWE sufficient to his standards:

I'm respecting you enough here to give you what I believe is the straight truth. In this country, SWE is perceived as the dialect of education and intelligence and power and prestige, and anybody . . . who wants to succeed in American culture has got to be able to use SWE. This is just How It Is. You can be glad about it or sad about it or deeply pissed off. You can believe it's racist and unfair and decide right here and now to spend every waking minute of your adult life arguing against it, and maybe you should, but I'll tell you something—if you ever want those arguments to get listened to and taken seriously, you're going to have to communicate them in SWE, because SWE is the dialect our nation uses to talk to itself.

Earlier in the essay he makes an analogy between this argument, as a relation to power, and the impossibility, in his view, of allowing boys to wear skirts to school, even if the parent and the boy both believe skirts are objectively better than pants: "In modern America any little boy who comes to school in a skirt . . . is going to get stared at and shunned and beaten up and called a total geekoid by a whole lot of people whose approval and acceptance are important to him." It could be a compelling statement of what used to be a normative belief system—call it liberal antipluralism—that positions itself at the rational center of a political sphere available to others only through certain conditions, or standards, of membership. In certain circles (those associated with Obama and his admiration of Reinhold Niebuhr, for example) it's known as "realism," though more radical thinkers like Roberto Unger would describe it as the essence of false necessity: staring at what exists and representing that stare as insight. Wallace's language, in expected and unexpected places, is saturated with this cynical use of realism, a variety of code switching meant to display, and also arbitrate, total linguistic fluency; and I can't think of the Wardine section of *Infinite Jest* outside of this aesthetic posture, an elitist exuberance some people would call slumming. What lingers about this displaced fragment over the novel as a whole, other than the voice and the sound, as if Wallace is spinning the dial on the radio?

# 7

*Signifying Rappers* came about while Wallace was living in Cambridge in the summer of 1989 with his former college roommate, the lawyer and future novelist Mark Costello; they wrote it in tandem, at the suggestion of the editor Lee Smith, as an argument for why hip hop should be taken "seriously." (In a 2013 preface to the reprinted edition, Costello says the original title might have been "How Rap, Which You Hate, Is Not What You Think, and Is Interesting as Hell, and, If Offensive, a Useful Sort of Offensive Given What Is Happening Today.") For Costello the book is an occasion for earnest reportage (a visit to a recording session in progress; a Slick Rick concert at a

Roxbury high school) and for pontificating on the political contradictions of Public Enemy. But Wallace dwells on the listening itself, and
the absurdity of *his* listening, as a "white Boston male," a proto-yuppie,
a gentrifier:

> Because serious rap has, right from the start, presented itself as
> a Closed Show. . . . There's an aura of cohesion-in-competence,
> of an exclusive and shared universe in the present rap relation-
> ship between black artists and black audience not enjoyed by a
> music especially of and for people of color in something like the
> last 80 years. To mainstream whites it's a tight cohesion that can't
> but look, from outside the cultural window, like occlusion, clan-
> nishness . . . and inbreeding, a kind of reverse snobbery. . . . Serious
> rap's a musical movement that seems to revile whites as a group or
> Establishment and simply to ignore their possibility as distinct in-
> dividuals. . . . The music's paranoia, together with its hermetic ra-
> cial context, maybe helps explain why it appears just as vibrant
> and impassioned as it does alien and scary, to us, from outside.

For a writer so obsessed with reflexivity in all its forms, Wallace never
seems to recognize how profoundly he's being played: how he's participating in what Ralph Ellison, in "On Bird, Bird-Watching, and Jazz,"
called "a grim comedy of racial manners," the mimetic dance of desire, resentment, projection, and fantasy that has always character-
ized the American white relationship to black cool. The posture of
*Signifying Rappers* is that of an ironized field report on an alien semiotics, not unlike Umberto Eco's *Travels in Hyperreality*, with its pretend-
serious hermeneutic exegesis of Disneyland; but for Wallace the pose
can't be as detached as he wants it to be. Hip hop makes him feel excluded, angry, and baffled, never more so than when he sees rappers
playing his own game of postmodern evasion-and-replacement:

> Serious rap's so painfully real because it's utterly mastered the
> special '80s move, the "postmodern" inversion that's so much sad-
> der and deeper than just self-reference: rap resolves its own con-

tradictions by *genuflecting* to them. . . . A music less "against" than simply scornful of the cold blank caucasian System of special hypocrisies can't but be of compelling interest to those white of us who stand all scrubbed and eager at that magnifying impediment of glass that rappers—like all U.S. young—have built themselves into. It may be, as avant-avant-gardists were arguing, gee, only 70 or 80 years back, that "self-reference" itself is like anything that defines a genre, a Scene, a place-and-time—just another window, thick and unclean, bulletproof and parallax, where where you stand informs what you look at, where sound and gesture split and everything Outside's quiet and everyone's alone, and free.

It's necessary to stay with Wallace at this unhappy moment of frustration, because it's precisely that: a failure of his most potent ability and fervent belief, a failure to connect, even a failure of reciprocal recognition or love, only a few months after he had finished the final edits on "Westward," with that last line, "You are loved," still firmly in place. "Westward" is story-as-sample, plundering and mangling and reusing Barth's text and his authorial persona in a way that is (according to Wallace's own description) shamelessly hip hop in its affect and style. But somehow he can't see that. What he can see, at least in this moment, is his own whiteness: where "everything Outside's quiet and everyone's alone, and free."

*Signifying Rappers* came and went in an instant, in 1990, likely because, for those who cared, there was much more nuanced and better-informed criticism available; but this passage contains the tablature for a generational affect of white sadness and antisocial isolation that only rarely, if ever, named itself in racial terms. In this way Wallace was, unironically, peerlessly, Nostradamus, not only the voice but the prophet of his generation. The mimetic effect of rap's perceived rejection, I would venture to say, was to make white hipsters hermetic, congealed into a depressive pose, and even, in some cases, ironically racist. Or sometimes, as Wallace was, as "The Depressed Person" was, just depressed.

# 8

In her 2017 collection of poems *Field Theories*, Samiya Bashir quotes an interview with Albert Murray:

> I finally hit upon what was going to be my metaphor, that is, my basic approach to what life is. It's the second law of thermo-dynamics, which adds up to the blues, the tendency of all phenom-ena to become random. In other words, ain't nothing nothing. . . . It's a matter of articulating the blues, not the blues that gets con-fused with an art song, but a confrontation with the nothingness of the universe. . . . Go to a planetarium and sit there and look at the planetarium, and then think of the people, the lies they've told and so forth. [Sings] "It don't mean a thing 'cause it ain't got that swing." Because swing is elegance, and elegance is what makes human life worth having.

"Where you stand informs what you look at," Wallace wrote in *Signifying Rappers*, paraphrasing Heisenberg's uncertainty principle in idiomatic American, and contradicting his earlier argument that "the heavens, that best chiaroscuro, are color-blind." Paraphrase, translation, analogy, relation, restatement—the way Murray restates Galileo's argument for elegance in astronomical models, *natura nihil frustra facit* (Nature does nothing in vain)—are necessary, but also forms of necessary compromise that leave a residue. You can describe this as the basic problem of difference-in-interpretation, as Ricoeur and Gadamer did, or as the unresolvable presence of the Other, via Levinas, or the problem of other minds (Ayer, Ryle), or Wittgenstein's proof of the impossibility of a private language, but to phrase it in philo-sophical terms, while useful (Wallace devotes two pages in "Authority and American Usage" to unpacking Wittgenstein's argument), doesn't address the actual problem of the residue, which surrounds us and coats us and can't be washed off. The white blues is not the same as Murray's blues, though it is still the same shared problem of the same shared universe. Americanness, that ugly word, is sameness-within-difference, difference-within-sameness, blah blah blah, and this is a problem that is not—contra DeLillo, contra Wallace, contra the academy of critics and theorists surrounding them—reducible to technology and a naive McLuhanian/Debordian theory of mass culture and the spectacle. Nor is it reducible to a theoretical notion of "pluralism." The problem has to do with the act of mutual understanding: understanding my own subjectivity in relation to another's, across conditions of power.

Here is a place where cynicism, as a posture, departs from irony as a procedure. Irony, in this case, never forgets that words carry residue with them, as Bashir writes in "Consequences of the Laws of Thermodynamics":

> When Albert Murray said
> the second law adds up to
> the blues that in other words
> ain't nothing nothing he meant it
>
> not quite the way my pops says
> nomads don't show emotions
> but more how my grandmother
> warned that men like women
>
> with soft hands blood red
> nails like how Mingus meant
> truth if you had time for it
> facts if you got no time that
>
> years pass. . . .

I think I know what the cynicism blues looks like: it looks like Colson Whitehead's *Apex Hides the Hurt*. The unnamed protagonist of this novel, a young black branding consultant for a major advertising firm, is hired to choose a name for a small midwestern town that has split into three political camps: entrepreneurs, who want to rename the town New Prospera; descendants of the town's dominant family, who want to keep the name Winthrop; and descendants of the town's original black residents, who want to restore the long-discarded original name, Freedom. Whitehead's consultant is an embodiment of Sloterdijk's definition of cynicism—able to work under any circumstances, happy to embrace the vacuousness of his profession, while silently satirizing it at every turn—who made his reputation by rebranding a down-market bandage as Apex, available in a variety of flesh tones to "hide the hurt." But when he applies an Apex bandage to his injured toe, it becomes hideously infected and has to be amputated. In pain, physically compromised for the first time, he chooses a new name for the town, deposits it with his clients in an envelope, and leaves before they have time to react: Struggle. "He heard the conversations they will have," Whitehead writes. "They will say: I was born in Struggle. I live in Struggle and come from Struggle."

Is the reader supposed to laugh? Or feel that something has actually changed? In this moment, the veil of cynicism lifts: the reader is not stuck in the endgame, the telos, of failure, but returned to the vivid present as the protagonist wanders out of the frame. "There had been a moment . . . when he thought he might be cured. Rid of that persistent mind-body problem. That if he did something, took action, the hex might come off. . . . As the weeks went on and he settled into his new life, he had to admit that actually, his foot hurt more than ever."

Is that enough? It may never be. Can anyone fully say that they've snapped out of their illusions? On the other hand, *Apex* seems to be saying, to give suffering a name, a source, a trajectory, may also be a way to imagine its ending. Or not. Maybe it will hurt more. As if in the end all this pain might amount to something.

# 9

And what are feelings supposed to amount to? This is the point, as far as I understand it, of writing about affect, the public, relational language of emotions. Feelings matter: everybody has them, even in their apparent absence (as in the "rational actor" fantasy of classical economics); they tend to follow patterns and form structures; they operate at cross-purposes, influence decisions even when not acknowledged (this is the supposed antidote to classical economics, "behavioral economics"); but most of all, in questions of political struggle, the politics of liberation (which I'll describe in Buddhist terms as freeing living beings from the effects and the causes of suffering), they play an essential and complicated role, especially in an American context. You could say this is the project of going beyond living in the world to relating to the world, or, in other terms, turning feelings into agency. This is not a question I'm trying to superimpose on the practice of writing, or the texts discussed here: it's the question these texts ask of me, none more so than *Harold and Maude*. If we—whoever feels addressed by a text—can allow open endings to remain open, then the questions *Harold and Maude* ask are actual questions: where are we going to go, and what are we going to do, and what will the music sound like then?

When I ask "what would it mean to call this a white blues," I'm asking, is it possible to turn the affect of white sadness into a form with an object, from *sadness* to *sadness about*? This would mean turning the occult object of white hipster culture into the actual object of the lost address, the absent way of talking across the color line. It might involve a form of the Brechtian alienation effect, where the author has to disclose the text's own preconditions, ironizing the form itself. It would run the risk of an attempt at actual psychological insight, or (provisionally) answering the question, as *Harold and Maude* does, "Why is _____ unhappy?" Or "Why can't _____ be happy?"

It needs to be said, at the same time, what the white blues can never be: not historical, not epic, not nostalgic, not about loss. White nostalgia, the state of mourning for the supremacist regime as a form of innocence, is already bountifully present and recognizable in many of the texts mentioned in this book: in the post-2016 era, there's J. D. Vance's best-selling *Hillbilly Elegy*. Another way to put this would be that the white blues is not about "the blues" at all as a cultural cliché representing pre-1960 black music or the stylings of Dan Ackroyd and John Belushi in *The Blues Brothers*. The blues, as a musical form, exists in and for the present. (If you associate the blues only with Muddy Waters or B. B. King, listen to Prince's "Kiss," or Kanye's "Gold Digger," or more recent work by, say, Tank and the Bangas.) As a work like *Field Theories* demonstrates, writers fluent in the blues are constantly reading it outward without constraints, as a paradigm, not simply a style. Like any paradigm it defeats easy description. It constantly recirculates. The pain and pleasure in it are immediate, or, rather, constant. It represents an inoculation against resentment and rage.

It may be that the white blues, if it ever existed, could do the imaginative work of pointing toward a nonexistent racial politics without deferring it. It could be another way of operating, as Lauren Berlant says, "juxtapolitically": not investing all my emotional energy in the national electoral system—which has been in my lifetime a source of almost constant disappointment, leaving the majority of Americans poorer, sicker, and less free than they were forty years ago—but rather looking toward parallel or contiguous movements that may not look like politics at all. This is a kind of poetics of the gap, which is never going to be satisfying, but may be productively *un*satisfying.

I'm thinking about Young Jean Lee's 2014 play *Straight White Men*. This is a case where the alienation effect starts with the title, which might be called antimetonymic, starting with the whole instead of the part (a more normative title being something like *Dinner at the Andersons*, or *A Pair of Gloves*). Titles that "give away" the subject matter are common in theater that deals with so-called identity politics (*The Colored Museum*, *The Death of the Last Black Man in the Whole Entire World*). The reversal here is a calculated transgression; one of Lee's previous plays, *Song of the Dragons Flying to Heaven*, features characters like "Korean 2" and "White Person 1." But *Straight White Men* could be performed or read with no relation to the title; it would work as self-contained, realist, "straight" theater. Three adult brothers gather with their widowed father at Christmas, in an unidentified midwestern town. Their mother was a liberal activist who left them with a retitled game of Monopoly called "Privilege." Everything is jovial banter and awkward high fives until the oldest brother, Matt, inexplicably breaks down crying in the middle of the second act. He's crying, the audi-

ence learns—once the family has re-formed itself around him, in crisis mode, as a kind of encounter group—because he still lives at home,
having never fulfilled the high hopes the family had for him. His life
is meaningless because he hasn't "contributed" anything; because he
hasn't been useful or productive; but he doesn't want to *be* productive.
He sees no need to be. Try as they do, his father and brothers can't
convince him otherwise, and the play descends into a fugue state of
disappointment and recrimination.

What work is the title doing? Lee's characters, particularly the
middle brother, Ed, who works in finance but is guilty about it, are absolutely certain of the meaning of whiteness: it has only negative use
value that has to be defended through work and success. When it fails,
it collapses:

> [Ed speaking] Women and minorities may get to pretend they're
> doing enough to make the world a better place just by getting ahead,
> but a white guy's pretty hard pressed to explain why the world
> needs him to succeed. Matt's just trying to stay out of the way.

*Straight White Men* is sort of like how *Death of a Salesman* would feel if
Bartleby replaced Willy Loman: it replaces the pretense of popular
tragedy with the existential question of what work actually means,
how it constitutes "the self." In an economic system where work is intrinsically racialized, in a country that was founded on a racial division
of labor, Lee is telling us that work is not just a trap of white self-
esteem (the argument over white unemployment or semiemployment
that has fueled a thousand circular debates since Trump's election):
work is something like the ground of white existence itself, the one
thing standing between it and death. It's easy to feel, in this subject
position, that something else—color, feeling, taste, happiness—is other,
is elsewhere.

Here I'm thinking of another narrative in which white self-abasement
is even keener than it is in *Straight White Men*: Lorrie Moore's 1986
novel *Anagrams*, which follows the unraveling of Benna Carpenter, a
young woman whose life is recounted, or reconstituted, in several

different ways—as a nightclub singer, a young wife and homemaker, and an adjunct college professor. In another novel these multiple pathways might make for a dissonant, fragmentary text, but in *Anagrams* they're hardly noticeable, because Benna's voice—a mixture of mordant self-pity, lacerating self-criticism, and a constant, puckish drumbeat of jokes, puns, witticisms, and cutting analogies—never varies:

> "Love is the cultural exchange program of futility and eroticism," I said. And Eleanor would say, "Oh, how cynical can you get," meaning not nearly cynical enough. I had made it sound dreadful but somehow fair, like a sleepaway camp. "Being in love with Gerard is like sleeping in the middle of the freeway," I tried.
> "Thatta girl," said Eleanor. "Much better."

Benna, like many of Moore's protagonists, is locked within the double bind Berlant describes in *Cruel Optimism*, where "adjustment seems like an accomplishment." (As *Anagrams* proceeds, the reader sees that Benna's "adjustment" is itself a fiction: the child she describes so vividly is an invention she uses as a coping mechanism.) But it's important not to undervalue her optimism, the sometimes-furtive way she demonstrates, and simultaneously undermines, a capacity and desire for love. Though she has an on-again, off-again boyfriend, the sad-sack wannabe opera singer Gerard, the focus of her desire turns out to be Darrel, a black Vietnam veteran and student in her creative writing class. Darrel grew up middle class; Benna lived in a trailer. When he tells her he wants to be an orthodontist, she remembers how "she had nightly pressed her front teeth hard against the heel of her hand, to push them back: orthodontia for the poor." As I read the novel the first time I kept expecting Moore to expel Darrel from the story, the way black characters are so often expelled from American narratives: as glimpsed figures of moral authority or emblems of a characters' bad conscience, but always as what Henry James called the ficelle, an instrumental figure with no central dramatic significance. But Benna stays stubbornly attached to him, grappling with a churning mixture of resentment, inferiority, and almost fetishistic desire:

Where are Darrel's sneakers? He is wearing what my brother Louis used to call "hard shoes"—leather shoes. And a slick shirt, slippery and nice. It has a dry, sweet smell, like bubblegum and cedar.

Whenever I have danced this way with Gerard, it's always been sort of a joke: I lead and he pretends to swoon. With Darrel, there's no joking. . . . I turn back, look up at Darrel, and feel my heart fluttering. It's a Tennessee Williams heart. A bad Tennessee Williams heart. I don't know what to say. The music urges love on you like food. . . .

What is this jazz? I grew up in the country, in a trailer. We did things like stand far apart and ripple our stomachs in and out.

Darrel is too good for Benna to turn away from, in every way that Gerard isn't: he's earnest, sensual, a talented poet with aspirations for a stable future. When they have sex, Benna thinks, "I know if I can keep feeling like this I'll be okay, if I can feel like this I'm not dead, I won't die. Life is sad. Here is someone." But the desperation of her need for him is also, transparently, a refusal to take him seriously; after a few months of intense intimacy, their relationship implodes in a breakup scene worth quoting at length:

Here we are on the god-knows-what anniversary of John Lennon's death and Darrel is saying he wants to be an orthodontist. Maybe I am hearing things wrong. This sometimes happens this time of year: People hear things wrong. The night John Lennon died I was standing in a deli and someone burst in and shouted, "Guess who's been shot? *Jack Lemmon!*" . . . Darrel has meant something else all along. Surely he doesn't want to become a jeweler of teeth, a bruiser of gums. It's a joke. "Yeah, right," I laugh. "I can see you as an orthodontist."

Darrel looks suddenly irritated, screws up his leathery face into a fist, bunched like one of those soft handbags. "What, isn't that good enough for you, Benna? Upward mobility for the oppressed? Is that just not angry enough for you?"

It's true. That's what I want for Darrel, from Darrel. He should be angry like Huey Newton. Or in a wheelchair making speeches, like Jon Voight.

"You want me to be a little black boy vet with a Ph.D. and a lot of pissed-off poetry?"

"Why not?" I say. It doesn't sound bad, it's just the way he's saying it. Darrel stands up and paces peevedly about the living room.

"I can't believe it. You're just like everyone else. You want me to be your little cultural artifact. Like a Fresh-Air child. Come off it, Benna."

"*You* come off it," I say. This is the old children's strategy of retort. I've learned it from Georgianne or remembered it or simply saved and practiced it. "You're being so, well . . . *bourgeois.*"

This is the word that intelligent, twentieth-century adults use when they want to criticize each other. It is the thinking man's insult. It is the wrong word. Don't let your mouth write a check your ass can't cash, Darrel said once, and this time I truly have. Darrel's been storing up for it and leaps on it like a wild man. "*Bourgeois!?*" He's pacing quick and hard, left to right. "You!" he shouts, freezes, points to me.

The sterile tent of ironic defensiveness, the imprimatur of cynical cool, the reflexive habit of turning tragedy into verbal junk that Benna has maintained her entire life, is finally breached: John Lennon may be Jack Lemmon, but Huey Newton, somehow, is still Huey Newton. For her, Darrel is not just an emblem of psychological health and sexual healing; he represents an entirely different order of redemption as well. Darrel, on the other hand, can take a joke, but he can't ironize away his desire for a solid income, a professional career, the terminally uncool, unexceptional, bourgeois life Benna has till now mocked so relentlessly as a way of inoculating herself against the shame of downward mobility.

When Benna has lost Darrel, her life plunges swiftly toward rock bottom: she loses her precarious teaching job, and Gerard dies in a freak accident. In the novel's final moments, observing Georgianne, her imaginary daughter, Benna thinks again, "Life is sad. . . . Here is someone"—as if to say that Darrel is this fiction's fiction, its object of cruel optimism, the object that, when desired, becomes impossible to attain.

An anagram is a word formed by rearranging the letters of another word. The title suggests multiple and presumably equal possibilities or versions, as in a game, where there's no value placed on "cinema" as opposed to "iceman." The pathos of *Anagrams* comes from the failure of the game, or its failure to *be* a game: no rearrangement of the givens can produce actual love, or justice, what Cornel West says love looks like in public. It's easy to describe this—as many critics did in 1986—as incoherent, murky, and depressing. What happens if I call it, instead, a different order of blues? Would this be a way of saying what I think of as failure, if I recognize it as such, is not actually the end of the story? Go sit and look at the planetarium, Albert Murray says, and ask: where can Benna and Darrel find their own elegance? The universe is multiple in nature. If I can't see it, I'm not looking hard enough.

# 10

In 1971, the same year *Harold and Maude* was released, the Dutch American performance artist Bas Jan Ader produced a three-minute silent film, *I'm too sad to tell you*, which consists of a close-up of his face passing through a variety of sad or confused expressions, with tears rolling down his cheeks, as well as a postcard mailed to his friends with the same message.

This was a departure from his other works of the period, which showcased his obsession with gravity: in one, he bicycles off the bank of a canal in Amsterdam; in another, he balances a chair atop the roof of a house in Los Angeles and then rolls down the roof, landing in some bushes on the ground. The work Ader is most famous for, *In search of the miraculous*, occurred in 1975, when he set out from New England to sail across the Atlantic in a thirteen-foot open boat, the smallest boat ever used for that purpose. Ader disappeared at sea; his boat was found off the coast of Ireland ten months later.

It's possible to trace, in a minimalist register, the trajectory of a white blues in Ader's work. You could call it the escape from the presumption of normativity into silence. (By which I don't mean the passive-aggressive silence of aggrieved withdrawal, which is something else entirely, like a pause in an argument that is at its midpoint, where the rage will always return.) Of course, in a sense, it's unfair even to try to describe a work in which the artist vanishes and is presumed dead; there's no way of knowing, on a simple level, whether this is the complete work as the artist intended. On the other hand, in a Schrödinger's cat analysis: *In search of the miraculous* obviously was meant to include the risk of Ader's death; it can be read as the openest of all open endings, the one where the artist doesn't witness its completion.

I've been haunted by *In search of the miraculous* since I encountered a reference to it, years ago, because it represents a horizon of white art making, namely, the choice to stop, to absent oneself. Which is to say: the question of whether to write at all is one white writers should take seriously. To produce art—even explicitly antiracist art—under conditions that reward white subjectivity, center it, and render it harmless and neutral, is, arguably, a way of collaborating with and sustaining those conditions. This is a case where the argument that "the solution to the problems within the work of art is to produce more art" may actually be the root of the problem. Because it may be that white writers can never escape the horror of performing within the family romance of whiteness and the white state. It may be that Harold's choice is to have no more performances at all, but to just resume ordinary life, which for the artist is a kind of death. (Even Max Fischer, in *Rushmore*, undertakes this option, briefly dropping out of school and becoming a barber in his father's shop.) The other side of the coin, unfortunately, is that Ader's suicide is a potent act of mythmaking, part of the cult of romantic early death of the white male that goes back through Ian Curtis and Nick Drake to Rimbaud to Keats and Kleist all the way to Orpheus. It takes on an ersatz profundity summed up by the wonderful name of a new emo band, formed in 2007: The World Is a Beautiful Place and I Am No Longer Afraid to Die.

The real point of emo, for me, at any rate, was not to die but to go on living in a new key. I'm interested in the ways artists can put their bodies on that line, not necessarily over it. In September 2008, a few days after Wallace's suicide, James Wood, Daniel Mendelsohn, and Pico Iyer were asked at a public event to comment on whether his death was a literary gesture—"or is that just too distasteful a suggestion?" Mendelsohn replied, "I'm so dumbfounded by the question I don't—I'm not sure what to say. The only literary gesture is writing." Without saying anything about the circumstances of Wallace's life, about which I know nothing outside the public record, I can say this: Mendelsohn's words are the prison Wallace felt we inhabited, and wanted us all to escape. I don't know if he felt he failed or succeeded; but I don't want to go the same way. I want us all to go together. He would never have wanted us to feel so alone.

# White Out

This bitter earth is the one place we all have standing.

Fred Moten

# 1

## On Bad Timing

On the morning after the election we were up early; it was a school day, an ordinary Wednesday. When I went into the kids' room (or maybe it was Sonya who went in first) and told them the news, they were very quiet. We had an almost soundless morning. It was too warm for November; there was sunlight spilling everywhere; but the weather always feels unbearable in a catastrophe. The streets seemed virtually empty. Everything was still in place. You glanced at strangers and then looked away, seeing the same thing: I am still here, this is really happening.

"After great pain," Dickinson wrote, "a formal feeling comes— / The Nerves sit ceremonious, like Tombs." Like many people I'm still grasping for a form, for the right words, to describe what happened in November 2016—not only on Election Day but the days that followed, the first few weeks, as the country and the world recoiled from the shock of an event that seemed impossible, even if it was, in retrospect, clearly predictable.

These feelings of facing the impossible—terror, horror, anger, astonishment—were widespread after the election among people I knew, including those who had remained detached and skeptical (rightfully so) while the campaign was under way. Even among my friends who insisted that whatever the outcome, the fundamental conditions of American life wouldn't change, especially for the people who were most vulnerable, impoverished, and subject to violence—they, too, were overcome with rupture and shock. A sense of slippage, of losing the thread, or being forced back into crisis and catastrophic time. Maybe all conflict comes from the urge to superimpose one timeline over another, to force one story in and another out.

The obvious words are all, in one way or another, about time. "Catastrophe," *kata* meaning "down" and *strophē*, "to turn," originally a synonym for denouement, the end of the story. The final stroke or turn that concludes a series of events. "Inevitable." "The last." "The end of." "Backlash." ("Whitelash.")

For years I've been interested in the elasticity of time: not time as a phenomenon in physics—which may or may not exist—but human perceptions of time, which may be the only "time" there is. Political, historical time, the matrix, or really matrices, humans operate in, consciously or not. (I use the word "matrix" intentionally: a constructed world, an internally coherent system that may or may not resemble the world outside it.) There are too many of these constructs to keep track of. Hegel, Freud, Nietzsche, Marx (and Lenin, Mao, the Weather Underground, the Khmer Rouge); the Cultural Turn; Late Capitalism; the End of History; Moore's Law; the Mayan Calendar; the Great Singularity; Queer antifuturists (exemplified by Lee Edelman's *No Future*) and utopians (exemplified by Jose Muñoz's *Cruising Utopia*).

Take one beloved, often-quoted example, a saying by Martin Luther King Jr: "The arc of history is long, but it bends toward justice." Which presupposes that I see myself in time as a point on a curve, progressing in one direction.

Or this, from Roy Scranton's *Learning to Die in the Anthropocene*: "Once the methane hydrates under the oceans and permafrost begin to melt . . . we face the imminent collapse of the agricultural, shipping, and energy networks upon which the global economy depends, a large-scale die-off in the biosphere that's already well under way, and our own possible extinction as a species. . . . If, as Montaigne asserted, 'To philosophize is to learn how to die,' then we have entered humanity's most philosophical age. . . . The rub now is that we have to learn to die not as individuals, but as a civilization."

You can live in one of these matrices but not, properly speaking, in both of them. That itself is terrifying. But to live in a plural world is to live among people who inhabit many different time lines, who are living out entirely different stories. And perhaps even to inhabit different time lines yourself, without thinking much about the contradictions between them.

I'm interested in what people are most afraid of. This seems necessary to the task of a novelist. It would seem obvious that people are afraid of dying, of the end of the world, civilization's collapse, disaster, the worst-case scenario, the zombie apocalypse, "race war"; but there's the less obvious but still palpable fear of having chosen the wrong matrix, and misunderstood time and the historical conditions in which you live.

"In Trump Time, the clock moves backward," the novelist Brit Bennett wrote in an essay published on the first anniversary of the election. "The feeling that time itself is reversing might be the most unsettling aspect of a most unsettling year. What else is Make America Great Again but a promise to re-create the past? . . . He creates a fantasy for his base of white Americans but a threat for many others. After all, in what version of the past was America ever great for my family?"

It's easy to read catastrophe as the end, as time stopped or reversed, when it has not actually stopped or reversed. (Maybe this is the root of Beckett's refusal to end *The Unnameable*: "I can't go on, I'll go on.") When I say "elasticity of time," this is what I mean: the feeling that chronological time is unbearable and the future is unbearable; which is also to say that karma and consequences are unbearable.

Or: not just unbearable but unreadable.

It seems obvious that to find something unbearable is to want to prevent it, or forestall it, and also shun it, curse its name. But the opposite is true, Frank Kermode argues in *The Sense of an Ending*. Since the advent of Christianity, the West has held its theories about the end of time close, played with them, embellished them, obsessed over them. Thinking about the end of days has shaped Western culture's sense of what it means to end. Fictions of the end—which is the only kind of apocalypse that actually exists—are always threatening to become real.

"Perhaps if we have a terrible privilege it is merely that we are alive and are going to die, all at once or one at a time," Kermode writes. "Other people have noticed this, and expressed their feelings about it in images different from ours, armies in the sky, for example, or a palpable Antichrist; and these we have discarded. But it would be childish to argue, in a discussion of how people behave under eschatological threat, that nuclear bombs are more real and make one experience more authentic crisis-feelings than armies in the sky. There is nothing at all distinguishing about eschatological anxiety. . . . Crisis is a way of thinking about one's moment, and not inherent in the moment itself."

Which also means (Kermode doesn't quite go on to say) that politics often amounts to a kind of eschatology, always reading the present for signs of one or another imminent end. He fails to say, in turn, that politics, like eschatology, like fiction, is a form of entertainment.

"Every language on the apocalypse is also apocalyptic," says Derrida, "and cannot be excluded from its object."

I want to resist this idea, in the following small way: fictions, consciously fictional narratives, end without ending everything around them. Fiction reminds the reader that the end is not really the end. ("'Strophe' . . . is not only the Greek word for 'turn,'" Sonya Posmentier writes in *Cultivation and Catastrophe*, "but also for the poetic unit of a stanza. . . . Catastrophe, then, is always involved with art making. It contains . . . the making of form in the first place.") I'm looking for, and hoping for, a literature that resists death, that resists the identification of "death" and "ending." Our lives end in death, but the world and the culture do not have to die. One does not require the other. Time does not have to pull incessantly in the direction of oblivion.

This is an improvised essay for the time being. I wrote it without a form or an end in mind. Later, I might add to it. Or not. It could be an afterthought, a capsule, a thread, a broken thread. All these words are also about time, and of course themselves take time. In the time it takes to read this, another impossible thing may have happened.

## White Out

As a construct for classifying human beings, whiteness is always seeing its own end, its obsolescence. ("Indeed I tremble for my country when I reflect that God is just," Jefferson wrote in *Notes on the State of Virginia*. "That his justice cannot sleep for ever.")

In the early twentieth century the end of whiteness—white dominance of the world—became a widespread cultural obsession. "Civilization's going to pieces," Tom Buchanan says in *The Great Gatsby*. "I've gotten to be a terrible pessimist about things. Have you read 'The Rise of the Coloured Empires' by this man Goddard?" He goes on to explain:

> "The idea is if we don't look out the white race will be—will be utterly submerged. It's all scientific stuff; it's been proved."
>     "Tom's getting very profound," said Daisy with an expression of unthoughtful sadness. "He reads deep books with long words in them. What was the word we—"
>     "Well, these books are all scientific," insisted Tom, glancing at her impatiently. "This fellow has worked out the whole thing. It's

up to us who are the dominant race, to watch out or these other races will have control of things."

The book Fitzgerald alludes to, Lothrop Stoddard's *The Rising Tide of Color Against White World-Supremacy*, was one of many popular titles of the 1920s (most famously Oswald Spengler's *The Decline of the West*) that made versions of the same argument. In 1929 Stoddard debated W. E. B. Du Bois in Chicago. Contemporary newspaper accounts described Stoddard as being "outclassed" and "speechless."

Fitzgerald writes of Tom Buchanan: "There was something pathetic in his concentration, as if his complacency, more acute than of old, was not enough to him any more."

After the rise of fascism in the 1930s, explicit theories of white eclipse fell out of fashion in American and European mainstream political discourse; they became associated with far-right parties and groups like the John Birch Society, Aryan Nations, and the National Front, and paranoid, dystopian fantasies, like William Pierce's *The Turner Diaries* or Jean Raspail's *The Camp of the Saints*. (Implicitly, during the same period, fears of white eclipse permeated every aspect of American life; that's a different story.) But in the early twenty-first century—a period now coming to a close—public interest in the end of whiteness returned, in what was, ostensibly, an entirely different, more rigorous, "objective," even celebratory form.

In 2012 the Census Bureau reported that, for the first time, more than half of United States children under age one were nonwhite minorities, using the following categories: "Hispanic," "Black," "Asian," "American Indian and Alaska Natives," "Native Hawaiians and Other Pacific Islanders." In 2013, and then 2015, the bureau concluded that more whites were dying than being born, and that non-Hispanic whites would cease to be the American majority in 2044.

If you looked at a newspaper anytime in the late Obama years it was hard to miss these findings. They made headlines. There was a feeling of acceleration about them. There were concurrent reports, in 2015 and 2016, that life expectancy for white Americans, particularly middle-aged white men, was declining. "This change reversed decades of progress in mortality and was unique to the United States; no other rich country saw a similar turnaround," Anne Case and Angus Deaton wrote in the *Proceedings of the National Academy of Sciences.* "This increase for whites was largely accounted for by increasing death rates from drug and alcohol poisonings, suicide, and chronic liver diseases and cirrhosis. . . . Rising midlife mortality rates of white non-Hispanics were paralleled by increases in midlife morbidity. Self-reported declines in health, mental health, and ability to conduct activities of daily living, and increases in chronic pain and inability to work . . . all point to growing distress in this population."

What exactly does it mean to say "this population"? In a 2015 *New York Times* essay, "The Myth of a White Minority," the sociologist Richard Alba wrote that "the predictions make sense only if you accept the outdated, illogical methods used by the census, which define as a 'minority' anyone who belongs to 'any group other than non-Hispanic White alone.' In the words 'group' and 'alone' lie a host of confusions."

The census, Alba observed, refuses to account for the growing demographic of mixed-race Americans, at least some of whom will identify as white, or the likelihood that (following the trajectory of other ethnic groups) some "Hispanics," a highly diverse category, will begin to identify as white. "Some of the mixed children now classified as minorities surely will think of themselves mainly as whites when they grow up," he wrote. "Researchers have already found a significant group of American adults who declare themselves as non-Hispanic whites to the census, but acknowledge having some Mexican ancestry. Others may have mixed or even minority identities, but will be 'sociologically white,' integrated into white communities and family networks and seen as essentially no different from anyone else."

Alba concluded: "We cannot abandon ethno-racial categories. They register legacies of slavery, conquest and oppression that have enduring effects. They are still useful, to measure and redress inequalities. But we need to admit that these categories are at best rough approximations when it comes to understanding who we are becoming. Our society, transformed by immigration and new forms of assimilation, hasn't yet developed the vocabulary to capture the nuanced realities of this evolution."

When I read Alba's response I was thinking: the idea of population itself is a form of catastrophic thinking. Because a population is always, consciously or not, defined against its limit. The concept of the limit is built into race itself.

"Figures of massified life, in the forms of multitudes, crowds, and overpopulation, have been persistently racializing figures," Michelle Murphy writes in *The Economization of Life.* "*Population* . . . is profoundly entangled with designations of surplus life, of life unworthy, of life contained, of life open to destruction."

There's no way to do political work of any kind without numbers and measurements; there's no way to do political work without understanding that numbers are objects of projection and desire. Fixed in the mind, taken as objectively real and final, a number can be a melancholy thought and a rageful thought, but also, for the people thinking it, a moment of exultation.

## Necropolitans

Here's an unoriginal thought: people who feel closer to death, in any available sense—the death of life on earth, the death of people who live down the street, the death of *their kind of people*—act differently for that reason. See themselves differently, imagine the future differently.

In the late 1990s Achille Mbembe coined the term "necropolitics" to describe an alternate way of thinking about the power of the state. Enlightenment thought, he argued, has always assumed that the political subject—the citizen—achieves a good life, a fully moral life, by the "exercise of reason in the public sphere." "The romance of sovereignity," he writes, "in this case, rests on the belief that the subject is the master and the controlling author of his or her own meaning." Only by giving up this romance can we see the state as it actually is. Politics is the "work of death." The sovereign state exercises the power of life and death over its subjects; subjects exercise their agency only by choosing how and when to die. Death is not a negative value: referring to Georges Bataille's concept of the accursed share, the way societies give off excess energy and productivity by way of warfare, elaborate ritual, or art making, Mbembe writes, "What connects terror, death, and freedom is an *ecstatic* notion of temporality and politics. The future, here, can be authentically anticipated, but not in the present. The present itself is but a moment of vision—vision of the freedom not yet come. Death in the present is the mediator of redemption."

He goes on to say this: "In our contemporary world, weapons are deployed in the interest of maximum destruction of persons and the creation of *death-worlds*, new and unique forms of social existence in which vast populations are subjected to conditions of life conferring upon them the status of *living dead*."

Mbembe's principal example was the figure of the Palestinian suicide bomber. He also drew examples from slave revolts, from the Nazi death camps, from analyses by Arendt, Agamben, Hegel, Foucault. As a political theorist, he did not invoke necropolitics as a state of the imagination, say, in *Rambo II*, or *The Terminator*, or *Robocop*.

A few years ago, watching *Mad Max: Fury Road* on a flight to China, I wondered if I was seeing necropolitics in a pure, unadulterated form, not as a theory but as a stimulant. The movie seemed to me set on permanent fast-forward. Every scene ended as soon as it began. The enemy, Immortan Joe, is a masked bionic man with horns who controls a slave state in the desert. The slaves are virtually naked and spray-painted white and chrome to mark their status. The hero, played by Charlize Theron, instigates a rebellion to free the slaves, which becomes a vast battle among vehicles speeding across the desert.

During the battle, slaves die, seemingly happily, in order to free themselves and their comrades; they've been promised they will be reborn in "Walhalla," a central tenet of their religion, the Cult of the V8.[5]

"That *race* . . . figures so prominently in the calculus of biopower is entirely justifiable," Mbembe writes. "Race has been the ever present shadow in Western political thought and practice. . . . In the economy of biopower, the function of racism is to regulate the distribution of death and to make possible the murderous functions of the state."

Intercontinental jet airplanes, like the Boeing 777, burn approximately one gallon of fuel per second. In a thirteen-hour flight, like the flight I took from New York to Shanghai, the plane uses 46,800 gallons of fuel. According to "radiative forcing"—quantitative models that aggregate the varying effects of different stimuli on the climate—airplane emissions are thought to be particularly bad for short-term climate change: "Aviation emissions include water vapor, which creates clouds, and releases of ample black carbon, nitrous oxide and sulphur oxide," the Yale Center for Climate Communications reports: "These in turn contribute even more to a greenhouse effect and the trapping of heat."

I wonder if people privileged enough to ride in 777s watch a movie like *Mad Max: Fury Road* and see it not as fantasy, not as allegory, but as predictive, near-future, dystopian realism, in which the most dehumanizing acts are taken for granted. Why are these people driving so fast? Where are they going? What is the relation between speed, fossil fuels, enslavement, and death?

I'm no longer clear about where the imagination ends and politics begins, or what it means to do political analysis apart from the imagined worlds of individual subjects. I can only say this much: whenever

---

5. The term "Cult of the V8" isn't used in the movie; it's a description fans use in the Mad Max Wiki, based on the many V-8-associated icons within the Citadel, Immortan Joe's temple.

I travel by plane I feel reduced to a passport and a credit card. This is a perverse reversal of Agamben's most famous concept, the idea of the dehumanized noncitizen, reduced to "bare life." I go from duty-free shop to duty-free shop, a profit center in transit, a purchasing agent. I'm reminded that I'm participating in climate change on a massive scale; that the capital I accumulate and invest—my retirement account in TIAA, invested in arms manufacturers, and energy companies, despite years of customer protests—takes part in transactions I never authorized, to say nothing of my taxes, which have paid for KBR-Halliburton's kidnapping of Nepalis to work in the Green Zone during the Gulf War, extraordinary renditions and drone strikes, deportations and private prisons and the world's largest nuclear stockpile.

Which is why I've always had a hard time limiting Mbembe's concept of necropolitics and its philosophical ground to the conditions of state violence and indiscriminate death in Gaza, Syria, Kashmir, the Congo. I wonder if the concept even necessarily depends on the involvement of a state at all, or if it's a general feature of a transactional, global free market; if it exists in decentralized, local, improvisatory situations that feel more like freedom. It matters in this context that "necropolitics" describes not just one but an entire canon of action movies and dystopian novels, circulated around the world, beginning in the 1970s. It matters that the formulation can be reversed so easily to serve as a something like a policy platform, not a means of critique. Or even a way of life.

Maybe the way to say this is: necropolitics is not just about the living dead (a state of negation) but living death (a state of affirmation), being not a noncitizen but a citizen of the necropolis, which makes you a necropolitan. Which means (among other things) getting used to death—administered, systematic, programmatic death, random and predictable—as a condition of life, and getting along with life in spite of it. In the United States, in 2018, this means acclimating to mass shootings and police killings as an ordinary condition within a larger

matrix of planetary death and possible governmental collapse. A necropolitan can live in a condition of dread, or boredom, or even localized
hope, or more likely, passing through all of these states, with the underlying assumption that catastrophe is inevitable, that one day the world
will revert to masters and slaves. This particular outcome is never spoken out loud, but revealed over and over in dystopian narratives that
also feel like fantasies.

(In September 2017 the *New York Times* ran an article in the Style section called "How to Survive the Apocalypse." "Yes, the world is clearly
coming to an end," the reporter writes. "But is there anything you
can do to prepare? That is not a philosophical question, or a theo-
logical one. And if it is a question that seems to beg any explication,
you may stop reading now. But if you are among the swelling class of
weekend paranoiacs of affluent means who are starting to mull fantasies of urban escape following the endless headlines about disasters,
both natural and manufactured, you may be starting to see a different image in your mind when [you] think 'survivalist.' You may no
longer see the wild-eyed cave dweller in camouflage fatigues, hoard-
ing canned goods. You may even see one in the mirror.")

A necropolitan, like a cosmopolitan, is someone comfortable with moving from one place to another, carrying a private, distinct, if not always articulated, set of values. This is not a writerly but a therapeutic,
or sociotherapeutic, or whatever, kind of thought: having persistent
access to dystopian or apocalyptic narratives and sensory states (video
games, for example) doesn't necessarily make one more likely to kill,
but may make it easier to be a necropolitan. As a lifestyle. As fun. Or,
to be adjunct, to live among necropolitans with a sense of humor, and,
as Peter Sloterdijk says, to keep from crying.

## Resemblance: A Fugue

It's the spring of 1985 and I'm lying on the carpet in my living room,
watching the movie *First Blood*. In a dripping forest somewhere in the
Pacific Northwest, young Sylvester Stallone crouches alone, dressed

in a shapeless brown vest like a monk's habit, with a pulsing wound on his right arm. Helicopters chatter overhead, searching for him. He bites off a length of unraveled thread from his sleeve, and using a needle concealed in his boot heel, begins to suture the cut closed with his good hand.

With his shock of dark hair, short beard, and swarthy skin, not to mention the unfitted garment, he's a kind of guerrilla Christ. I'm eleven years old and even I can see it. ("Bodybuilding does . . . sometimes draw on Christian imagery," Richard Dyer writes in *White*, referring to Stallone and Schwarzenegger. "The activity itself involves pain, bodily suffering, and with it the idea of the value of pain. This may be echoed in film images of bodybuilders crucified . . . combining as they do 'passivity offset by control, humiliation offset by nobility of sacrifice, eroticism offset by religious connotations of transcendence.'") Even Rambo's weapon of choice, the five-foot-long, belt-fed M-50 machine gun—designed not to be fired upright, but lying or sitting down, balanced on a V-shaped stand—is a version of the cross Jesus carried to Golgotha. It's Rambo's cross to bear.

In the flickering blue light, my cousins narrate the movie in low voices. Every tenth round the M-50 fires is an incendiary, an explosive bullet. To sterilize a needle outdoors, hold it in the flame of a lighter till it turns black and shiny. The handle of the knife unscrews; the needle, the lighter, the thread fit inside it. A barbed arrowhead is designed to create massive tissue trauma; a hollowpoint bullet makes a fist-sized exit wound.

My cousins grew up in the Black Hills, half an hour from where our great-grandparents arrived in the gold rush in 1878. I hardly know them. They're working for my dad, doing construction on our new house in Maryland. The oldest and middle brother originally came to the East Coast as college students from the University of Wyoming, to work as interns for Alan Simpson, their Wyoming senator, and for Dick Cheney, at that time the sole Wyoming congressman. Later, all three of them will go on to establish careers, and families, in Houston, Dallas, Phoenix.

While my cousins are visiting we hardly talk about politics. We watch movies. We watch *Mad Max* and *Conan the Barbarian* and *Pale Rider* and *Dirty Harry* and *Commando* and *Red Dawn* and *The Terminator* and *Platoon*. My parents won't let us watch *Animal House* or *Taxi Driver* or *Death Wish*, but my cousins know all the best lines, and soon, so do we.

My parents won't let me handle or fire a gun, but I have a stack of *Guns & Ammo* magazines in my room (bought with my allowance, at supermarkets and gas stations), and a mental arsenal, beginning with Travis Bickle's tiny hidden wrist-pistols and moving up to all the various assault rifles.

Only years later did I connect *Mad Max*—set in a dystopian future, but filmed in the ordinary Australian outback—with the landscape of western South Dakota and Wyoming, which my cousins knew as ordinary. I remember Rob taking me and my brother for a ride in his Camaro once when we were visiting Rapid City. There were no seat belts in the back seat. He floored it on a straightaway; we hit a hundred in a huge cloud of dust.

"Speed is a question of how much you're willing to spend," reads a poster in the window of a mechanic's shop in *Mad Max*. "Have you got it in you?"

It's possible to experience your own family as a kind of suspension of disbelief. You can watch them, your older cousins, or siblings who have already grown and left the house, or younger uncles and aunts— people who occupy a half step between generations, relative to you— and imagine your life as a movie joined with theirs.

For example: I've always been small for my age, but it's this same year, when my cousins are around, after a series of hormone-challenge tests in the hospital, I'm assigned to inject myself with synthetic growth hormone, a newly invented drug. If I don't, the endocrinologists say, I may not reach more than five feet tall.

When I learn about my diagnosis—months after the initial tests—I begin having what I can only describe as internal, purely passive, fits of loneliness and rage. I keep seeing, in what I can only call my mind's eye, not only images of myself armed, massacring my enemies, but because I can't heal myself, as Rambo sutures himself in the forest, I am also the figure of Willem Dafoe dying in *Platoon*, on his knees, his arms outspread.

"The cinema of action is a cinema of striking back—of restoration and reassurance," writes the film critic Harvey O'Brien. "Action movies are therefore also a cinema of crisis and *re*action—of attempting to restore agency through force of will. Though [they] seem to project hypermasculine triumphalism and redemption through violence, they . . . represent a profoundly anxious attitude."

A month after the release of *Rambo II*—where Rambo returns to Vietnam to rescue POWs—the army began placing posters for the movie outside its recruitment offices.

I think of these events in my life as a "phase." I did not become my liberal family's Alex P. Keaton. I had no interest in systematic cruelty toward the poor when it was pointed out to me. A year later I was listening to *Meat Is Murder* and *Sandinista!* and reading *Bury My Heart at Wounded Knee.*

My youngest cousin became an auto auctioneer in Phoenix. He was briefly part of a reality TV show: *Desert Car Auctions.* I watched him once: in a salvage lot on the edge of the desert, selling twenty cars an hour. "No matter what the price or the condition is," he said to me, "there's a customer for every car." After the November 2016 election I deleted him on Facebook. "By supporting him," I wrote, "you're effectively saying my family has no right to exist, that you would like to kill us all."

My eldest cousin went on to be an executive at Enron, then at El Paso Gas and Electric, and now, according to LinkedIn, at Entoro, an energy investment company. He is the most openly racist person I've ever known; the only one, for example, who would say, looking at a black man passing on the sidewalk, "Look at that gorilla." I had to look him up online because I haven't spoken to him in fifteen years. Yet there he is, my first cousin, my father's brother's son.

What does it mean to have a family? I've never known the answer to this question. I'm writing about the part of my family I know the least—intentionally—because it's important to pay attention to peripheries. I am peripheral in their world and they are peripheral in mine.

Wittgenstein, explaining the concept of family resemblance in section 67 of *Philosophical Investigations*: "Why do we call something a 'number'? Well, perhaps because it has a—direct—relationship with several things that have hitherto been called number; and this can be said to give it an indirect relationship to other things we call the same name. And we extend our concept of number as in spinning a thread we twist fibre on fibre. And the strength of the thread does not reside in the fact that some one fibre runs through its whole length, but in the overlapping of many fibres."

I may be most closely related to my cousins in the sense that we are all beneficiaries of the same estate, my grandparents', which passed down to each of us a share of the fortune accumulated by my great-grandfather out of real estate holdings in Deadwood and Lead and stock in the Homestake Mine, that is to say, a fortune accumulated on the illegally occupied land belonging to the Great Sioux Reservation, established by the Fort Laramie Treaty of 1868.

When stock is sold, the capital gains tax is calculated based on the price of the stock when it was bought. Some of the stock I inherited from my grandparents had been held for so long that the date of purchase was no longer known.

I sold some of this stock to pay tuition the first year I was in graduate school for creative writing.

The aggregate wealth of white American families, by some estimates, is seventy times that of African American families.

Elements of family wealth dispersed over generations—houses, land, jewelry, investments, pensions—are sometimes called "invisible capital." To own investments whose purchase dates are forgotten makes them doubly invisible. When I write the sentence, "Jess Row received his MFA from the University of Michigan in 2001," without identifying the source of my capital, the capital is invisible three times over.

The image of the continuous thread made of discontinuous fibers twisted together is the opposite of precarity: whiteness, you could say, sticks together without making sense. I would like to unbind the thread and look at each fiber separately. But there are too many of them, and

I am one of them, and this writing could be a fraying, a slight loosening, at most. It will end and whiteness will not end.

This is one in a series of failed analogies. I can't come up with an encompassing theory that binds enslavement to societal collapse to climate change to the free movement of capital to Enlightenment theories of race to whiteness and white theories of its own demise, except to say this: it may be that a movie like *Mad Max: Fury Road* has gotten out ahead of more orthodox forms of interpretation in summarizing this era's worst instincts.

This is not a proper fugue, because the melodies don't harmonize; it's a death fugue, a tone cluster. The best I can do here is a kind of necropolitan free association, a sketch of a negative and (to me) ugliest possible version of freedom. It's the story I've been trying to tell about whiteness, and I don't know the words for it. I have these feelings of rage—I've had them nearly all my life—about my body and its inadequacies, but the world is such a large container for them that they wander and disperse, and I find them in unexpected moments, like when I'm watching a movie, or when I pass a billboard for a firing range and wish I could go inside. These feelings are unreal, in the sense that they feel most powerful when I don't have responsibility for them.

It matters that many of the Charlottesville protesters, when tracked and identified by online antifascist activists, claimed they went to the protests because they wanted to have fun, that they didn't necessarily believe what they were saying. They were lifestyle apocalyptics. They were shocked and defensive and fragile at being called to account.

It matters that most of the AR-15-style assault rifles sold in the United States (under many different brand names) live in closets and basements and gun cabinets and are never used, the way panic rooms and apocalypse retreats sit and gather dust. They are ritual objects in a death cult; they're fun to play with. In the 1980s there was a popular bumper sticker that read, "The one who dies with the most toys wins."

My cousins loved that idea and lived by it. No one at the time, as far as I know, noted it was a slogan that would also apply to the pharaohs, or the early Chinese emperors. Just as no one likes to talk about the godlike feeling of flying six miles up, in the stratosphere, with a credit limit and a passport that admits you nearly everywhere.

## On the Evening Redness in the West

In high school I fell under the spell of a novel called *Suttree*. I didn't know who Cormac McCarthy was; I plucked the book off the shelf at random, because I liked the title and the strange, forbidding typeface. *Suttree* was like Faulkner on hallucinogens: it didn't seem like a book anyone could have written outside of an altered state. The protagonist lives in a houseboat underneath a bridge in Knoxville, Tennessee. In nearly five hundred pages, relatively little happens: Suttree has given up his family and inherited wealth, he lives among homeless and derelict men, and his life seems made up of small encounters, some violent, that lead nowhere. The narrator punctuates these observations with dense, visionary passages that may come from Suttree himself, or not; it's never clear who is speaking, exactly, or why:

> The path cut through heatstricken lots and fallow land and passed under a high trestle that crossed the river. A tramp's midden among the old stone footings where gray bones lay by rusted tins and a talus of jarshards. A ring of blackened bricks and the remains of a fire. . . . Pieces of burnt foil sunburst in blue and yellow. Dredging charred relics from the ashy sleech. Melted glass that had reseized in the helical bowl of a bedspring like some vitreous chrysalis or chambered whelk from southern seas.

It never occurred to me—as far as I remember—that *Suttree* closely resembled *First Blood*. Obviously it was not framed as an action movie. Suttree is not hunted. But that may be only because he has successfully escaped; he has cut all ties with his past. I remember a feeling of giddiness as I read these passages, thinking I was getting away with something; but what?

Suttree's emotional life—to use a word McCarthy might appreciate—
is cauterized; the stumps burned shut, the nerve endings sealed off,
not because of actual trauma but because of some existential wound:
maybe the threat of its opposite, domestic castration. ("We've all got
holes to fill," Townes Van Zandt sang, in "To Live Is to Fly," his 1971
ode to masculine self-pity. "Them holes are all that's real.")

The next year I read *Blood Meridian, or The Evening Redness in the West.*
If *Suttree* never moved, *Blood Meridian* was all movement: the kid, another unknown, pastless hero, joins forces with a gang of murderous
outlaws, led by an enigmatic prophet, "the judge," on the Texas-
Mexico border, supposedly in the 1850s. The gang receives a commission from the Mexican government to massacre Indians on the
frontier, payable by the count of scalps, and the novel begins what
feels like an endless, inexorable movement from one holocaustic scene
to another:

> The bodies of the dead were stripped and their uniforms and
> weapons burned along with the saddles and other gear and the
> Americans dug a pit in the road and buried them in a common
> grave, the naked bodies with their wounds like the victims of sur-
> gical experimentation lying in the pit gaping sightlessly at the des-
> ert sky as the dirt was pushed over them.

*Blood Meridian* has been compared to Sam Peckinpah's films, particularly *The Wild Bunch*, which makes it similar also to John Yoo's films,
and Takeshi Kitano's and Quentin Tarantino's, but also *Rambo III*, in
which John Rambo kills dozens of Afghan soldiers single-handedly,
and *Death Wish II*, which features Charles Bronson killing scores of
drug dealers with a MAC-10 submachine gun. This is not to diminish
its importance as literature.

"The reader is snatched, yanked, thrown into an environment entirely
foreign," Toni Morrison wrote about the technique of *Beloved*, "and I
want it as the first stroke of the shared experience that might be possible between the reader and the novel's population."

When *Beloved* was chosen by a 2006 *New York Times* poll as the "Best American Novel of the Last 25 Years," *Blood Meridian* was the runner-up, along with *American Pastoral*, *Underworld*, and the *Rabbit* novels.

"Both novels treat primordial situations of American violence . . . in compressed, lyrical language that rises at times to archaic, epic strangeness," A. O. Scott wrote in an accompanying article. "Some of their power . . . arises from the feeling that they are uncovering ancient tales, rendering scraps of a buried oral tradition in literary form. . . . 'Beloved' . . . concerns itself with the recovery of origins, the isolation of a primal trauma whose belated healing will be undertaken by the narrative itself. And while 'Blood Meridian' is far too gnomic and nihilistic to claim such a therapeutic function for itself, it nonetheless shares with 'Beloved' a vision of the past as an alien realm of extremity, in which human relations are stripped to the bare essentials of brutality and tenderness, vengeance and honor. In some ways, the mode of fiction McCarthy and Morrison practice is less historical than pre-historical."

Missing from Scott's analysis is this observation: *Beloved* is narrated from the perspective of the human being escaping genocide; *Blood Meridian* from the perspective of the human perpetrating genocide.

Everyone involved can be called "American," for lack of a better word.

One novel is "therapeutic," the other is "gnomic and nihilistic." I can't decide which of these is the prehistory Scott refers to, or what it means for the nineteenth century to be prehistoric. Or which is truly "strange."

In McCarthy's most recent novel, *The Road*, a father and son journey across a postapocalyptic America, pursued by roving gangs of cannibals who may also be zombies. They're trying to make it to the southern coast, though it's not clear whether they intend to flee overseas to a safer location. "We're carrying the fire," the father assures his son, with no further explanation. "Because we're the good guys." The father is injured and then dies; the son continues the journey with another family of "good guys."

After the Las Vegas mass shooting in September 2017, Peggy Noonan wrote, in the *Wall Street Journal*, "Americans have so many guns because drug gangs roam the streets, because they have less trust in their neighbors, because they read Cormac McCarthy's 'The Road.' Because all of their personal and financial information got hacked in the latest breach, because our country's real overlords are in Silicon Valley and appear to be moral Martians who operate on some weird new postmodern ethical wavelength. . . . Our leaders don't even think about this technological revolution. They're too busy with transgender rights."

This is unfair. Very few of the nation's gun owners have read Cormac McCarthy. (More may have seen the movie version of *The Road*, starring Viggo Mortensen, though its box office sales were disappointing.) But the cultural work novels like *The Road* do is not negligible, either; it exists on a continuum. It's traceable, as much as critics like Scott seem not to want to acknowledge it; it's therapeutic.

Which means, for critics, a note of caution: novels are more like ritual than professional readers imagine them to be; more performative, in ways that are hard to predict.

"As war becomes dishonored and its nobility called into question," says the judge in the last pages of *Blood Meridian*, "those honorable men who recognize the sanctity of blood will become excluded from the dance, which is the warrior's right, and thereby the dance will become a false dance and the dancers false dancers. . . . Only that man who has offered up himself entire to the blood of war, who has been to the floor of the pit and seen horror in the round and learned at last that it speaks to his inmost heart, only that man can dance."

Suggestions that white people can't dance as well as blacks is a common trope in American comedy, rooted in the nineteenth century, when minstrel shows first began copying the dances of enslaved people and representing them for white audiences.

I'm not suggesting that McCarthy *necessarily* intends the scene to be read as one of envy. I'm suggesting that this is not a new dance; it's a dead metaphor readers may not want to revive.

In second grade, at my elementary school's spring festival, I danced the Cakewalk and won. This is not a joke. The Cakewalk, in this case, was less like a dance than a game: you hopped from one numbered square to another until the music stopped and a number was drawn. The prize was an actual chocolate cake, in a box. Everything was in pastels, and the music was something slow, with swing, to allow small children to move and think they were dancing. Maybe someone was wearing a straw boater hat. I remember thinking, the whole time, that something was wrong. Something about being given a whole cake, in the heat, glistening and soft in its box, at a fair, where I had no way of eating it. It wasn't a cake, it was a message. But what message, and for whom? My parents must have been there, though I don't remember them. I don't remember if we got it home in time to eat it.

## On Bullets Fired at Ghosts

The Ghost Dance movement of the 1880s began with a Paiute shaman, Wovoka, who claimed to have had a vision of Jesus Christ as the messiah and redeemer of all Indian tribes, who had come to North America to bring judgment on the whites for their brutality and greed. The Lakota leaders who traveled to Nevada to meet Wovoka in 1889 reported that he himself was Jesus, and that he still bore the scars and holes of his crucifixion. Wovoka, they said, told them he could sweep away the whites with his own arm.

The Lakota were starving; their government rations had been cut in half, and they had no other means to survive. Wovoka's instructions were to purify themselves, pray, and dance, wearing no metal or other item manufactured by whites, in order to receive their own visions. They should begin farming, Wovoka said, and practice complete nonviolence, among themselves and toward outsiders. The dances went on for days and weeks. The Lakota dancers moved out of their government-sponsored houses and schools and back into tipis to be closer to the dance grounds.

"Alarming reports," writes Rani-Henrik Andersson in *The Lakota Ghost Dance of 1890*, "included accusations that the ghost dancers promised to beat out children's brains and drink the white man's blood. . . . They claimed that during the ceremony the Lakota ghost dancers resorted to cannibalism." It was this climate of fear, rather than any threat of an armed revolt, Andersson concludes, after surveying all surviving historical accounts, that led the military commanders in the area to authorize a campaign, including the use of brand-new mounted machine guns, against family groups of dancers who were lightly armed, if at all. There was no possibility that the Lakota could pose a threat to any whites, either the soldiers stationed close by, or the settlers, like my great-grandparents, living fifty or a hundred miles away.

Those bullets were fired at ghosts; they were fired at the impossible figure of a shaman who could sweep away white people with a movement of his arm. It's possible that, in this way, the white soldiers, the white community, the white media, took Wovoka even more seriously than the Lakota ghost dancers. Which makes sense: the narrative of judgment was their narrative, the story of Christ reappearing at the Day of Judgment. The massacre at Wounded Knee, in this way, was a real event, the killing of humans sick and limping in the snow, performed like a play for an absent audience who wanted to imagine themselves being—almost—swept away.

## On Tombs

In a 2010 essay, "People-of-Color-Blindness," Jared Sexton took issue with Mbembe's theory of necropolitics by arguing that Mbembe's description of plantation slavery, which allowed for the possibility that enslaved people could assert their own subjectivity in certain limited ways, did not go nearly far enough in stressing how the living death enslavement represented extends into the lives of black people in the present. Borrowing a phrase from Frank Wilderson, Sexton argued for an entirely new "political ontology of race." "It is racial blackness as a necessary condition for enslavement that matters most, rather than whiteness as a sufficient condition for freedom," Sexton wrote, "and because blackness serves as the basis of enslavement in the logic of a transnational political and legal culture, it *permanently destabilizes the position of any nominally free black population*" (italics mine).

"If the position of the Black is . . . a paradigmatic impossibility in the Western Hemisphere, indeed, in the world," Wilderson writes in *Red, White, and Black*, "in other words, if a Black is the very antithesis of a Human subject . . . then his or her paradigmatic exile is not simply a function of repressive practices on the part of institutions":

> Put another way: no slave, no world. And, in addition, no slave is *in* the world. If, as an ontological position, that is, as a grammar of suffering, the Slave is not a laborer but an anti-Human, a position against which Humanity establishes, maintains, and renews its coherence, its corporeal integrity; if the Slave is . . . a being outside of relationality, then our analysis cannot be approached through the rubric of gains or reversals in struggles with the state and civil society, not unless and until the interlocutor first explains how the Slave is of the world.

I started reading the Afro-pessimists and their sources—Saidiya Hartman, Hortense Spillers, Orlando Patterson, Mbembe, Frantz Fanon—during the winter of the 2016 election, while I had a visiting teaching job at NYU, and an office window that faced another gray office building, which happened to be the building where the Triangle Shirtwaist fire killed 141 people, mostly young female garment workers, in 1911. When you search for "Triangle Shirtwaist fire," Google also provides links to the Dhaka fire, which killed 117 garment workers at the Tazreen clothing factory in 2012, and the 2013 Rana Plaza building collapse, in a different district of Dhaka, where at least 1,134 garment workers died.

What does it mean to say that nothing changes and nothing will ever change, unless and until the world itself is destroyed?

Wilderson quotes from the psychoanalyst and critic David Marriott, who argues in *On Black Men* that just as black subjectivity is forever erased by the social death of slavery, white subjectivity never leaves the scene of lynching, and particularly the dismemberment of the black man's genitals. "The lynching, and the scene of lynching preserved in photography and in cinema, is a gift which Whites exchange, libidinally and literally, among themselves," Wilderson writes. "As such, Whites experience lynching, whether 'live' on the tree, or fragmented through the prism of photography . . . as the gift of filiation, the capacity to have and inherit parental 'legacies,' and as the gift of affiliation, the capacity to be recognized, and act as a community."

What is there to do with this thought? After I read this passage, for days afterward, I felt upset. I felt gloomy. I couldn't stop thinking about it. It had accomplished its goal; I felt hopeless and paranoid. My language reduces to a series of modifiers, stacked up like bricks. The person who posted quotes from Wilderson on Facebook, a black woman writer I know from conferences and readings, surely hated me. I felt stripped of a capacity to respond. This was intentional, I thought: intended for me. This not thinking-into the image of the castration of the black man, which I had "seen," read, mostly recently in Colson Whitehead's *The Underground Railroad*; not inquiring into how it feels to read those images, not actually thinking at all, but recoiling into a defensive posture.

"All concepts of race," Richard Dyer writes in *White*, "are always concepts of the body and of hetero-sexuality."

One core problem with Afro-pessimism, as Sexton and Wilderson have defined it—a critique made by Spillers, Hartman, and many others in the field—is precisely this masculinism, this obsession with symbolic and actual castration, which places the phallus at the center of the discourse. Again.

As a man, a heterosexual man, I experience speaking—writing—and being heard—being "received"—with the phallus. I experience being silenced, being deprived of the right to speak, with castration. How many metaphysical systems—or antimetaphysical critiques—are rooted in the symbolic castration of the opponent, the denial of his (it's always a "his") right to speak?

The last word. The last analysis. The analysis of the end, which is to say, the final word on the subject, after which no other words will be spoken, because the world has ended.

I put this passage by Frank Wilderson among Wittgenstein's discontinuous fibers that make up, together, a family resemblance. (But I'm no longer clear: a resemblance to what? Or to more than one thing?) Along with the feeling of paralysis that comes from staring too long at the stone columns of a building that shows no signs of ever being a tomb.

# 2

## On Know How

I apply for a job. It's not a job I can easily imagine taking; it would mean starting fresh in a new part of the country. It's a long shot. But I still apply, because it's the kind of job I want; a step up from where I am now. I make it to the first round of interviews, via Skype, but no further. Afterward, a friend of mine who was on the search committee says, You would have been a finalist, but we had to hire a person of color.

I've looked at the department website and I know exactly what she means.

A white friend of mine who doesn't have a full-time job, who's moved to a city where his wife works, applies to the only two teaching jobs within the greater metro area and tells me he heard, through the grapevine, that in both cases, they would only seriously consider people of color.

Another white writer I know says to me, apropos of nothing, it's actually *easier* now for minority writers to get published than white writers, don't you know that?

I should know what to say to him, but I don't. There's a gap in the conversation, an uncomfortable silence.

While working on a piece about whiteness in the aftermath of the 2016 election I came across a study, conducted by a psychologist at Harvard in 2011, that questioned a broad sample of white Americans about the consequences of gains in civil rights by nonwhite Americans. The majority of respondents believed that any gain in civil rights by nonwhites—overcoming hiring discrimination, for example— had to result in a loss of power for white people. There was no other possibility.

White people—even those committed, in theory, to the struggle against white supremacy—do not know how to share power. White people do not know how to let white supremacy die without feeling they themselves are dying.

When I have thoughts like this, I want to drink expensive whiskey, the kind you can buy in duty-free shops in airports. I developed a taste for single malts—Islay single malts—in my twenties, in graduate school, when it seemed to me that I needed to develop those subtle gestures of connoisseurship male writers like to display at cocktail parties and in hotel bars. I like the taste of peat fires releasing carbon into the atmosphere. That's the flavor of my white melancholy and regret.

I use the phrase "know how" in order to imagine the roots of the words, *gnosis* and *technē*, the understanding or inner knowledge and the means or technique to carry something out. This basic skill of sharing power, you would think, would be the object of study, would have its own institutes and subfields and euphemisms. Instead of "disempowerment," you could say "collective empowerment"; instead of "surrender," you could say "re-allocate" or "adaptive integration"; instead of "scarcity and competition," you could say "sharing and mutuality." Only you don't say any of these things, because this field does not exist. There is no public body of knowledge and also no body to look at other than an emasculated body.

Which doesn't mean that giving up or sharing power never happens; in small ways it happens all the time. Awkwardly. Every time, as if a little world is ending.

I give a reading from *Your Face in Mine*, which is about race but not about redistribution, at a bar in Prospect Heights, and afterward, in the back of the bar, a white guy in his fifties urgently needs to talk to me. He wants to tell me about what he calls "weebees and weebos," women-owned and minority-owned businesses, which are protected classes in New York City contracting, and what a scam they are. I can't tell what the point of his story is. I have this experience often. I meet white people with one story to tell about race, often while drinking, and as hard as I try to listen, I don't get the point, because there isn't a point to be stated out loud. These stories always seem to be about failure, good intentions going wrong, naive bureaucrats or programs. No one wants to tell me their success stories. The underlying point actually isn't so hard to discern at all: it goes, I tried to be a good non-racist person but I gave up because the world disappointed me. Or because I wasn't met with enough gratitude. Or because racial differences or divisions are a reality polite people don't want to recognize or concede.

*It's twice as hard for white people to get a job. It's twice as hard for white writers to get published.*

It's not, actually; the latest numbers from the *Chronicle of Higher Education* indicate that the number of people of color with full-time academic jobs has hardly changed in the past forty years. And while there are only incomplete statistics on racial representation in literary publishing, try this simple test: find a retail bookstore, go to the fiction or poetry section, and select any fifty titles by American writers currently on the shelves in alphabetical order. Read the current catalogs of major US literary publishers. Black people, Latinx, Native American, and Pacific Islanders make up 38% of the current population, in US Census terms; are they represented, or overrepresented, at a rate of four in ten, six in ten, eight in ten?

Numbers—while always open to critique—should be a counterweight to fantasy and paranoia. It's a question of *technē*. I was not prepared to use them; I avoided statistics, never took economics. My father was an economist who could never explain math problems to me sequentially, because he solved them too easily in his head. But I've come to the conclusion that not having to count, or not bothering to count accurately, or verify a calculation, is itself a form of power and deniability. "How much are you worth?" Jack Nicholson, playing the detective Jake Gittes, asks John Huston, playing the land baron Noah Cross, in *Chinatown*, and Huston replies, spreading his hands, "I've no idea."

Rob Spillman, the editor of *Tin House*, explained on a panel in 2010 that he began keeping statistics on the gender ratio of authors published in the magazine, before the organization VIDA started its industry-wide count, and consciously decided that *Tin House* had to publish more women to change its ratios.

This is simple and embarrassing math that seems arbitrary and unliterary. It's nonadministered math. But without it, words like "representation" and "inclusion" and "diversity," which exercise tremendous weight, are completely weightless, open to almost any interpretation.

On the other hand, numbers are no substitute for the *gnosis*, the guiding principle, the way of thinking that is leading us somewhere. If representation happens: then what? If the space becomes inclusive:

then what? If the magazine publishes in numbers reflecting a break-down of the census, and all the things the census doesn't count: then what?

My mouth runs dry.

I want to say to my friend, make sure your facts are correct. And then: you and I are part of a history we didn't start and will not see end; we're here only for this episode.

I want to say something ridiculous, like, *courage*. Not because white courage, or moral suasion, or sacrifice, or martyrdom is the answer; not because white people's feelings are the issue; but because the bottom layer of an antiracist consciousness has to be, as in *The Hitchhiker's Guide to the Galaxy*, a commitment not to panic, overread, or catastrophize. For white people, at least the white people I know, this is counter-intuitive. It takes work.

I want to say to my friend: what do we mean, the two of us, when we say the word "freedom"? When we say it to one another, when we say it in public? How have we gone so long without knowing what we mean?

## Literature and Survival

A friend writes me and wants to know if I would agree that we're living in "a golden age for diverse books."

It's the second week of April 2018, and I'm sitting at a mezcal bar on the Lower East Side with an editor, who's wondering if one of her authors, Jesmyn Ward, who's won the National Book Award twice, might also win the Pulitzer. It could happen. It happened last year to Colson Whitehead. She doesn't, but Kendrick Lamar does, for music. Beyoncé is singing at Coachella; she performs "Lift Every Voice and Sing." *Black Panther* is still the highest-grossing movie of the year.

Danny Ray Thomas, a black man in Houston, was shot and killed by a police officer, at an intersection in Houston on March 22, 2018. He was not armed. He had been fighting with another man; he was clearly in an altered state. His pants were around his ankles. He was unarmed. His pants were around his ankles. A photograph at the scene establishes this. In 2016 his wife drowned their two children, five and seven years old, in a bathtub, while he was in prison on a drug offense. He struggled with severe depression. In another time and place, he might have been called "grief-mad." His pants were around his ankles when he was shot.

I'm thinking about the word *relief*. In the OED the fourth definition of relief is "the state of being clearly visible or obvious due to being accentuated." As in the stock phrase, "thrown into sharp relief."

Relief, from the Latin *relevare*, "to raise again, to make light, to alleviate."

There is something here I want to tease out. The lives of black people, Palestinians, undocumented US residents, Latinx people, queers, the vulnerable and precarious, those once thought to be "marginalized," appear in sharp relief. Those words are raised off the page. Precarity, vulnerability, the condition or possibility of death in life: it changes the way I say the word "people" or "we" or "you." Precarity is like an extra dimension in language. This is where the interest of the average reader lands, for obvious reasons. Not by accident, not by natural occurrence, but because the culture has been shifted by the work of generations of academics, editors, writers, activists, and then met with a confluence of forces: the Black Lives Matter movement, resurgent, activist white supremacists and Nazis, global authoritarianism, the European refugee crisis, and the 2016 election. Sharp relief.

It's the fall of 2017, a year after the election, and I'm at a poetry reading in Tucson. Javier Zamora, who was born in El Salvador, says he hasn't been back in Tucson since he crossed through the city after being smuggled across the border when he was nine. He says he still feels traumatized, right at that moment, remembering how he hid from the sound of helicopters in Tucson. And then he goes on to read his poems. This is writing in sharp relief, and now I read a Facebook post by a white poet in her seventies, who has been publishing books for forty years: "I find I dislike quite a lot of contemporary poetry. Not all of it, of course. But some poetry is just a shrill whine."

A shrill whine is the sound of helicopters passing overhead.

Put Zamora's collection of poems, *Undocumented*, alongside *Blood Meridian*. This is where American literature has to locate itself in the present: no longer at the point where marked divides from unmarked, where interest and subject matter separate themselves from pure disinterested art.

It matters to me that the definition of "relief" comes apart in this way: (1) something that is raised so that it's harder to ignore, or (2) to make light, as in to help someone pick up something heavy, to provide support or what my Zen master used to call "together action," a literal translation of the phrase 同行, meaning "cooperation" or "to work in concert." Not because one definition necessarily includes the other, but because the language could be altered to include both possibilities. Relief demands relief. Relief draws relief to itself.

Artists, as human beings, need to be involved, primarily, in the struggle to protect life, provide relief and sanctuary, aid other people's survival. And then, because they're artists, secondarily, they have to struggle with the word "as." What it means to be called, included, invoked, seen, named.

It seems so palpably obvious to me, saying this, that one way of answering the question—"Is this a golden age?"—is to say, as the video artist Hito Steyerl says in *Duty Free Art*, that this is an age of planetary civil war. Which is not the same thing as learning how to die. It may even be the opposite. There are as many ways of responding to this situation as there are artists, but if you work with no sense of crisis at all, that is, for example, if you work in a realist mode and still insist on isolating characters artificially from the news, the shouting in the streets, the feelings of panic or dread or stifled or unstifled rage, your work may seem like a series of limited formal gestures and be read as much for what it leaves out as what it gathers in. Or, if you create fantastic landscapes (of whatever kind, not just in the orthodox realm of "fantasy"), your landscapes will be read historically, because so many other fantasies preceded you. Including the fantasies that brought about the Enlightenment, progress, nationhood, personhood. This is an era of making things imperfectly legible.

Ten years ago, when I won an award for young American novelists, a well-known editor remarked that fiction was becoming as relevant to the culture as landscape painting. I never got to ask him what he meant—what landscapes he was imagining, or whose fiction he had in mind. It may be that he was simply saying novels rarely are a subject of public discussion unless they're adapted into film or TV, which is true. The private act of novel reading doesn't lend itself to the instant-feedback cycle of social media the way that, strikingly, poetry does. (This is excellent news for poets, and novelists shouldn't begrudge them their success.) But I think he was saying something else: the form of the novel is too conservative, too dependent on nineteenth-century conventions, for this era; the tools it uses, the representational devices, are almost embarrassing. I wanted to ask him: are these landscapes with people running through them, pursued by helicopters? He was speaking with a kind of determined sadness. I wonder if what he really meant was " . . . as relevant as that evening redness in the West."

## On the Reading Public

In high school, instead of *Suttree*, I wish I'd read Samuel R. Delany's *Dhalgren*. (Which is not to say *Suttree* isn't worth reading; *First Blood* is still worth seeing.) *Dhalgren* is as screwy, baroque, and gloriously pointless as *Suttree*, but much more fun to read, because in the ruined city Delany describes (Bellona, a city abandoned in the middle of an otherwise-functioning United States) people are, strangely, everywhere. The novel is full of scabrous descriptions of gay and straight sex; long philosophical dialogues, utopian fantasies, all kinds of narrative tricksterism. There are black and white characters, and many unidentified characters, too; race is as hard to follow as any other thread in *Dhalgren*. The ruined, apocalyptic city turns into a carnival. There's much more you could say about this novel; I would like to quote from it endlessly. But it needs to be read. For all its chaos and fragmentation and tangential logic, it feels essential and (in an American context) still completely unknown.

Sold as a cheap paperback, labeled "science fiction," *Dhalgren* sold more than a million copies in the 1970s; went out of print, was rescued once by Wesleyan University Press, then finally published in a Vintage paperback edition in 2000.

"Of the half-dozen or so fellow readers I know who have attempted to scale [this] 800-page Matterhorn . . . none have succeeded," Garth Risk Hallberg wrote in a "Difficult Books" column in *The Millions* in 2010. "Still, when I tackled it myself last month, I kept encountering people in parks and coffee shops and on the subway who would glance down at the jacket, blurt, 'Great book,' and then vanish into the urban landscape."

I want to meet those people who will not be met.

## On Tenderness

When we drove up to the hotel in Deadwood my uncle Burt was waiting for us on a bench outside the lobby. He stood up to greet us, and his face went slack; he couldn't lift his arms. I'm not feeling well, he said. In another minute he had collapsed back onto the bench. It's a stroke, a nurse said, who'd rushed over to help. The EMTs had already applied EKG pads and a pulse oxidation monitor when his eyes fluttered and he muttered, Not a stroke. Narcolepsy. Cataplexy. Don't you know what that is?

The last time I'd seen Burt, four years previous, was at my father's side, in his last week of life, when he was only semiconscious, unable to lie still, in bouts of intense pain. Burt brought him ice chips, spoke to him soothingly, and kept him calm. He and my father had never been close; now he seemed to know exactly what to do.

Cataplexy, according to the National Sleep Foundation, is "a sudden and uncontrollable muscle weakness or paralysis that comes on during the day and is often triggered by a strong emotion. . . . Without much warning, the person loses muscle tone and can have a slack jaw, broken speech, buckled knees or total weakness in their face, arms, legs, and trunk. A person experiencing total cataplexy stays awake and is aware of what is happening, but cannot move. These episodes last up to a minute or two, and some people may fall asleep afterwards. . . . Some individuals avoid emotions that may bring on cataplexy."

In Burt's double-wide trailer, filled with my grandparents' furniture, a rifle leaned on the couch next to the door. A stack of Bill O'Reilly's books sat next to his easy chair, facing the TV. In the stack of mail on the kitchen counter was a letter from "The Sheriff Joe Arpaio Legal Fund."

In the town my great-grandparents helped build, on land that by federal treaty and Supreme Court affirmation still belongs to the seven bands of the Lakota, I spoke to my cousin Rob, with whom I'd cut off all contact nine months before, after he'd posted a meme of young women crying after Trump's victory. I said, he's fine, it looked like a stroke but it wasn't. This happens all the time, he said, and he needs to start planning to come live with me in Phoenix.

When I tell people on the East Coast that my father grew up in Deadwood, that my family came there in the gold rush, that my great-grandfather once owned half its real estate, they often say, "Deadwood is a real place?"

The last members of my family to live in the Black Hills are Burt—who is eighty-six—and my father's cousin Bill, a retired school bus driver and local historian who helped found the Black Hills Mining Museum. Bill tells me he doesn't want any of his children to inherit his house, which his grandfather built by hand in 1901. None of them should live in the Black Hills, he says. He doesn't say why, as if it's obvious.

I drove back from Burt's trailer through the streets of Deadwood late at night, returning to the hotel where my children were sleeping—the sixth generation of my family to have some presence here, if only for a few days and possibly, probably, never again. I felt exhausted and angry. Fuck you, you bloody nightmare town, I wanted to say, I didn't choose you.

In December 2016, three weeks after the election, during the continuing protests over the Dakota Access Pipeline on the Standing Rock Lakota reservation, a group of United States Army veterans performed a ceremony of asking forgiveness from the Lakota. "In the presence of hundreds of veterans and Lakota medicine people, elders and leaders," *Indian Country Today* reported, "Wes Clark Jr. donned the uniform of the Seventh Cavalry and spoke of the history of his unit. With tears in his eyes, Clark said: 'Many of us, me particularly, are from the units that have hurt you over the many years. We came. We fought you. We took your land. We signed treaties that we broke. We stole minerals from your sacred hills. We blasted the faces of our presidents onto your sacred mountain. When we took still more land and then we took your children and then we tried to make your language and we tried to eliminate your language that God gave you, and the Creator gave you. We didn't respect you, we polluted your Earth, we've hurt you in so many ways but we've come to say that we are sorry. We are at your service and we beg for your forgiveness.'"

This was a request for forgiveness, the reporter noted, "140 years in the making."

What is the social function of tenderness? To do what a person can't do privately, I want to say. So that we're not trapped within a family resemblance. Justice makes love manifest in public what it can't do in private. I wish I could have told my father that while he was still alive, just to hear what he would say. He left the Black Hills, without ever explaining why. I want to say it's because he didn't know how to ask for forgiveness, or ask what justice actually requires. But I can't say that for him, so I say it for myself, because I'm still here, and there's no time like the present.

## No Hope

"What would it be . . . to think from no standpoint?" Fred Moten asks in "Blackness and Nothingness," a response to Jared Sexton and Frank Wilderson's work. "To think outside the desire for a standpoint?"

The arguments associated with Afro-pessimism, Moten says, invoke views of nonexistence and nonself—in Buddhist terms, *prajna* (insight), *sunyata* (emptiness), *nisvabhava* (no self-nature)—but don't define them in enough detail. "Nothingness," Moten says, and the paradoxical statement "I am nothing," are not new or self-evident terms. (Think of how they occur, just to choose one subset of examples, in Dickinson, Whitman, Wallace Stevens, Amiri Baraka.) It's not necessary, or even possible, to think of nothingness as some kind of pure negation or voidness; to say "nothing" is to invoke something, to create an opposition and a duality.

*Sunyata*, the Buddhist concept of emptiness, is something quite different: in the Madhyamaka or Middle Way tradition, *sunyata* is a non-affirming negative: it contains "nothing" and "something" but doesn't rest on either one. It arises without relying on concepts at all; it contains all relative relationships within it.

If all concepts break down under pressure, how does healing take place? "Conventional things exist precisely *as that which is empty*, the very bases of emptiness," writes Guy Newland, articulating the position of Tsongkhapa, founder of the Gelugpa tradition, represented today by the Dalai Lama. "Ultimate emptiness is not self-existent, but simply the empty quality . . . that characterizes these conventional things. Without real conventional things, there could be no emptiness. Awakened wisdom here entails recognition of the conventional *as* conventional; knowledge of emptiness matters because it strips away false superimpositions about how these conventional things exist."

Buddhist teachings on emptiness, Moten says, help "prepare us to consider . . . that blackness is the place that has no place. . . . Things are in, but they do not have, a world, a place. . . . Nothing is not absence. Blackness is more and less than one in nothing. This, informal, informing, insolvent insovereignity is the real presence of the nothing we come from, and bear, and make."

About ten years ago, when someone asked me to sum up my philosophy of fiction, I borrowed a line from Liz Phair's song "Flower": "Everything you say is so obnoxious, funny, true, and mean."

I'm thinking of *Dhalgren*, and I'm thinking: you could replace Liz Phair's line with: informal, informing, insolvent, insovereign.

"It's not that I want to enclose things in the dialectical movement between beginning and end," Moten writes. "Invention and passage denote an already existing alternative for which we are not constrained to wait. We are already down here on and under the ground, the water, as worked, unwrought nothingness working fleshly releasement in a privation of feasting, a fragility of healing."

In years of reading Moten's work I've struggled, like many other readers, to find a footing in it. I don't believe in fetishizing difficulty, but

I also believe in the struggle to make language do new things. And I think one of the things he's trying to do—and not alone; accompanied by many other writers, in different ways—is find a new way to say, "We need to gather together," with a strained emphasis on the *we*, which is also: *we?*

In his 2008 essay "Black Op," Moten makes the challenge even clearer: "It is obvious . . . that blackness has always emerged as nothing other than the richest possible combination of dispersion and permeability in and as the mass improvisation and protection of the very idea of the human. . . . Ultimately, the paraontological force that is transmitted in the long chain of life and death performances that are the concern of black studies is horribly misunderstood if it is understood as exclusive. Everyone whom blackness claims, which is to say everyone, can claim blackness."

(I wrote a novel to try to understand this particular use of the verb "to claim.")

At the end of the film *Take This Hammer*, which follows James Baldwin on a trip to San Francisco in the spring of 1963, Baldwin faces the camera and says, speaking to white America, "I give you the problem back. You're the nigger, baby, it isn't me."

I thought, at one time, that this reciprocity, the fundamental interrelatedness, the invagination of the color line, was a multidimensional, complicated, nuanced thing. (It is.) I failed to think of it as not only reciprocal but recursive and bound to repeat itself, under the right conditions. I failed to imagine the right conditions.

But I still say: it isn't wrong to do this work.

I'm sitting in the audience, and the poet and performance artist Tracie Morris says, "All of us, black people, people of color, our white allies, friends, we know how to survive this, because we've done it before. These things are not new."

Fanon says, at the end of *Black Skin, White Masks*:

> Superiority? Inferiority?
> Why not simply try to touch the other, feel the other, discover each other?
> Was my freedom not given me to build the world of *you*, man?

"Today, what I want to talk about is having no hope," the Zen teacher Charlotte Joko Beck once said, in an informal talk to her students. "All hope, of course, is about sizing up the past and projecting it into the future. Anyone who sits for any length of time sees that there is no past and no future except in our mind." She went on to say, "We are usually living in vain hope for something or someone that will make my life easier, more pleasant. We spend most of our time trying to set life up in a way so that will be true; when, contrariwise, the joy of our life is just in totally doing and just bearing what must be borne, in just doing what has to be done. It's not even what *has* to be done; it's there to be done so we do it."

She ended by saying, "So if we practice like this, what reward will we get? If we really practice like this, it takes everything we have. What will we get out of it? The answer, of course, is nothing. So let's not have hope. We won't get anything. We'll get our life, of course, but we've got that already.... We can be rewarded with this nothing at all."

Is there anything useful about thinking this way? Or to try it a different way: what is a politics of no hope? Mbembe would say, that's just what necropolitics is: not trusting the state to do anything but kill, negotiating with it only over the time and manner of my own death. Or the manner in which I will become a killing instrument of the state. Or both.

I refuse to sit with this formulation. "No hope" is a nonaffirming negation; it doesn't mean "despair." Just as "no more white supremacy" doesn't mean "replaced with _____ supremacy."

Or, to try it another way: when we—those of us taught to be white people—imagine the end of the world, what we see is a mirror: our own cataplexy, a false death, a death-in-life. But we have not died and whiteness has not died. We are back on this same bitter earth with nothing solved.

Or, to try it another way: because whiteness happened, the worst has already happened. It is not yet-to-come. The question isn't: why does the death exuberance of racism, of white supremacy, of necropolitics, keep coming back? The question is: why do we keep being surprised? To invent a category, a figure of "massified life," as Michelle Murphy says, is to invent something that has to be maintained, which is to say, something one can imagine disappearing, losing its potency, inverting and becoming its opposite. ("The forms of multitudes, crowds, and overpopulation, have been persistently racializing figures," she says.)

But there is no "other hand," no way of unwinding the history, no "if only." We're stuck with the images we have, the materials we're given. This stuckness is something like what Emily Apter calls "small-p politics," which is to say, the messiness of ordinary life as we live it together, the opposite of grand homogenizing theories.

Surely everyone has an image of "the messiness of life": I think about my uncle, who is neither entirely alive nor dead to me, not incorporated or eliminated, just there, stuck to me, and me to him. What good does it do to wish it were otherwise?

I've been reading Denis Johnson's *Fiskadoro*, a book for some reason I saved till the end. Sixty years after a nuclear war destroyed most of the United States, tiny communities of survivors live on in the Florida

Keys, a place they call "Quarantine," without quite knowing what that means; Key West is now known as Twicetown, because two missiles landed there but didn't explode. Mr. Cheung, one of the few musicians left, remembers nothing of the previous world, but his hundred-year-old grandmother does; she hovers in the background, unable to speak, consumed with her memories of fleeing Saigon in the last days of 1975. Fiskadoro, a fisherman's son, studies the clarinet with Mr. Cheung until his father's death at sea ends his lessons; in his grief he goes on a kind of vision quest. He finds a band of outcasts who live in the swamps outside Twicetown; they initiate him with a crude, self-inflicted circumcision, and a drug that removes his memories.

There are recognizably white people in *Fiskadoro*, but not many; Mr. Cheung, Fiskadoro, and virtually all the survivors are what would today be called "multiracial." They speak a Creolized mixture of English and Spanish and worship Allah (though vaguely, without specifically Muslim practices) and/or Bob Marley. Mr. Cheung belongs to the Society for Knowledge, which searches the few remaining books for clues about the former world; only at the end of the novel, in a climactic moment, does he hear a description of nuclear war. Now, he realizes, he's learned all he needs to learn about the past: enough to stop wishing he'd been born a hundred years earlier.

"You know," he says, "in this past I long for, I don't remember how even then I longed for the past."

There's an astonishing passage at the very end of the novel, after Fiskadoro's capacity for memory is gone, and Mr. Cheung has given up his search for the past; Mr. Cheung allows himself to consider, for a moment, the future:

> He and Fiskadoro were standing, as a matter of fact, between two
> civilizations, standing together at the southern edge of the crowd
> of people and at the northern edge of the crowd of seagulls, who'd
> come around to see what was happening through eyes too tiny

to hold any questions. The seagulls walked back and forth at the border of water, all bellies and beaks, throwing out their chests with an air of flat assumption like small professors. Fiskadoro looked back and forth between these seagulls and Mr. Cheung, and Mr. Cheung guessed what he was seeing.

The Cubans will come, [he] recited to himself, the Quarantine won't last forever. Everything we have, all we are, will meet its end, will be overcome, taken up, washed away. But everything came to an end before. Now it will happen again. Many times. Again and again. Something is coming and something is going— but that isn't the issue. The issue is that I failed to recognize myself in these seagulls.

Is this a place where whiteness has run its course, without disappearing, no longer attached to capital, power, or a transcendent signifier? I don't know. I don't feel qualified to answer the question. But I can observe this: It's a gesture of the imagination that also reminds us of the limits of our self-importance as imagining agents. To write fictions, you throw out your chest with an air of assumption like a small professor.

But this is the opposite of saying the imagination isn't important.

"There may even be a real relation between certain kinds of effectiveness in literature and totalitarianism in politics," Kermode writes in *The Sense of an Ending*. "We have to distinguish between myths and fictions. Fictions can degenerate into myths whenever they are not *consciously held to be fictive*" (italics mine).

Maybe, Johnson is saying, the work of the white writer, in particular, is to recognize where I failed to recognize myself, partly, but also to see myself recognized. It's like saying: the self doesn't always have to constitute itself *by* itself. Which is just a fancier way of saying: we are all part of one bigger picture.

## On Bullets Fired in Dreams

The book has to end; I don't want it to end, because nothing is decided; there's no crescendo and no payoff.

Throughout the Obama administration, Emily Apter observes, the American right supported and applauded impolitic behavior of all kinds, from birtherism to Joe Wilson's "You lie!" to Twitter memes comparing Michelle Obama to a gorilla. But what does being impolitic actually reveal? "Politics itself ends up resembling an art of diplomacy that conceals a relationship of natural enmity in courteous forms of etiquette, tact, and civil behavior," Roberto Esposito says. Impolitics, on the other hand, Apter says, exposes "the latent insecurity underwriting even the most casual or anodyne political transactions."

Politics, in one formulation, means giving up honesty to avoid violence. That's an obvious argument; that's the "civil" in civil society. Has it ever actually worked that way? And is violence the only possible outcome when a thread begins to loosen, and real talk breaks out? Or to put it another way, Apter says: what would happen if citizens stopped thinking of politics as a set of given terms, and began to ask questions of the terms themselves?

Think of Grace Paley in "The Immigrant Story":

> I made an announcement to the sixth-grade assembly thirty years ago. I said: I thank God every day that I'm not in Europe. I thank God that I'm American-born and live on East 172nd Street where there is a grocery store, a candy store, and a drug store on one corner and on the same block a shul and two doctors' offices.
>     One Hundred and Seventy-second Street was a pile of shit, [Jack] said. Everyone was on relief except you. Thirty people had t.b. Citizens and noncitizens alike starving until the war. Thank God capitalism has a war it can pull out of the old feed bag every now and then or we'd all be dead. Ha ha.

Why shouldn't fiction be the scene of a necessary impoliteness, of cross talk, of nakedness? "My dear," Paley's narrator says, "no one knows the power of good sense. It hasn't been built up or experimented with sufficiently."

If a world-ending apocalypse were really imminent (it isn't); if I had access to a titanium-lined concrete time capsule; if someone asked me to preserve some evidence of what happened during my lifetime, I would box up many of the books I've referred to here, and others I didn't have time to include (Paul Beatty's *The Sellout*; Joan Brady's *Theory of War*; C. E. Morgan's *The Sport of Kings*; Rosellen Brown's *Civil Wars*; Fran Ross's *Oreo*) and write a note saying, This was how one subset of American writers tried to work the trap they found themselves in. And it was okay. It was the beautiful opposite of a compromise.

In the first scene of Quentin Tarantino's *Reservoir Dogs*, Harvey Keitel says to Michael Madsen, "If you shoot me in a dream, you better wake up and apologize." This sounds ridiculous only if you maintain that there is some strict separation between reality and dreams, or, more specifically, between the lived world people inhabit and the world as they imagine it to be—in a dream, in a novel, in a film. This book has tried to advocate for a different view: to take fictions seriously, as if they actually matter. To say: there's no way of understanding "real life" without taking them into account. Which doesn't mean anyone has to feel trapped or governed by them; in fact, it's easier to relate to fictions, as Frank Kermode says, if you know when and how they end. I'm thinking of it not so much as waking up from a deep sleep as speaking the last line of a story out loud. The story's over, and I'm walking; my feet are on the ground; I have someone to my left and someone to my right. We're going somewhere; we haven't given up. Hello there. Good to see you. I'm walking on this bitter earth, and I'm not the only one.

# Acknowledgments

This book was shaped in every way by the interlocutory presence of my wife and best friend, Sonya Posmentier. As a scholar of African American literature, as a writer, as a human being, her contribution to this project is visible to me on every page.

I was lucky to have not one but three editors at Graywolf: Fiona McCrae, who acquired *White Flights* and has been the guiding force behind it; Steve Woodward, who joined us in the early stages and kept the process moving all along; and Yana Makuwa, who offered essential insights at the very end. Denise Shannon supported this project from the very beginning, as did Megan Lynch, my editor at Ecco Books. I'm grateful for their patience and encouragement.

Some of these essays are drawn from earlier versions published in *Boston Review* ("The Novel is [Not] Dead," 2011; "White Flights," 2013; and "No Crying," 2015), *Guernica* ("Native Sons," 2014), and the *New Republic* ("What Are White Writers For?" and "A Safe Space for Racism," 2016). The first two essays in *White Flights* started as "To Whom It May Concern," which appeared on Claudia Rankine's Open Letter website in 2011 and the anthology that grew out of it, *The Racial Imaginary* (Fence Books, 2015, edited by Claudia Rankine, Beth Loffreda, and Max King Cap). I'm particularly grateful to Deborah Chasman and Simon Waxman at *Boston Review* for their sentence-by-sentence work on the very first incarnations of this book.

Versions of these pieces were presented as lectures or papers at the "Thinking Its Presence: Race and Creative Writing" conferences in 2014 and 2015; at the University of Alabama, NYU, the Chautauqua Institution, and the "NonfictionNow" conference in 2017. Special thanks to Prageeta Sharma for her work in creating and sustaining "Thinking Its Presence"; John Keene, who responded to an earlier version of "No Bite"; Dorothy Wang, Thomas Sayers Ellis, Ailish Hopper, Farid Matuk, Tonya M. Foster, Tisa Bryant, Rae Paris and Django Paris, Ed Pavlić, Tracie Morris, and others who helped me think through my ideas in Missoula and Tucson (and beyond).

Much of *White Flights* was written while I was a visiting professor in the Department of English at NYU and while I was a Guggenheim fellow on leave from the College of New Jersey, for which I thank the Solomon R. Guggenheim Foundation and its staff. I'm grateful to Chris Cannon for helping to arrange my year at NYU, and to my NYU colleagues, as well as the department staff, particularly Alyssa Leál. My two years of leave from TCNJ wouldn't have been possible without the support of Glenn Steinberg, Jacqueline Taylor, Gregory Pogue, and Cynthia Bishop-Lyons.

I met Yahdon Israel in the early stages of writing *White Flights*, and throughout the process he's been a source of provocative questions, detours, clarifications, and unexpected insights. I'm grateful for his friendship and his commitment to enlarging the literary conversation by any means necessary.

Thanks to Mark St. Pierre and Tilda Long Soldier for hosting my family at the Odd Duck Inn on the Pine Ridge Reservation, and to Bill Stone for his guidance when we visited Lead and Deadwood. Thanks to Rob Foshay for digitizing our family recordings of George Bartholemew Brazil. And a special thanks to Mary Bordeaux and Peter Strong of Racing Magpie Gallery in Rapid City for their advice and support.

Others who contributed to *White Flights* in significant ways—a book recommendation, a conversation, a crucial question, a letter at the right time—are Adrienne Brown, Briallen Hopper, Fred Moten, Lauren Berlant, Lisa Lucas, Major Jackson, Martha Southgate, Katie Freeman, Layli Long Soldier, Victor LaValle, Jonathan Lethem, and Charles Baxter. Thank you all.

# Permission Acknowledgments

# Bibliography

## Books, Articles, and Dissertations

Aaron, Daniel. "How to Read Don DeLillo." In *Introducing Don DeLillo*, edited by Frank Lentricchia. Duke University Press, 1991.

Adorno, Theodor, et al. *Aesthetics and Politics: The Key Texts of the Classic Debate within German Marxism.* Verso, 1977.

Agamben, Giorgio. *The Coming Community.* University of Minnesota Press, 1993.

———. *Homo Sacer: Sovereign Power and Bare Life.* Stanford University Press, 1998.

Aitken, Robert. *The Mind of Clover: Essays in Zen Buddhist Ethics.* North Point Press, 1984.

Alba, Richard. "The Myth of a White Minority." *New York Times*, 11 June 2015, https://www.nytimes.com/2015/06/11/opinion/the-myth-of-a-white-minority.html.

Allison, Dorothy. *Trash.* Penguin Books, 1988.

Andersson, Rani-Henrik. *The Lakota Ghost Dance of 1890.* University of Nebraska Press, 2008.

Apter, Emily. "Impolitic." In *Unexceptional Politics: On Obstruction, Impasse, and the Impolitic.* Verso Books, 2018.

Bachelard, Gaston. *The Poetics of Space.* Penguin, 2014.

Baker, Barbara, ed. *Albert Murray and the Aesthetic Imagination of a Nation.* University of Alabama Press, 2010.

Baldwin, James. *Another Country.* Vintage Books, 1993.

Baraka, Amiri. *Dutchman and the Slave.* William Morrow, 1964.

Barth, John. *Lost in the Funhouse*. Doubleday, 1968.

Bashir, Samiya. *Field Theories*. Nightboat Books, 2016.

Bataille, Georges. *Blue of Noon*. Marion Boyars, 2002.

Beatty, Paul. *The Sellout*. Farrar, Straus and Giroux, 2015.

Beck, Charlotte Joko. *Everyday Zen: Love and Work*. HarperCollins, 1989.

Beckett, Samuel. *Three Novels*. Grove Press, 1958.

Bender, Aimee. *Willful Creatures*. Anchor Books, 2006.

Bennett, Brit. " 'I Thought It Would Be Better for You': A Mother, a Daughter, and Racism in America in 2017." *Vogue*, 8 November 2017.

Berger, John. *Ways of Seeing*. Penguin, 1977.

Berlant, Lauren. *Cruel Optimism*. Duke University Press, 2011.

Bernstein, J. M. Introduction to *The Culture Industry: Selected Essays on Mass Culture*, by Theodor Adorno. Routledge, 1991.

Berriault, Gina. *Women in Their Beds and Other Stories*. Counterpoint, 1996.

Biss, Eula. *Notes from No Man's Land: American Essays*. Graywolf Press, 2009.

Bonet, Clarissa. "Impolitic: Emily Apter." *Political Concepts*, February 2018, https://www.politicalconcepts.org/impolitic.

Brady, Joan. *Theory of War*. Simon and Schuster, 1997.

Brooks, Peter. *Reading for the Plot: Design and Intention in Narrative*. Harvard University Press, 1992.

Brown, Rosellen. *Civil Wars*. Random House, 1998.

Brown, William Wells. *Clotel, or The President's Daughter*. Penguin, 2003.

Butler, Judith. *The Psychic Life of Power: Theories in Subjection*. Stanford University Press, 1997.

Carver, Raymond. *Cathedral*. Random House, 1983.

———. "Letters to an Editor." *New Yorker*, 24 December 2007, https://www.newyorker.com/magazine/2007/12/24/letters-to-an-editor.

———. *What We Talk About When We Talk About Love*. Vintage Books, 1974.

———. *Where I'm Calling From: New and Selected Stories*. Vintage Books, 1988.

———. *Where Water Comes Together with Other Water*. Vintage Books, 1986.

Case, Anne, and Angus Deaton. "Rising Morbidity and Mortality in Midlife among White Non-Hispanic Americans in the 21st Century." *Proceedings of the National Academy of Sciences* 112, no. 49 (2015): 15078–83, https://doi.org/10.1073/pnas.1518393112.

"Cataplexy." *National Sleep Foundation*, 2010, https://sleepfoundation.org/narcolepsy/content/cataplexy.

Cha, Theresa Hak Kyung. *Dictee*. University of California Press, 2001.

Chabon, Michael. *Telegraph Avenue*. HarperCollins, 2012.

Chang, Jeff. *Can't Stop Won't Stop: A History of the Hip-Hop Generation*. St. Martin's Press, 2005.

————. *We Gon' Be Alright: Notes on Race and Resegregation*. Picador, 2016.

————. *Who We Be: The Colorization of America*. St. Martin's Press, 2014.

Cheever, John. *The Collected Stories of John Cheever*. Alfred A. Knopf, 1978.

Cheng, Anne Anlin. *The Melancholy of Race: Psychoanalysis, Assimilation, and Hidden Grief*. Oxford University Press, 2001.

Chesnutt, Charles. "What Is a White Man?" Charles Chesnutt Digital Archives, https://chesnuttarchives.org.

Clifton, Lucille. *The Collected Poems of Lucille Clifton*. BOA Editions, 2012.

Coates, Ta-Nehisi. "The Case for Reparations." *Atlantic*, June 2014, https://www.theatlantic.com/magazine/archive/2014/06/the-case-for-reparations/361631.

Coetzee, J. M. *Disgrace*. Viking, 1999.

————. "Jerusalem Prize Acceptance Speech." In *Doubling the Point: Essays and Interviews*, edited by David Attwell. Harvard University Press, 1992.

Conrad, Joseph. Preface to *The Nigger of the Narcissus*. Doubleday, 1914.

Crenshaw, Kimberlé. "Mapping the Margins: Intersectionality, Identity Politics, and Violence against Women of Color." *Stanford Law Review* 43, no. 6 (1991), www.jstor.org/stable/1229039.

Crouch, Stanley. "Black Like Huck." *New York Times Magazine*, 6 June 1999.

Debord, Guy. *Society of the Spectacle*. Black and Red, 2000.

Delany, Samuel R. *Dhalgren*. 1975. Vintage Books, 2000.

DeLillo, Don. *Americana*. Penguin, 1989.

————. *Underworld*. Scribner, 1997.

Derrida, Jacques. "The Law of Genre." In *Acts of Literature*, edited by Derek Attridge. Routledge, 1992.

————. "Of an Apocalyptic Tone Recently Adopted in Philosophy." *Oxford Literary Review* 6, no. 2 (1984).

————. "White Mythology: Metaphor in the Text of Philosophy." In *Margins of Philosophy*, translated by Alan Bass. University of Chicago Press, 1973.

DiAngelo, Robin. "White Fragility." *International Journal of Critical Pedagogy* 3, no. 3 (2011).

Dickinson, Emily. *Selected Poems of Emily Dickinson.* Modern Library, 2004.

Dillard, Annie. *An American Childhood.* Harper & Row, 1987.

Dixon, Thomas. *The Sins of the Father: A Romance of the South.* University Press of Kentucky, 2004.

Dyer, Richard. *White.* Routledge, 1997.

Edelman, Lee. *No Future: Queer Theory and the Death Drive.* Duke University Press, 2004.

Ellis, Bret Easton. *Less than Zero.* 1985. Vintage Books, 1998.

Ellis, Trey. *Platitudes.* Vintage Contemporaries Original, 1988.

Fanon, Frantz. *Black Skin, White Masks.* Rev. ed. Grove, 2008.

Fields, Karen E., and Barbara J. Fields. *Racecraft: The Soul of Inequality in American Life.* Verso, 2012.

Fitzgerald, F. Scott. *The Great Gatsby.* Scribner, 2003.

Ford, Richard. "In the Same Boat." *New York Times Magazine,* 6 June 1999.

———. *Independence Day.* Alfred A. Knopf, 1995.

———. *The Lay of the Land.* Alfred A. Knopf, 2006.

———. *Rock Springs.* Vintage Books, 1988.

———. *The Sportswriter.* Vintage Books, 1986.

Foucault, Michel. *"Society Must Be Defended": Lectures at the Collège de France,* edited by Mauro Bertani and Alessandro Fontana. Picador, 2003.

Frank, Thomas. "Why Johnny Can't Dissent." *Commodify Your Dissent: Salvos from "The Baffler."* W. W. Norton, 1997.

Franzen, Jonathan. *The Corrections.* Farrar, Straus and Giroux, 2001.

———. *How to Be Alone.* Farrar, Straus and Giroux, 2002.

Gardner, John. *On Becoming a Novelist.* Harper & Row, 1983.

Greenwald, Andy. *Nothing Feels Good: Punk Rock, Teenagers, and Emo.* St. Martin's Griffin, 2003.

Guglielmo, Jennifer, and Salvatore Salerno, eds. *Are Italians White? How Race Is Made in America.* Routledge, 2003.

Gurganus, Allan. *White People.* Alfred A. Knopf, 1991.

Hall, Edward T. *The Hidden Dimension.* Anchor Books, 1969.

Hallberg, Garth Risk. "Difficult Books: *Dhalgren* by Samuel R. Delany." *The Millions,* 29 June 2010, https://themillions.com/2010/06/difficult-books-dhalgren-by-samuel-r-delany.html.

Hartigan, John, Jr. *Odd Tribes: Toward a Cultural Analysis of White People.* Duke University Press, 2005.

Hofmannsthal, Hugo von. *The Lord Chandos Letter and Other Works.* New York Review Books, 2005.

Hurston, Zora Neale. "How It Feels to Be Colored Me." In *Folklore, Memoirs, and Other Writings*. Library of America, 1995.

Hunt, Erica. "All about You." *Los Angeles Review of Books*, 8 December 2014.

Isenberg, Nancy. *White Trash: The 400-Year History of Class in America*. Viking, 2016.

Iser, Wolfgang. *The Implied Reader: Patterns of Communication in Prose Fiction from Bunyan to Beckett*. Johns Hopkins University Press, 1978.

Ishiguro, Kazuo. *The Remains of the Day*. Vintage Books, 1988.

Jacobson, Matthew Frye. *Whiteness of a Different Color: European Immigrants and the Alchemy of Race*. Harvard University Press, 1998.

Jakobson, Roman, and Morris Halle. "Two Aspects of Language and Two Types of Aphasic Disturbances." In *Fundamentals of Language*. Mouton de Gruyter, 1971.

Jameson, Fredric. *Postmodernism, or, The Cultural Logic of Late Capitalism*. Duke University Press, 1991.

Jefferson, Thomas. *Notes on the State of Virginia*. Penguin Classics, 1998.

Johnson, Denis. *Fiskadoro*. HarperCollins, 1995.

Johnson, Mat. *Loving Day*. Spiegel & Grau, 2015.

———. *Pym*. Spiegel & Grau, 2010.

Jones, Edward P. *Lost in the City*. HarperCollins, 2012.

Kael, Pauline. *Deeper into Movies*. Marion Boyars, 1998.

Kennedy, Randall. *Interracial Intimacies*. Vintage Books, 2003.

Kermode, Frank. *The Sense of an Ending: Studies in the Theory of Fiction*. Oxford University Press, 1967.

Klein, Melanie. *The Selected Melanie Klein*. Edited by Juliet Mitchell. Free Press, 1986.

Koestenbaum, Wayne. *Humiliation*. Picador, 2011.

———. *My 1980s and Other Essays*. Farrar, Straus and Giroux, 2013.

Konstantinou, Lee. *Cool Characters: Irony and American Fiction*. Harvard University Press, 2016.

Lee, Chang-rae. *Aloft*. Riverhead Books, 2004.

———. *A Gesture Life*. Riverhead Books, 1999.

Lee, Young Jean. *Straight White Men*. Theater Communications Group, 2016.

Lentricchia, Frank, ed. *Introducing Don DeLillo*. Duke University Press, 1991.

Lerner, Ben. *The Hatred of Poetry*. Farrar, Straus and Giroux, 2016.

———. *10:04*. Farrar, Straus and Giroux, 2014.

Lethem, Jonathan. *The Fortress of Solitude*. Doubleday, 2003.

Lipsitz, George. *The Possessive Investment in Whiteness.* Temple University Press, 2006.

Lish, Gordon. *All Our Secrets Are the Same: New Fiction from "Esquire."* W. W. Norton, 1976.

———. *Zimzum.* 1993. Westview Press, 2005.

Lorde, Audre. *Zami: A New Spelling of My Name.* Crossing Press, 1982.

Lott, Eric. *Love and Theft: Blackface Minstrelsy and the American Working Class.* Oxford University Press, 1993.

Lovell, Joel. "George Saunders Has Written the Best Book You'll Read This Year." *New York Times Magazine,* January 3, 2013.

Lucarelli, Jason. "The Consecution of Gordon Lish: An Essay on Form and Influence." *Numero Cinq,* 4 February 2013, http://numerocinqmagazine.com/2013/02/04/the-consecution-of-gordon-lish-an-essay-on-form-and-influence-jason-lucarelli.

Lutz, Gary. "The Sentence Is a Lonely Place." *Baffler,* January 2009.

Marcus, Ben. *The Age of Wire and String.* Dalkey Archive Press, 1998.

Marriott, David. *On Black Men.* Edinburgh University Press, 2000.

Mason, Bobbie Ann. *Shiloh and Other Stories.* Modern Library, 2001.

Max, Daniel T. *Every Love Story Is a Ghost Story: A Life of David Foster Wallace.* Viking, 2012.

Mbembe, Achille, and Libby Meintjes. "Necropolitics." *Public Culture* 15, no. 1 (2003), muse.jhu.edu/article/39984.

McCarthy, Cormac. *Blood Meridian.* Vintage Books, 1985.

———. *The Road.* Knopf, 2006.

———. *Suttree.* Vintage Books, 1979.

McGurl, Mark. *The Program Era: Postwar Fiction and the Rise of Creative Writing.* Harvard University Press, 2009.

McPherson, James Alan. *Elbow Room.* Scribner, 1987.

———. *A Region Not Home: Reflections from Exile.* Simon and Schuster, 2000.

Michaels, Walter Benn. *The Trouble with Diversity.* Holt, 2006.

Mitchell, W. J. T. *Seeing through Race.* Harvard University Press, 2012.

Moore, Lorrie. *Anagrams.* Alfred A. Knopf, 1986.

Morgan, C. E. *The Sport of Kings.* Farrar, Straus and Giroux, 2016.

Morris, Tracie. Oral presentation at Thinking Its Presence: Race and Creative Writing conference, University of Arizona, November 2017.

Morrison, Toni. *Playing in the Dark: Whiteness and the Literary Imagination.* Harvard University Press, 1992.

———. "Rootedness: The Ancestor as Foundation." In *The Norton Anthology of African American Literature*, edited by Henry Louis Gates and Nellie Y. McKay. W. W. Norton, 2004.

———. "The Site of Memory." In *The Norton Anthology of African American Literature*, edited by Henry Louis Gates and Nellie Y. McKay. W. W. Norton, 2004.

Moten, Fred. "Black Op." *Modern Language Association* 123, no. 5 (2008): 1743–47, http://www.jstor.org/stable/25501981.

———. "Blackness and Nothingness (Mysticism in the Flesh)." *South Atlantic Quarterly* 112, no. 4 (2013): 737–80, https://doi.org/10.1215/00382876-2345261.

———. *Stolen Life: Consent Not to Be a Single Being*. Duke University Press, 2018.

Muñoz, José Esteban. *Cruising Utopia: The Then and There of Queer Futurity*. New York University Press, 2009.

———. "Feeling Brown, Feeling Down: Latina Affect, the Performativity of Race, and the Depressive Position." *Signs: Journal of Women in Culture and Society* 31, no. 3 (Spring 2006): 675–88.

Murphy, Michelle. *The Economization of Life*. Duke University Press, 2017.

Murray, Albert. *Blue Devils of Nada: A Contemporary American Approach to Aesthetic Statement*. Vintage Books, 1996.

———. *Collected Essays and Memoirs*. Library of America, 2016.

———. "Improvisation and the Creative Process." In *The Jazz Cadence of American Culture*, edited by Robert G. O'Meally. Columbia University Press, 1998.

———. *The Omni-Americans: Some Alternatives to the Folklore of White Supremacy*. Outerbridge and Dienstfrey, 1970.

Nancy, Jean-Luc. *Being Singular Plural*. Stanford University Press, 2000.

Naylor, Gloria. *Linden Hills*. Penguin Books, 1986.

Nelson, Maggie. *The Argonauts*. Graywolf Press, 2015.

———. *The Art of Cruelty*. W. W. Norton, 2011.

Newland, Guy. "How Does Merely Conventional Karma Work?" In *Moonpaths: Ethics and Emptiness*, edited by the Cowherds. Oxford University Press, 2016.

Ngai, Sianne. *Ugly Feelings*. Harvard University Press, 2005.

Noonan, Peggy. "The Color of Death—and of Disdain." *Wall Street Journal*, 5 October 2017.

Nyong'o, Tavia. *The Amalgamation Waltz: Race, Performance, and the Ruses of Memory*. University of Minnesota Press, 2009.

O'Connor, Flannery. *Mystery and Manners*. Farrar, Straus and Giroux, 1961.

———. *A Prayer Journal*. Farrar, Straus and Giroux, 2013.

Obama, Barack, and Marilynne Robinson. "President Obama and Marilynne Robinson: A Conversation in Iowa." *New York Review of Books*, 5 November 2015.

O'Brien, Harvey. *Action Movies: The Cinema of Striking Back*. Columbia University Press, 2012.

Paley, Grace. "The Immigrant Story." In *The Collected Stories*. Farrar, Straus and Giroux, 1994.

Peckinpah, Sam. *The Wild Bunch*, edited by Stephen Prince. Cambridge University Press, 1999.

Pierce, William. *The Turner Diaries*. National Vanguard Books, 1999.

Pietila, Antero. *Not in My Neighborhood: How Bigotry Shaped a Great American City*. Ivan R. Dee, 2010.

Poe, Edgar Allan. *The Narrative of A. Gordon Pym of Nantucket*. Dover Publications, 2005.

Posmentier, Sonya. *Cultivation and Catastrophe: The Lyric Ecology of Modern Black Literature*. Johns Hopkins University Press, 2017.

Powers, Richard. *The Time of Our Singing*. Farrar, Straus and Giroux, 2003.

Rankine, Claudia. *Citizen: An American Lyric*. Graywolf Press, 2014.

———. *Don't Let Me Be Lonely*. Graywolf Press, 2004.

Raspail, Jean. *The Camp of the Saints*. Social Contract Press, 1995.

Robinson, Marilynne. *Gilead*. Farrar, Straus and Giroux, 2004.

———. *Home*. Farrar, Straus and Giroux, 2008.

———. *Housekeeping*. Farrar, Straus and Giroux, 1980.

Roediger, David. *Towards the Abolition of Whiteness*. Verso, 1991.

Ross, Fran. *Oreo*. Northeastern University Press, 1974.

Roth, Phillip. *American Pastoral*. Houghton Mifflin, 1997.

———. *The Human Stain*. Houghton Mifflin, 2000.

Row, Jess. *Your Face in Mine*. Riverhead Books, 2014.

Scott, A. O. "In Search of the Best." *New York Times*, 21 May 2006, https://www.nytimes.com/2006/05/21/books/review/scott-essay.html.

———. "Return of the Prodigal Son." *New York Times*, 19 September 2008, https://www.nytimes.com/2008/09/21/books/review/Scott-t.html.

Scott, Candice. "Tense and Aspect Markers in African American English." PhD diss., University of Michigan, 2016.

Scranton, Roy. *Learning to Die in the Anthropocene*. City Lights Books, 2015.

Sedgwick, Eve Kosofsky. "Paranoid Reading and Reparative Reading." In *Touching Feeling: Affect, Pedagogy, Performativity*. Duke University Press, 2003.

Senna, Danzy. *Caucasia*. Riverhead Books, 1999.

Sexton, Jared. "People-of-Color-Blindness: Notes on the Afterlife of Slavery." *Social Text* 28, no. 2 (2010): 31–56, https://doi.org/10.1215/01642472-2009-066.

Sloterdijk, Peter. *Critique of Cynical Reason*. University of Minnesota Press, 1987.

Smith, Anna Deveare. *Fires in the Mirror*. Anchor Books, 1993.

———. *Twilight: Los Angeles, 1992*. Anchor Books, 1994.

Smith, Valerie, and Adrienne Brown, eds. *Race and Real Estate*. Oxford University Press, 2016.

Sollors, Werner. *Interracialism: Black-White Intermarriage in American History, Literature, and Law*. Oxford University Press, 2005.

———. *Neither Black Nor White Yet Both: Thematic Explorations of Interracial Literature*. Oxford University Press, 1997.

Southgate, Martha. *The Fall of Rome*. Scribner, 2002.

Spengler, Oswald. *The Decline of the West*. Oxford University Press, 1991.

Spillers, Hortense J. "Mama's Baby, Papa's Maybe: An American Grammar Book." *Diacritics* 17, no. 2 (1987): 65–81, www.jstor.org/stable/464747.

Stein, Gertrude. "Composition as Explanation." In *Selected Writings of Gertrude Stein*. Vintage, 1990.

Sterne, Laurence. *The Life and Opinions of Tristram Shandy, Gentleman*. Penguin, 2003.

Steyerl, Hito. *Duty Free Art: Art in the Age of Planetary Civil War*. Verso, 2017.

Stoddard, Lothrop. *The Rising Tide of Color against White World-Supremacy*. University of Hawai'i Press, 2003.

Svenonius, Ian F. *Censorship Now!!* Akashic Books, 2015.

Taliman, Valerie. "Veterans Ask for Forgiveness and Healing in Standing Rock." *Indian Country Today*, 7 December 2016, https://newsmaven.io/indiancountrytoday/archive/veterans-ask-for-forgiveness-and-healing-in-standing-rock-k2fLUonhqEy6D-NjnhlJJw.

Tompkins, Jane. *West of Everything: The Inner Life of Westerns.* Oxford University Press, 1992.

Truong, Monique. *The Book of Salt.* Houghton Mifflin, 2004.

Tyler, Anne. *The Accidental Tourist.* Alfred A. Knopf, 1985.

Unger, Roberto Mangabeira. *False Necessity: Anti-Necessitarian Social Theory in the Service of Radical Democracy.* Verso, 2001.

Unger, Roberto Mangabeira. *The Religion of the Future.* Verso, 2016.

Wallace, David Foster. *Brief Interviews with Hideous Men.* Little, Brown, 1999.

———. *Consider the Lobster.* Little, Brown, 2006.

———. *Girl with Curious Hair.* W. W. Norton, 1996.

———. *Infinite Jest.* Little, Brown, 2009.

———. *A Supposedly Funny Thing I'll Never Do Again.* Little, Brown, 1998.

Wallace, David Foster, and Mark Costello. *Signifying Rappers.* Little, Brown, 2013.

Whitehead, Colson. *Apex Hides the Hurt.* Anchor Books, 2007.

———. *The Intuitionist.* Anchor Books, 2000.

———. *The Underground Railroad.* Little, Brown, 2016.

Wihbey, John. "Fly or Drive: Parsing the Evolving Climate Math." Yale Center for Climate Communications, 2 September 2015.

Wilder, Laura Ingalls. *Little House on the Prairie.* HarperCollins, 2008.

Wilderson, Frank. *Red, White, and Black: Cinema and the Structure of U.S. Antagonisms.* Duke University Press, 2010.

Williams, Alex. "How to Survive an Apocalypse." *New York Times*, 23 September 2017, https://www.nytimes.com/2017/09/23/style/how-to-survive-the-apocalypse.html.

Williams, Patricia. *Rabbit: A Memoir.* HarperCollins, 2017.

Winters, David. "An Interview with Gordon Lish." *Critical Quarterly* 57, no. 4 (December 2015). *Wiley Online Library*, https://doi.org/10.1111/criq.12228.

Wittgenstein, Ludwig. *Philosophical Investigations*, edited by P. M. S. Hacker and Joachim Schulte, 4th ed. Wiley-Blackwell, 2009.

Wolff, Tobias. "Heart of Whiteness." Cultural Comment, *New Yorker*, 15 August 2014, https://www.newyorker.com/culture/cultural-comment/tobias-wolff-on-race.

Young, Coleman, with Lonnie Wheeler. *The Hard Stuff: The Autobiography of Coleman Young.* Viking, 1994.

Young, Kevin. *The Grey Album: On the Blackness of Blackness.* Graywolf Press, 2012.

Zamora, Javier. *Unaccompanied.* Copper Canyon Press, 2018.


## Films and Recordings

Beyoncé. "Lift Every Voice and Sing." YouTube, uploaded by Maverick, 4 May 2018, https://www.bing.com/videos/search?q=beyonce+lift+every +voice+and+sing&view=detail&mid=789A524EB6EB5047B905789 A524EB6EB5047B905&FORM=VIRE.

*Black Panther.* Directed by Ryan Coogler. Performances by Chadwick Boseman, Lupita Nyong'o, Michael B. Jordan. Marvel Studios, 2018.

Cat Stevens. *Harold and Maude Original Soundtrack Recording.* Vinyl Films, 1972.

*Chinatown.* Directed by Roman Polanski. Performances by Jack Nicholson, Faye Dunaway, John Huston. Paramount Pictures, 1974.

*Death Wish II.* Directed by Michael Winner. Performances by Charles Bronson, Jill Ireland, Vincent Gardenia. MGM Home Entertainment, 1982.

*Dirty Harry.* Directed by Don Siegel. Performances by Clint Eastwood, Andrew Robinson, Harry Guardino. Warner Brothers, 1978.

*First Blood.* Directed by Ted Kotcheff. Performances by Sylvester Stallone, Brian Dennehy, Richard Crenna. Orion Pictures, 1982.

*Harold and Maude.* Directed by Hal Ashby. Performances by Bud Cort, Ruth Gordon. Paramount Pictures, 1971.

Indian Summer. *Hidden Arithmetic.* Future Recordings, 2006.

Liz Phair. "Flower." *Exile in Guyville.* Matador Records, 1993.

*Mad Max: Fury Road.* Directed by George Miller. Performances by Charlize Theron, Tom Hardy. Warner Bros. Pictures, 2015.

*Platoon.* Directed by Oliver Stone. Performances by Charlie Sheen, Tom Berenger, Willem Dafoe. MGM Home Entertainment, 1986.

*Rambo II.* Directed by George P. Cosmatos. Performances by Sylvester Stallone, Richard Crenna, Charles Napier. Artisan Entertainment, 1985.

*Reservoir Dogs.* Directed by Quentin Tarantino. Performances by Harvey Keitel, Tim Roth, Michael Madsen. Live America Inc., 1992.

Rites of Spring. *End on End.* Dischord Records, 1987.

*Robocop.* Directed by Paul Verhoeven. Performances by Peter Weller, Nancy Allen, Daniel O'Herlihy. Orion Pictures, 1987.

*Rushmore.* Directed by Wes Anderson. Performances by Jason Schwartzman, Bill Murray. Touchstone Pictures, 1998.

Sideshow. *Lip Read Confusion.* Flydaddy Records, 1995.

Swing Kids. *Discography.* Three One G Records, 1996.

*Take This Hammer.* Directed by Richard O. Moore. Performance by James Baldwin. National Educational Television, 1963.

*The Terminator.* Directed by James Cameron. Performances by Arnold Schwarzenegger, Linda Hamilton, Michael Biehn. Pacific Western, 1984.

Townes Van Zandt. "To Live Is to Fly." *Rear View Mirror,* Sundown Records, 1993.

# Illustration Credits

Page 28: Edward Hopper, *Pennsylvania Coal Town*, 1947. © 2018 Heirs of Josephine Hopper. Licensed by VAGA at Artists Rights Society (ARS), NY. Photo supplied by the Butler Institute of American Art.

Page 123: *The Beating of Reginald Denny*, video still. Reproduced with the permission of Los Angeles News Service.

Page 151: Marie-Shirine Yener, *Harassment Graphic*. © 2018 Artists Rights Society (ARS), New York / ADAGP, Paris.

Page 155: Ryan Southen, *Detroit Central Station*. Reproduced with the permission of the photographer.

Page 176: *Peoples Temple children, Jonestown, Guyana, circa 1977–1978*. Photographs of Peoples Temple in the United States and Guyana, PC010. Reproduced with the permission of the California Historical Society.

Page 181: Samuel Weber and John Michael. *Glyph VII*. Copyright © 1980 The Johns Hopkins University Press. Reprinted with the permission of Johns Hopkins University Press. Reproduced with the permission of Johns Hopkins University Press.

Page 184: Adrian Piper, *My Calling (Card) #1 (for Dinners and Cocktail Parties)*, 1986–present. Performance prop: brown business card with printed text on cardboard. Dimensions: standard business card size. Collection of the Adrian Piper Research Archive Foundation Berlin. © APRA Foundation Berlin.

Page 201: Frank Wojciechowski, *Anna Deveare Smith in "Fires in the Mirror."* Reproduced with the permission of the photographer.

Page 201: *Fires in the Mirror* (1993 TV movie), video still. Directed by George C. Wolfe. Shown: Anna Deavere Smith. Reproduced with the permission of PBS/Photofest.

Page 213: Pat Graham, *Frodus.* Reproduced with the permission of the photographer.

Page 259: Willem Dafoe in *Platoon,* film still, 1986. Movie Store Collection Ltd / Alamy Stock Photo.

Jess Row is the author of the novel *Your Face in Mine* and two collections of short stories, *The Train to Lo Wu* and *Nobody Ever Gets Lost*. His fiction has appeared in the *New Yorker*, the *Atlantic*, *Granta*, and *Tin House*, as well as three times in *The Best American Short Stories*; he's received a Whiting Writers Award, two Pushcart Prizes, and NEA and Guggenheim fellowships, and was named a "Best Young American Novelist" by *Granta* in 2007. His essays and criticism have appeared in the *New York Times*, the *New Republic*, *Bookforum*, *Boston Review*, and elsewhere. He teaches at NYU and the College of New Jersey, and is a senior dharma teacher in the Kwan Um School of Zen.

The text of *White Flights* is set in Janson.
Book design by Rachel Holscher.
Composition by Bookmobile Design and Digital
Publisher Services, Minneapolis, Minnesota.
Manufactured by Versa Press on acid-free,
30 percent postconsumer wastepaper.